The Mint

THE
MINT

A Miscellany
of
Literature, Art
and Criticism

EDITED BY GEOFFREY GRIGSON

ROUTLEDGE AND SONS LTD

Published in 1946 by George Routledge
and Sons Limited, 68 Carter Lane,
London, E.C.4, and printed in Great
Britain by Butler and Tanner Limited,
Frome and London

Typography by Seán Jennett

Foreword

THE MINT is what it states itself to be—a miscellany of
literature, art and criticism. And it is a miscellany which
will reappear from time to time, and which needs and will
be glad of contributions under those three heads. Without being
narrow, it is not 'political': it does not favour one set of collective
impulses against another. Nothing that has happened so far in a
world now rather grey proves the liveliness of the individual human
spirit to have lost its value, the honesty of the man of letters, the
'literary conscience', not to be the criterion still by which an editor
should edit, so far as he can. If an editor looks round just now, it is
true that he sees few considerable English talents, at least in writing,
while at the same time he sees all the temptations to natural frailty
much enlarged. Good writers are aloof from scholarship, good
scholars aloof from the good writing of their time, or else opposed
to it. And a vast quantity of paper can be found for every kind of
propaganda, very little as good as none for founding a new
periodical.

All of us have seen the variety of possible expedients, or lifebelts.
For example, one can conclude that the English are pigs, buy a
bottle of French perfume, and trot resolutely from the smell of the sty
towards Paris. One can be a neo-romantic, which nowadays is
less to become something so delicate as a passive Æolian harp
emitting a harmony in the breezes of the world than to become
an Æolian cinema-organ, on which the wind plays the fool.
One can say (at least it implies some control), I will concern myself
with delicate writing, avoid violence and sex, cultivate gentility,
and inhabit a frail, clean parlour of tasteful liberalism. One
can revolt, and become a Roaring Boy. One can React, one can
Progress, with a moral fanaticism, also thinking the disciplines
of an art to be a subterfuge. Or, as I say, one can be oneself:

be open, as an individual, to the diversity of humanity and of experience; believe that there are certain timeless, over-riding values, timelessly visible in a way of life, in a poem or painting of one's own time, in a Sardinian bronze, in a story by Turgenev or by Crabbe, in a street ballad, or in Mantegna's 'Agony in the Garden' in a newly-opened National Gallery; one can believe that art implies effort, is not a fashionable æsthetic eclecticism, not a surrender, not a wallow, but a matter of this literary conscience, this conscious control of doing excellently and honestly, according to one's powers, something big or something small, with all the individual talent and receptivity one has the luck to possess and the duty to develop.

That, at least, is the kind of writer, younger or older, known or unknown, English or European or of any other country, that I should prefer, in the age of the journalist and the publicity agent and the thousand-word article, to publish in *The Mint*. Contributions need not be short and they will not be censored.

G.

Contents

Contents

Illustrations

Illustrations

MARTIN BUBER

The Education of Character

*An Address to the National Conference of Palestinian Teachers
at Tel-Aviv in May 1939*

[I]

EDUCATION worthy of the name is essentially education of
character. For the genuine educator does not merely consider
individual functions of his pupil, as one intending to teach
him only to know or be capable of certain definite things; but his
concern is always the person as a whole, both in the actuality in
which he lives before you now and in his possibilities, what he
can become. But in this way, as a whole in reality and potentiality,
a man can be conceived either as personality, that is, as a unique
spiritual-physical form with all the forces dormant in it, or as character, that is, as the link between what this individual is and the
sequence of his actions and attitudes. Between these two modes of
conceiving the pupil in his wholeness there is a fundamental difference. Personality is something which in its growth remains essentially
outside the influence of the educator; but to assist in the moulding
of character is his greatest task. Personality is a completion, only
character is a task. One may cultivate and enhance personality, but
in education one can and one must aim at character.

However—as I would like to point out straightaway—it is advis-
able not to over-estimate what the educator can even at best do to
develop character. In this more than in any other branch of the
science of teaching it is important to realize, at the very beginning of
the discussion, the fundamental limits to conscious influence, even
before asking what character is and how it is to be brought about.

If I have to teach algebra I can expect to succeed in giving my
pupils an idea of quadratic equations with two unknown quantities.
Even the slowest-witted child will understand it so well that he will

amuse himself by solving equations at night when he cannot fall asleep. And even one with the most sluggish memory will not forget, in his old age, how to play with x and y. But if I am concerned with the education of character, everything becomes problematic. I try to explain to my pupils that envy is despicable, and at once I feel the secret resistance of those who are poorer than their comrades. I try to explain that it is wicked to bully the weak, and at once I see a suppressed smile on the lips of the strong. I try to explain that lying destroys life, and something frightful happens: the worst habitual liar of the class produces a brilliant essay on the destructive power of lying. I have made the fatal mistake of *giving instruction* in ethics, and what I said is accepted as current coin of knowledge; nothing of it is transformed into character-building substance.

But the difficulty lies still deeper. In all teaching of a subject I can announce my intention of teaching as openly as I please, and this does not interfere with the results. After all, pupils do want, for the most part, to learn something, even if not over-much, so that a tacit agreement becomes possible. But as soon as my pupils notice that I want to educate their characters I am resisted precisely by those who show most signs of genuine, independent character: they will not let themselves be educated, or rather, they do not like the idea that somebody wants to educate them. And those, too, who are seriously labouring over the question of good and evil, rebel when one dictates to them, as though it were some long established truth, what is good and what is bad; and they rebel just because they have experienced over and over again how hard it is to find the right way. Does it follow that one should keep silent about one's intention of educating character, and act by ruse and subterfuge? No; I have just said that the difficulty lies deeper. It is not enough to see that education of character is not introduced into a lesson in class; neither may one conceal it in cleverly arranged intervals. Education cannot tolerate such politic action. Even if the pupil does not notice the hidden motive it will have its negative effect on the actions of the teacher himself by depriving him of the directness which is his strength. Only in his whole being, in all his spontaneity can the educator truly affect the whole being of his pupil. For educating characters you do not need a moral genius, but you do need a man who is wholly alive and able to communicate himself directly to his fellow beings. His aliveness streams out to them and affects them most strongly and purely when he has no thought of affecting them.

The Greek word character means *impression*. The special link between man's being and his appearance, the special connexion between the unity of what he is and the sequence of his actions and attitudes is impressed on his still plastic substance. Who does the impressing? Everything does: nature and the social context, the house and the street, language and custom, the world of history and the world of daily news in the form of rumour, of broadcast and newspaper, music and technical science, play and dream—everything together. Many of these factors exert their influence by stimulating agreement, imitation, desire, effort; others by arousing questions, doubts, dislike, resistance. Character is formed by the interpenetration of all those multifarious, opposing influences. And yet, among this infinity of form-giving forces the educator is only one element among innumerable others, but distinct from them all by his *will* to take part in the stamping of character and by his *consciousness* that he represents in the eyes of the growing person a certain *selection* of what is, the selection of what is 'right', of what *should* be. It is in this will and this consciousness that his vocation as an educator finds its fundamental expression. From this the genuine educator gains two things: first, humility, the feeling of being only one element amidst the fullness of life, only one single existence in the midst of all the tremendous inrush of reality on the pupil; but secondly, self-awareness, the feeling of being, besides this, the only existence that *wants* to affect the whole person, and thus the feeling of responsibility for the selection of reality which he represents to the pupil. And a third thing emerges from all this, the recognition that in this realm of the education of character, of wholeness, there is only *one* access to the pupil: his *confidence*. For the adolescent who is frightened and disappointed by an unreliable world, confidence means the liberating insight that there is human truth, the truth of human existence. When the pupil's confidence has been won, his resistance against being educated gives way to a singular happening: he accepts the educator as a person. He feels he may trust this man, that this man is not making a business out of him, but is taking part in his life,

3

accepting him before desiring to influence him. And so he learns to *ask*.

The teacher who is for the first time approached by a boy with somewhat defiant bearing, but with trembling hands, visibly opened-up and fired by a daring hope, who asks him what is the right thing in a certain situation—for instance, whether in learning that a friend has betrayed a secret entrusted to him one should call him to account or be content with entrusting no more secrets to him—the teacher to whom this happens realizes that this is the moment to make the first conscious step towards education of character; he has to answer, to answer under a responsibility, to give an answer which will probably lead beyond the alternatives of the question by showing a third possibility which is the right one. To dictate what is good and evil in general is not his business. His business is to answer a concrete question, to answer what is right and wrong in a given situation. This, as I have said, can only happen in an atmosphere of confidence. Confidence, of course, is not won by the artificial endeavour to win it, but by direct and spontaneous participation in the life of the people one is dealing with—in this case in the life of one's pupils and by assuming the responsibility which arises from such participation. It is not the educational intention but it is the meeting which is educationally fruitful. A soul suffering from the contradictions of the world of human society, and of its own physical existence, approaches me with a question. By trying to answer it to the best of my knowledge and conscience I help it to become a character that actively overcomes the contradictions.

If this is the teacher's standpoint towards his pupil, taking part in his life and conscious of responsibility, then everything that passes between them can, without any deliberate or politic intention, open a way to the education of character: lessons and games, a conversation about quarrels in the class, or about the problems of a world-war. Only, the teacher must not forget the limits of education; even when he enjoys confidence he cannot always expect agreement. Confidence implies a break-through from reserve, the bursting of the bonds which imprison an unquiet heart. But it does not imply unconditional agreement. The teacher must never forget that conflicts too, if only they are decided in a healthy atmosphere, have an educational value. A conflict with a pupil is the supreme test for the educator. He must use his own insight wholeheartedly; he must not blunt the piercing impact of his knowledge, but he must at the same time have in readiness the healing ointment for the heart pierced by it. Not for a moment may he conduct a dialectical manœuvre instead of the real battle for truth. But if he is the victor he has to help the vanquished to endure defeat; and if he cannot conquer the self-willed soul that faces him (for victories over souls are not so easily won), then he has to find the word of love which alone can help to overcome so difficult a situation.

[2]

So far I have referred to those personal difficulties in the education of character which arise from the relation between educator and pupil, while for the moment treating character itself, the object of education, as a simple concept of fixed content. But it is by no means that. In order to penetrate to the real difficulties in the education of character we have to examine critically the concept of character itself.

Kerschensteiner in his well-known essay on *The Concept and Education of Character* distinguished between 'character in the most general sense', by which he means 'a man's standpoint to his human circumstances, which is constant and is expressed in his actions', and real 'ethical character', which he defines as 'a special standpoint, and one which in action gives the preference before all others to absolute values'. If we begin by accepting this distinction unreservedly—and undeniably there is some truth in it—we are faced with such heavy odds in all education of character in our time that the very possibility of it seems doubtful.

The 'absolute values' which Kerschensteiner refers to cannot, of course, be meant to have only subjective validity for the person concerned. Don Juan finds absolute and subjective value in seducing the greatest possible number of women, and the dictator sees it in the greatest possible accumulation of power. 'Absolute validity' can only relate to universal values and norms, the existence of which the person concerned recognizes and acknowledges. But to deny the presence of universal values and norms of absolute validity—that is the conspicuous tendency of our age. This tendency is not, as is sometimes supposed, directed merely against the sanctioning of the norms by religion, but against their universal character and absolute validity, against their claim to be of a higher order than man and to govern the whole of mankind. In our age values and norms are not permitted to be anything but expressions of the life of a group which translates its own needs into the language of objective claims, until at last the group itself, for example a nation, is raised to an absolute value—and moreover to the only value. This splitting up into groups so pervades the whole of life that it is no longer possible to re-establish a sphere of values common to mankind, and a commandment to mankind is no longer observed. As this tendency grows the basis for the development of what Kerschensteiner means by moral character steadily diminishes. How, under these circumstances, can the task of educating character be completed?

At the time of the Arab terror in Palestine, when there were single Jewish acts of reprisal, there must have been many discussions between teacher and pupils on the question: Can there be any suspension of the Ten Commandments, i.e. can murder become a good deed if committed in the interest of one's own group? One such discussion was once repeated to me. The teacher asked: 'When the commandment tells you "Thou shalt not bear false witness against thy neighbour", are we to interpret it with the condition, "provided that it does not profit you"?' Thereupon one of the pupils said, 'But it is not a question of my profit, but of the profit of my people.' The teacher: 'And how would you like it, then, if we put our condition this way: "Provided that it does not profit your family"?' The pupil: 'But family—that is still something more or less like myself; but the people—that is something quite different; there all question of *I* disappears.' The teacher: 'Then if you are thinking, "we want victory", don't you feel at the same time, "I want victory"?' The pupil: 'But the people, that is something infinitely more than just the people of to-day. It includes all past and future generations.' At this point the teacher felt the moment had come to leave the narrow compass of the present and to invoke historical destiny. He said: 'Yes; all past generations. But what was it that made those past generations of the Exile live? What made them outlive and overcome all their trials? Wasn't it that the cry "Thou shalt not" never faded from their hearts and ears?' The pupil grew very pale. He was silent for a while, but it was the silence of one whose words threatened to stifle him. Then he burst out: 'And what have we achieved that way? This!' And he banged his fist on the newspaper before him, which contained the report on the British White Paper. And again he burst out with 'Live? Outlive? Do you call that life? We want to live!'

I have already said that the test of the educator lies in conflict with his pupil. He has to face this conflict and, whatever turn it may take, he has to find the way through it into life, into a life, I must add, where confidence continues unshaken—more, is even mysteriously strengthened. But the example I have just given shows the extreme difficulty of this task, which seems at times to have reached an impassable frontier. This is no longer merely a conflict between two generations, but between a world which for several millennia has believed in a truth superior to man, and an age which does not believe in it any longer—will not or cannot believe in it any longer.

But if we now ask, 'How in this situation can there be any education of character?' something negative is immediately obvious: it is senseless to want to prove by any kind of argument that nevertheless the denied absoluteness of norms exists. That would be to assume that the denial is the result of reflection, and is open to argument, that is, to material for renewed reflection. But the denial is due to the disposition of a dominant human type of our age. We are justified in regarding this disposition as a sickness of the human race. But we must not deceive ourselves by believing that the disease can be cured by formulæ which assert that nothing is really as the sick person imagines. It is an idle undertaking to call out, to a mankind that has grown blind to eternity: 'Look! the eternal values!' To-day host upon host of men have everywhere sunk into the slavery of collectives, and each collective is the supreme authority for its own slaves; there is no longer, superior to the collectives, any universal sovereignty in idea, faith, or spirit. Against the values, decrees and decisions of the collective no appeal is possible. This is true, not only for the totalitarian countries, but also for the parties and party-like groups in the so-called democracies. Men who have so lost themselves to the collective Moloch cannot be rescued from it by any reference, however eloquent, to the absolute whose kingdom the Moloch has usurped. One has to begin by pointing to that sphere where man himself, in the hours of utter solitude, occasionally becomes aware of the disease through sudden pain: by pointing to the relation of the individual to his own self. In order to enter into a personal relation with the absolute, it is first necessary to be a person again, to rescue one's real personal self from the fiery jaws of collectivism which devours all selfhood. The desire to do this is latent in the pain the individual suffers through his distorted relation to his own self. Again and again he dulls the pain with a delicate poison and thus suppresses the desire as well. To keep the pain awake, to waken the desire—that is the first task of everyone who regrets the obscuration of eternity. It is also the first task of the genuine educator in our time.

The man for whom absolute values in a universal sense do not exist cannot be made to adopt 'a standpoint which in action gives the preference over all others to absolute values'. But what one can inculcate in him is the desire to attain once more to a real standpoint, and that is, the desire to become a person following the only way that leads to this goal today.

But with this the concept of character formulated by Kerschensteiner and deriving, as we know, from Kant is recognized to be useless for the specifically modern task of the education of character. Another concept has to be found if this task is to be more precisely defined .

We cannot conceal from ourselves that we stand to-day on the ruins of the edifice whose towers were raised by Kant. It is not given to us living to-day to sketch the plan for a new building. But we can perhaps begin by laying the first foundations without a plan, with only a dawning image before our mind's eye.

[3]

According to Kerschensteiner's final definition character is 'fundamentally nothing but voluntary obedience to the maxims which have been moulded in the individual by experience, teaching, and self-reflection, whether they have been adopted and then completely assimilated or have originated in the consciousness through self-legislation'. This voluntary obedience 'is, however, only a form of self-control'. At first, love or fear of other people must have produced in man 'the *habit* of self-conquest'. Then, gradually, 'this outer obedience must be transformed into inner obedience'.

The concept of habit was then enlarged, especially by John Dewey in his book, *Human Nature and Conduct*. According to him character is 'the interpenetration of habits'. Without 'the continued operation of all habits in every act' there would be no unified character, but only 'a juxtaposition of disconnected reactions to separated situations'.

With this concept of character as an organization of self-control by means of the accumulation of maxims, or as a system of interpenetrating habits, it is very easy to understand how powerless modern educational science is when faced by the sickness of man. But even apart from the special problems of the age, this concept can be no adequate basis for the construction of a genuine education of character. Not that the educator could dispense with employing useful maxims or furthering good habits. But in moments that come perhaps only seldom, a feeling of blessed achievement links him to the explorer, the inventor, the artist, a feeling of sharing in the revelation of what is hidden. In such moments he finds himself in a sphere very different from that of maxims and habits. Only on this, the highest plane of his activity, can he fix his real goal, the real concept of character which is his concern, even though he might not often reach it.

For the first time a young teacher enters a class independently, no longer sent by the training college to prove his efficiency. The class before him is like a mirror of mankind, so multiform, so full of contradictions, so inaccessible. He feels 'These boys—I have not sought them out; I have been put here and have to accept them as they are —but not as they now are in this moment, no, as they *really* are, as they can become. But how can I find out what is in them and what can I do to make it take shape?' And the boys do not make things easy for him. They are noisy, they cause trouble, they stare at him with impudent curiosity. He is at once tempted to check this or that trouble-maker, to issue orders, to make compulsory the rules of decent behaviour, to say No, to say No to everything rising against him from beneath: he is at once tempted to start from beneath. And if one starts from beneath one perhaps never arrives above, but everything comes down. But then his eyes meet a face which strikes him. It is not a beautiful face nor particularly intelligent; but it is a real face, or rather, the chaos preceding the cosmos of a real face. On it he reads a question which is something different from the general curiosity: 'Who are you? Do you know something that concerns me? Do you bring me something? What do you bring?'

In some such way he reads the question. And he, the young teacher, addresses this face. He says nothing very ponderous or important, he puts an ordinary introductory question: 'What did you talk about last in geography? The Dead Sea? Well, what about the Dead Sea?' But there was obviously something not quite usual in the question, for the answer he gets is not the ordinary schoolboy answer; the boy begins to *tell a story*. Some months earlier he had stayed for a few hours on the shores of the Dead Sea and it is of this he tells. He adds: 'And everything looked to me as if it had been created a day before the rest of creation.' Quite unmistakably he had only in this moment made up his mind to talk about it. In the meantime his face has changed. It is no longer quite as chaotic as before. And the class has fallen silent. They all listen. The class, too, is no longer a chaos. Something has happened. The young teacher has started from above.

The educator's task can certainly not consist in educating great characters. He cannot select his pupils, but year by year the world, such as it is, is sent in the form of a school class to meet him on his life's way as his destiny; and in this destiny lies the very meaning of his life's work. He has to introduce discipline and order, he has to establish a law, and he can only strive and hope for the result that discipline and order will become more and more inward and autonomous, and that at last the law will be written in the heart of his pupils. But his real goal which, once he has well recognized it and well remembers it, will influence all his work, is the great character.

The great character can be conceived neither as a system of maxims nor as a system of habits. It is peculiar to him to act from the whole of his substance. That is, it is peculiar to him to react in accordance with the uniqueness of every situation which challenges him as an active person. Of course there are all sorts of similarities in different situations; one can construct types of situations, one can always find to what section the particular situation belongs, and draw what is appropriate from the hoard of established maxims and habits, apply the appropriate maxim, bring into operation the appropriate habit. But what is untypical in the particular situation remains unnoticed and unanswered. To me that seems the same as if, having ascertained the sex of a new-born child, one were immediately to establish its type as well, and put all the children of one type into a common cradle on which not the individual name but the name of the type was inscribed. In spite of all similarities every living situation has, like a new-born child, a new face, that has never been before and will never come again. It demands of you a reaction which cannot be prepared beforehand. It demands nothing of what is past. It demands presence, responsibility; it demands you. I call a great character one who by his actions and attitudes satisfies the claim of situations out of deep readiness to respond with his whole life, and in such a way that the sum of his actions and attitudes expresses at the same time the unity of his being in its willingness to accept responsibility. As his being is unity, the unity of accepted responsibility, his active life, too, coheres into unity. And one might perhaps say that for him there rises a unity out of the situations he has responded to in responsibility, the indefinable unity of a moral destiny.

All this does not mean that the great character is beyond the acceptance of norms. No responsible person remains a stranger to norms. But the command inherent in a genuine norm never becomes a maxim and the fulfilment of it never a habit. Any command that a great character takes to himself in the course of his development does not act in him as part of his consciousness or as material for building up his exercises, but remains latent in a basic layer of his substance until it reveals itself to him in a concrete way. What it has to tell him is revealed whenever a situation arises which demands of him a solution of which till then he had perhaps no idea. Even the most universal norm will at times be recognized only in a very special situation. I know of a man whose heart was struck by the lightning flash of 'Thou shalt not steal' in the very moment when he was moved by a very different desire from that of stealing, and whose heart was so struck by it that he not only abandoned doing what he wanted to do, but with the whole force of his passion did the very opposite. Good and evil are not each other's opposites like right and left. But the evil approaches us as a whirlwind, the good as a direction. There is a direction, a 'yes', a command, hidden even in a prohibition, which is revealed to us in moments like these. In moments like these the command addresses us really in the second person, and the Thou in it is no one else but one's own self. Maxims command only the third person, the each and the none.

One can say that it is the unconditioned nature of the address which distinguishes the command from the maxim. In an age which has become deaf to unconditioned address we cannot overcome the dilemma of the education of character from that angle. But insight into the structure of great character can help us to overcome it.

Of course, it may be asked whether the educator should really start 'from above', whether, in fixing his goal, the hope of finding a great character, who is bound to be the exception, should be his starting-point; for in his methods of educating character he will always have to take into consideration the others, the many. To this I reply that the educator would not allow himself to adopt this method if it were inapplicable to these others. In fact, however, his very insight into the structure of a great character helps him to find the way by which alone (as I have indicated) he can begin to influence also the victims of the collective Moloch, pointing out to them the sphere in which they themselves suffer—namely, their relation to their own selves. From this sphere he must elicit the values which he can make credible and desirable to his pupils. That is what insight into the structure of a great character helps him to do.

A section of the young is beginning to feel to-day that, because of their absorption by the collective, something important and irreplaceable is lost to them—personal responsibility for life and the world. These young people, it is true, do not yet realize that their blind devotion to the collective, e.g. to a party, was not a genuine act of their personal life; they do not realize that it sprang, rather, from the fear of being left, in this age of confusion, to rely on themselves, on a self which no longer receives its direction from eternal values. Thus they do not yet realize that their devotion was fed on the unconscious desire to have responsibility removed from them by an authority in which they believe or want to believe. They do not yet realize that this devotion was an escape. I repeat, the young people I am speaking of do not yet realize this. But they are beginning to notice that he who no longer, with his whole being, decides what he does or does not, and assumes responsibility for it, becomes sterile in soul. And a sterile soul soon ceases to be a soul.

This is where the educator can begin and should begin. He can help the feeling that something is lacking to grow into the clarity of consciousness and into the force of desire. He can awaken in young people the courage to shoulder life again. He can bring before his pupils the image of a great character who denies no answer to life and the world, but accepts responsibility for everything essential that he meets. He can show his pupils this image without the fear that those among them who most of all need discipline and order will drift into a craving for aimless freedom: on the contrary, he can teach them in this way to recognize that discipline and order too are starting-points on the way towards self-responsibility. He can show that even the great character is not born perfect, that the unity of his being has first to mature before expressing itself in the sequence of his actions and attitudes. But unity itself, unity of the person, unity of the lived life, has to be emphasized again and again. The confusing contradictions cannot be remedied by the collectives, not one of which knows the taste of genuine unity and which if left to themselves would end up, like the scorpions imprisoned in a box, in the witty fable, by devouring one another. This mass of contradictions can be met and conquered only by the rebirth of personal unity, unity of being, unity of life, unity of action—unity of being, life and action together. This does not mean a static unity of the uniform, but the great dynamic unity of the multiform in which multiformity is formed into unity of character. To-day the great characters are still 'enemies of the people', they who love their society, yet wish not only to preserve it but to raise it to a higher level. To-morrow they will be the architects of a new unity of mankind. It is the longing for personal unity, from which must be born a unity of mankind, which the educator should lay hold of and strengthen in his pupils. Faith in this unity and the will to achieve it is not a 'return' to individualism, but a step beyond all the dividedness of individualism and collectivism. A great and full relation between man and man can only exist between unified and responsible persons. That is why it is much more rarely found in the totalitarian collective than in any historically earlier form of society; much more rarely also in the authoritarian party than in any earlier form of free association. Genuine education of character is genuine education for community.

In a generation which has had this kind of upbringing the desire will also be kindled to behold again the eternal values, to hear again the language of the eternal norm. He who knows inner unity the innermost life of which is mystery, learns to honour the mystery in all its forms. In an understandable reaction against the former domination of a false, fictitious mystery, the present generations are obsessed with the desire to rob life of all its mystery. The fictitious mystery will disappear, the genuine one will rise again. But a generation which honours the mystery in all its forms will no longer be deserted by eternity. Its light seems darkened only because the eye suffers from a cataract; the receiver has been turned off, but the resounding ether has not ceased to vibrate. To-day, however, in the hour of upheaval, the eternal is sifted from the pseudo-eternal. That which flashed into the primal radiance and blurred the primal sound will be extinguished and silenced, for it has failed before the horror of the new confusion and the questioning soul has unmasked its futility. Nothing remains but what rises above the abyss of to-day's monstrous problems, as above every abyss of every time: the wing-beat of the spirit and the creative word. But he who can see and hear out of unity will also behold and discern again what can be beheld and discerned eternally. The educator who helps to bring man back to his own unity will help to put him again face to face with God.

(This Address was originally given in Hebrew, and has been translated from the Author's German by Ronald Gregor Smith.)

W. H. AUDEN

Four Poems

I

IN SICKNESS AND IN HEALTH

(for Maurice and Gwen Mandelbaum)

Dear, all benevolence of fingering lips
That does not ask forgiveness is a noise
  At drunken feasts where Sorrow strips
To serve some glittering generalities:
Now, more than ever, we distinctly hear
The dreadful shuffle of a murderous year
And all our senses roaring as the Black
Dog leaps upon the individual back.

Whose sable genius understands too well
What code of famine can administrate
  Those inarticulate wastes where dwell
Our howling appetites: dear heart, do not
Think lightly to contrive his overthrow;
O promise nothing, nothing, till you know
The kingdom offered by the love-lorn eyes
A land of condors, sick cattle, and dead flies.

And how contagious is its desolation,
What figures of destruction unawares
  Jump out on Love's imagination
And chase away the castles and the bears;
How warped the mirrors where our worlds are made;
What armies burn up honour, and degrade
Our will-to-order into thermal waste;
How much lies smashed that cannot be replaced.

W. H. Auden

O let none say I Love until aware
What huge resources it will take to nurse
   One ruining speck, one tiny hair
That casts a shadow through the universe:
We are the deaf immured within a loud
And foreign language of revolt, a crowd
Of poaching hands and mouths who out of fear
Have learned a safer life than we can bear.

Nature by nature in unnature ends:
Echoing each other like two waterfalls,
   Tristan, Isolde, the great friends,
Make passion out of passion's obstacles;
Deliciously postponing their delight,
Prolong frustration till it lasts all night,
Then perish lest Brangaene's worldly cry
Should sober their cerebral ecstasy.

But, dying, conjure up their opposite,
Don Juan, so terrified of death he hears
   Each moment recommending it,
And knows no argument to counter theirs;
Trapped in their vile affections, he must find
Angels to keep him chaste; a helpless, blind,
Unhappy spook, he haunts the urinals,
Existing solely by their miracles.

That syllogistic nightmare must reject
The disobedient phallus for the sword;
   The lovers of themselves collect,
And Eros is politically adored:
New Machiavellis flying through the air
Express a metaphysical despair,
Murder their last voluptuous sensation,
All passion in one passionate negation.

Four Poems

Beloved, we are always in the wrong,
Handling so clumsily our stupid lives,
    Suffering too little or too long,
Too careful even in our selfish loves:
The decorative manias we obey
Die in grimaces round us every day,
Yet through their tohu-bohu comes a voice
Which utters an absurd command—Rejoice.

Rejoice. What talent for the makeshift thought
A living corpus out of odds and ends?
    What pedagogic patience taught
Pre-occupied and savage elements
To dance into a segregated charm?
Who showed the whirlwind how to be an arm,
And gardened from the wilderness of space
The sensual properties of one dear face?

Rejoice, dear love, in Love's peremptory word;
All chance, all love, all logic, you and I,
    Exist by grace of the Absurd,
And without conscious artifice we die:
O, lest we manufacture in our flesh
The lie of our divinity afresh,
Describe round our chaotic malice now,
The arbitrary circle of a vow.

The scarves, consoles, and fauteuils of the mind
May be composed into a picture still,
    The matter of corrupt mankind
Resistant to the dream that makes it ill,
Not by our choice but our consent: beloved, pray
That Love, to Whom necessity is play,
Do what we must yet cannot do alone
And lay your solitude beside my own.

W. H. Auden

That reason may not force us to commit
That sin of the high-minded, sublimation,
   Which damns the soul by praising it,
Force our desire, O Essence of creation,
To seek Thee always in Thy substances,
Till the performance of those offices
Our bodies, Thine opaque enigmas, do,
Configure Thy transparent justice too.

Lest animal bias should decline our wish
For Thy perfection to identify
   Thee with Thy things, to worship fish,
Or solid apples, or the wavering sky,
Our intellectual motions with Thy light
To such intense vibrations, Love, excite,
That we give forth a quiet none can tell
From that in which the lichens live so well.

That this round O of faithfulness we swear
May never wither to an empty nought
   Nor petrify into a square,
Mere habits of affection freeze our thought
In their inert society, lest we
Mock virtue with its pious parody
And take our love for granted, Love, permit
Temptations always to endanger it.

Lest, blurring with old moonlight of romance
The landscape of our blemishes, we try
   To set up shop on Goodwin Sands,
That we, though lovers, may love soberly,
O Fate, O *Felix Osculum*, to us
Remain nocturnal and mysterious:
Preserve us from presumption and delay;
O hold us to the voluntary way.

Four Poems

II

Jumbled in the common box
Of their dark stupidity,
Orchid, swan, and Caesar lie;
Time that tires of everyone
Has corroded all the locks
Thrown away the key for fun.

In its cleft the torrent mocks
Prophets who in days gone by
Made a profit on each cry,
Persona grata now with none;
And a jackass language shocks
Poets who can only pun.

Silence settles on the clocks;
Nursing mothers point a sly
Index finger at a sky,
Crimson with the setting sun;
In the valley of the fox
Gleams the barrel of a gun.

Once we could have made the docks,
Now it is too late to fly;
Once too often you and I
Did what we should not have done;
Round the rampant rugged rocks
Rude and ragged rascals run.

III

Lady, weeping at the crossroads
Would you meet your love
In the twilight with his greyhounds,
And the hawk on his glove?

Bribe the birds then on the branches,
Bribe them to be dumb,
Stare the hot sun out of heaven
That the night may come.

Starless are the nights of travel,
Bleak the winter wind;
Run with terror all before you
And regret behind.

Run until you hear the ocean's
Everlasting cry;
Deep though it may be and bitter
You must drink it dry.

Wear out patience in the lowest
Dungeons of the sea,
Searching through the stranded shipwrecks
For the golden key.

Push on to the world's end, pay the
Dread guard with a kiss;
Cross the rotten bridge that totters
Over the abyss.

There stands the deserted castle
Ready to explore;
Enter, climb the marble staircase
Open the locked door.

Cross the silent empty ballroom,
Doubt and danger past;
Blow the cobwebs from the mirror
See yourself at last.

Put your hand behind the wainscot,
You have done your part;
Find the penknife there and plunge it
Into your false heart.

IV

CANZONE

When shall we learn, what should be clear as day,
We cannot choose what we are free to love?
Although the mouse we banished yesterday
Is an enraged rhinocerous today,
Our value is more threatened than we know:
Shabby objections to our present day
Go snooping round its outskirts; night and day
Faces, orations, battles, bait our will
As questionable forms and noises will;
Whole phyla of resentments every day
Give status to the wild men of the world
Who rule the absent-minded and this world.

We are created from and with the world
To suffer with and from it day by day:
Whether we meet in a majestic world
Of solid measurements or a dream world
Of swans and gold, we are required to love
All homeless objects that require a world.
Our claim to own our bodies and our world
Is our catastrophe. What can we know
But panic and caprice until we know
Our dreadful appetite demands a world
Whose order, origin, and purpose will
Be fluent satisfaction of our will?

W. H. Auden

Drift, Autumn, drift; fall, colours, where you will:
Bald melancholia minces through the world.
Regret, cold oceans, the lymphatic will
Caught in reflection on the right to will:
While violent dogs excite their dying day
To bacchic fury; snarl, though, as they will,
Their teeth are not a triumph for the will
But utter hesitation. What we love
Ourselves for is our power not to love,
To shrink to nothing or explode at will,
To ruin and remember that we know
What ruins and hyaenas cannot know.

If in this dark now I less often know
That spiral staircase where the haunted will
Hunts for its stolen baggage, who should know
Better than you, beloved, how I know
What gives security to any world,
Or in whose mirror I begin to know
The chaos of the heart as merchants know
Their coins and cities, genius its own day?
In my own person I am forced to know
How much must be forgotten out of love,
How much must be forgiven, even love.

Dear flesh, dear mind, dear spirit, O dear love,
In the depths of myself blind monsters know
Your presence and are angry, dreading Love
That asks its images for more than love;
The hot rampageous horses of my will,
Catching the scent of Heaven, whinny: Love
Gives no excuse to evil done for love,
Neither in you, nor me, nor armies nor the world
Of words and wheels, nor any other world.
Dear fellow-creature, praise our God of Love
That we are so admonished, that no day
Of conscious trial be a wasted day.

Or else we make a scarecrow of the day,
Loose ends and jumble of our common world,
And stuff and nonsense of our own free will;
Or else our changing flesh may never know
There must be sorrow if there can be love.

SEAN O'CASEY

The Raid

An Autobiographical Sketch

THE cold beauty of frost glittered everywhere outside, unseen, unfelt, for the slum was asleep. An uneasy silence echoed over the house, for awake or asleep, everyone knew that death with his comrade, the inflictor of wounds, roamed the darkened streets. Stretched out in a truckle bed in a tenement room, its murky window facing on to the street, Seán thought of the tapestry of the day. He could see the street stretching along outside, its roughly cobbled roadway beset with empty matchboxes, tattered straws, tattered papers, scattered mounds of horsedung, and sprinkled deep with slumbering dust waiting for an idle wind to come and raise it to irritating life again. Lean-looking gaslamps stood at regular intervals on the footpaths, many of them deformed from the play of swinging children, bending over like old men standing to gasp, and wait for a pain in the back to go. The melancholy pathway meandered along by the side of the tall houses, leading everywhere to tarnishing labour, to consumption's cough, to the writhings of fever, to bitter mutterings against life, and frantic calls on St. Anthony, The Little Flower, and Bernadette of Massabielle to be absent helps in time of trouble. Upon this rock I will build my church.

There were the houses, too—a long, lurching row of discontented incurables, smirched with the age-long marks of ague, fevers, cancer, and consumption, the soured tears of little children, and the sighs of disappointed newly-married girls. The doors were scarred with time's spit and anger's hasty knocking; the pillars by their sides were shaky, their stuccoed bloom long since peeled away, and they looked like crutches keeping the trembling doors standing on their palsied feet. The gummy-eyed windows blinked dimly out, laquered by a year's tired dust from the troubled street below. Dirt and disease were the big sacraments here—outward and visible signs of an inward and spiritual disgrace. The people bought the cheapest things in food they could find, to live, to work, to worship: the cheapest spuds, the cheapest tea, the cheapest meat, the cheapest fat, and waited for unsold bread to grow stale that they might buy that cheaper, too. Here they gathered up the fragments so that nothing would be lost. The streets were long haggard corridors of rottenness and ruin. What wonderful mind of memory could link this shrinking wretchedness with the flaunting gorgeousness of silk and satin; with bloom of rose and scent of lavender? A thousand years must have passed since the last lavender lady was carried out feet first from the last surviving one of them. Even the sun shudders now when she touches a roof, for she feels some evil has chilled the glow of her garment. The flower that here once bloomed is dead forever. No wallflower here has crept into a favoured cranny; sight and sign of the primrose were far away; no room here for a dance of daffodils; no swallow twittering under a shady eave; and it was sad to see an odd sparrow seeking a yellow grain from the mocking dust; not even a spiky-headed thistle, purple-mitred, could find a corner here for a sturdy life. No Wordsworth here wandered about as lonely as a cloud.

> The decent dead provoke no blood-congealing fear,
> Like the dread death that lives to fester here.

> Here children, lost to every sense but life,
> Indulge in play that mimics social strife;
> And learn from strenuous practice that they may

> Act well their part at home some future day:
> The girl trains her lungs to scream and shout,
> The boy his arms to knock a wife about.

And yet this riddled horridness had given root to the passion flower. What had been lost was found; what had been dead came to life again. The spirit beneath the coat brocaded, with slender sword quivering, had come into being again; not in brocade, but in rags; not with sword or dainty phrases, elegant in comedy and satire; but with bitter curses, blows as hard as an arm can give, and a rank, savage spit into a master's face. Fought these frantic fools did, led by Larkin and by Connolly; fought till the day star arose in their shivering hearts, the new and glorious light, the red evangel, the light of the knowledge of the glory of God, manifested in the active mind and vital bodies of men and women and little children. And now something stronger than bare hands were in the battle. Many a spear-point-flame from a gun frightened a dark corner or a shadowy street, making armed men in Khaki or Black crouch low in their rushing lorries, firing rapidly back at the street grown shadowy again, or the corner now darker than ever before.

Now the old house was still. Comely Bessie Ballynoy, on her way up, had knocked; but finding Seán in bed, had bid goodnight, and gone. Lazy sleep had crawled in by the dark hallway to soothe restlessness and to hush the clamour from the attic above to the basement below. A lousy sleep, dreary-eyed, in loosely slippered feet, torn and muddy, calling in a shoddy whisper for quietness; creeping in yawning, leaving no-one on watch, though every night now was a perilous night for Dublin. In all the rooms, all the cheap crockery stood quiet on the shelves; the chairs leaned against the shaky walls; rosy-faced fires had all gone pale; the patter of children's feet had long since ceased; only dreams crept slyly in to fill the ugly rooms with sparkling peace for a few dark moments, clothing the sleepers with a cautious splendour; setting them, maybe, to sip rare wines from bulging bottles, or led them to yellow sands bordering a playful sea. A younger lass, perhaps, dreamed of scanty night attire between snowy sheets, with a colour-robed prince by the bedroom door in haste to come in, and bid her a choice goodnight; while the younger men saw themselves, sword in hand, driving the khaki cut-throats out of Eire's five beautiful fields.

Every guardian angel relaxed now, and nodded sleepily by tattered counterpane and ragged sheet, for sin usually curled up like a dog to sleep at their feet, waiting for the tenement to go on again in the morning. So after curfew the silent tenement slept, unconscious even that every whining wail of every passing motor sang a song of death to someone; for in sleep the slimy roof above them had slid aside, and left the stars but a hand's breadth out of reach.

When will the day break in Eirinn; when will her day star arise? How often had he heard these words sung in a languishing voice after an eight-hand reel or a high-cauled cap at *ceilidh* or *sgoruid-beacht!* Well, no day would ever break here, nor would the shadows ever flee away. Seán's eyes were closing, and dimming thoughts swooned faintly from his mind into the humming whine of motor-engines coming quick along the road outside. Up on his elbow he shot as he heard the sound of braking telling him that the lorries were outside of his house, or of those on either side. Then he shot down again to hide as a blinding beam from a searchlight poured through the window, skimming the cream of the darkness out of the room. It silvered the old walls for a few moments, then withdrew like a receding tide to send its beam on another part of the house. Then there was a volley of battering blows on the obstinate wooden door, mingled with the crash of falling glass that told Seán the panels on each side of it had been shattered by hammer or rifle butt. A mad rush of heavy feet went past his door, to spread over the house; for no-one had come from a room to risk sudden death in the dark and draughty hallway.

A raid! All the winsome dreams of the house had vanished; sleep had gone; and children dug arms and legs into the tensing bodies of their mothers.

What were they—the Tommies or the Tans? thought Seán, for the Tommies would not shout so soullessly, nor smash the glass panels so suddenly; they would hammer on the door with a rifle butt, and wait for it to be opened. No; these were the Tans.

He heard the quick pit put pit put of stockinged feet, faint as it was, coming down the stairs, turning left at the bottom of them, and hurrying along the hall towards the back-yard. His ears were so cocked that he heard the soft, silkly pad of the hurrying feet plainly through the storm of blows falling on the street door; then he thought he heard the back door open softly and gently close again.

Who could that be? he thought. Might be any one of the men. Those who didnt take part in ambushes often carried ammunition to those who did; and the dockers and seamen gave a ready hand to the smuggling in of arms. If it wasnt for his own poor sight, he'd probably be doing it himself. All were friendly, save the third and delicate husband of comely Mrs. Ballynoy, who cared for no manner of politics. Someone, anyway, slipping into the back to dodge over the wall into the dark lanes, with fear but without fuss. The Dublin slums at war with the British Empire; all the power of an army, flanked by gangs of ruthless ruffians; all the ordered honour of a regal cabinet and the mighty-moneyed banks fighting the ragged tits of the tenements. An unequal fight, by God, but the slums would win! There goes the door.

A great crash shook the old house and shook the heart of Seán, for well he knew the ordeal that might be in front of him once the light from a Tan's torch smote the darkness of the room. He remembered the two boys brought bound from Dublin Castle to a dump-field on the edge of the city by two Auxie-Tan officers, who set them sitting against an old stone wall, extinguishing each young head under an old bucket picked from a rubbish heap. Then going away forty paces or so, they fired away at the buckets till they were full of holes, leaving what they had done behind them to put the fear of the Tans into the hearts of the surviving I.R.A. men. He thought, too, of Clancy, Clune, and McKee, caught and brought to the Castle, where the Tans interviewed them with the stimulant of bayonets, prodding them gamely till none of the three could sigh any longer, for each at last was dead. Now he could hear neither sound nor murmur—all had gone quiet after the crashing fall of the door. No sound even of a child's protest, though that wasnt surprising, for all of them would be too frightened to squeal till a gun exploded some-where: all was quiet—the sad silence of a sleeping slum. Yet Seán knew that the house must be alive with crawling men, slinking up and down the stairs, hovering outside this door or that one, each with a gun tensed to the last hair, with a ready finger touching the trigger. He guessed that a part of them were the Auxies, the classic members of sibilant and sinister raiders. The Tans alone would make more noise, slamming themselves into a room, shouting to shake off the fear that slashed many of their faces. The Auxies were too proud to show a sign of it. The Tommies would be warm, always hesitant at knocking a woman's room about; they would even be jocular in their funny English way, encouraging the women and even the children to grumble at being taken away from their improper sleep.

All Seán could do was to try to lie dead still, digging down deeper without a sound into the hard mattress of his truckle bed; stifling any desire to steal to the door to listen; to try to modify his breathing till it became unnoticed by himself; for a profound silence might make the Tans disinclined to probe a way in to find out the cause of it; though the Auxies cared nothing for silence, but would lift a corpse from a coffin to search for a gun. He always left his door unlocked now, for past experience had shown him that the slightest obstacle to a swift entrance to a room always irritated them.

From the corner of an eye he could see through the window the searchlight gliding, now up, now down the street, and once for a few moments it blinded him by flooding the room. Then he heard sullen, but loud, thuds of heavy iron falling on heavy wood, coming from the back, and he guessed they were breaking in the entrance to the large shed that was said to be used as a carpenter's shop, and in which Mrs. Ballynoy's husband sometimes worked. Now he heard soft, sly steps going down the hallway to the back. After whomsoever had crept away before they broke down the door. He had climbed the wall, thought Seán, and somewhere—maybe just behind it—crouched silently in the darkest corner of the narrow lane, a revolver tight in his hand, his shoes slung round his neck, so that, if he had to run, no sound of running feet would give an enemy a cue of a direction through which to send a hail of bullets: a bitter night for a pair of bare feet.

Seán could sense the women, and, maybe, the men, praying while the hammering lasted, to cease at once when silence came again, for it wouldnt serve them to let the Auxies hear them trying to talk to God. These silences were the worst: during the hammering one knew where they were; throughout the silences one didnt. Then they might be anywhere; might be opening his very own door snakily, softly, now; some of them might be even in the room, for their black uniforms fitted the darkness they loved, and black juices, smeared over their cheeks and brows, mixed them cosily with the darker shadows of the night. Any moment a brilliant torch might blind his slatted eyes, and a string of shouted questions blast his ear; a pressed-in, cold pistol barrel make a tiny livid rim on his naked chest. He tried to forget thought, making his mind one with the darkness, losing his fear in the vastness of space; but it was no use, for thought never got farther than that the Tans were there, and his mind came back to think of how it would feel to have a bullet burning a swift channel through the middle of his belly.

Azrael, Azrael, gentle, dignified being of spirit, graceful spirit of death, come, and minister unto us, and save us merry, gentlemen!

> Come lovely and soothing death,
> Undulate round the world, serenely arriving,
> Arriving
> In the day, in the night, to all, to each,
> Sooner or later, delicate death.

Ah! Whitman, Walt Whitman, you never knew the Tans! Death doesnt arrive serenely here, his hands are desperate, and neither is delicately formed. Here the angel of death is a biting bitch!

The silence was startled by the sound of a motor-engine warming up, getting ready to go. He heard steps now in the hall, and the sound of bravura jests from a few voices. They were going. They mightnt be, though: they pretended that at times, driving the lorries away a bit, but leaving the men behind, to come with a rush into the house again among foolish people hurrying in their nightclothes out of their rooms to ask questions of each other. Stay still; dont move; not a stir: some of them still might be just beyond the door.

He lay there for what seemed a long time, the sweat of fear damping his body, and making him shiver. Stay still; dont move—someone was beside the door. He heard the handle giving a faint, brassy murmur. Soon, a black-clothed arm would thrust itself within, and a shot might go off that he would never hear. He silently squirmed deeper into the bed, and left the rest to God.

—Eh! he heard the voice of Mrs. Ballynoy whisper from the darkness, Are you there, or did they take you? Are you gone, or are you asleep, or wha'?

—That woman again! he thought resentfully—what a fright she gave me! Awake, Mrs. Ballynoy, he whispered back.

—Well, she said softly, you can take your ayse now, an' sleep tranquil, or get up, an' talk about th' queer things done in a Christian age.

—Wait till I light a candle, he said, making a great creak as he heaved himself out of the bed's hollow.

The Raid

—You'll light no candle while I'm here, young man, said her voice, dressed in a titter, for a slip of an overall's th' only shelter between me and a piercin' look from a young man's eyes; an' it wouldnt be good to go from one exthreme to another on an identical night.

—Did they discover anything? asked Seán.

—Not a thing, though they took two o' th' men away with them. A sudden end to them all, an' a short fall to th' hottest hob that hell can heat! Dont light that candle yet, she added, for minds that have safely passed a danger near them are often reckless in their dealin' with an innocent female; though youre not that kind of a man, I know.

He heard the door softly closing and her hand fumbling with the lock. He hoped she wasnt going to stay. Ah! here's the key, for it's safer to put a locked door between eyes that pry into other people's affairs day an' night, tintin' everything with the colour of their own minds.

—Hadnt you better go back to your room, Mrs. Ballynoy, he warned. You need all the sleep you can get these days. We all do; and someone might be prowlin' round an' see an' think th' worst.

—Ay, she said; bad minds, th' lot o' them—that's why I've locked th' door. An' call me Nellie, for you know me well enough be now. Light th' candle now you can, but leave it on th' far side of where I'll be, for it's only a flimsy apron-overall I have between me an' all harm; and she tittered gaily as Seán very slowly lighted a candle on a box beside his bed.

She was a fine-looking heifer, right enough: long reddish hair coiled up into a bunch that rested neatly on the nape of a white neck; a well-chiselled, pale face, with large grey innocent eyes that seemed to be shrouded in a mist from the valley of the Missabielle; a fine figure set these charms off, and when she slyly waved this sweet figure in front of a man, he no longer saw, or wanted to see, the mist of Missabielle. A rose of Tralee, without the flower's serenity, maybe; but certainly a lovely rose of the tenements. But Seán was in no mood now to enjoy the charm of her fine figure and face. Once let a soul see she had been in his room, and the whole house would be declaring that he was carrying on with Mrs. Ballynoy. He should have had the

31

courage to get up and push her out. He almost wished now that the
Auxies had stayed a little longer.

In the sober light of the candle, he saw that she had just decorated
her delightful body in a pair of brown slippers and a flowered overall
reaching only halfway down her thighs, and showing a wide part of
her white swelling bosom; a show that was very charming, but
damned uncomfortable to one who was determined to take no notice
of it.

—Oh! There y'are, she said, when the candle-light got steady, nice
and snug an' all alone. She came over and sat down on the edge of
the bed beside him. I'm askin' meself why a land, overflowin' with
prayer an' devotion, should be so often plunged into dhread in the
dead o' night for nothin'? An' they tellin' me it's for Ireland's sake.
Them politics'll be the death of us some day. I feel terrible shy in this
get-up, she said, suddenly. Afther washin' the one good nightgown
I have, I was sleepin' in me skin, an' this overall was th' first thing
I laid hands on when the Tans came thundherin' at the door.
Pansies on it, she said, giggling, pulling it a little from her thigh,
pansies for thought! and she poked Seán in the breast, playfully, with
a hand reddened by the soda she used in the washing of clothes.

—Isnt Mr. Ballynoy at home, said Seán, trying to get her mind
away from the overall, while he thought of a way to get rid of
her.

—Didnt I tell you this mornin', on the stairs, that he was on a
counthry job! He would be when the Tans come; though it's little
good he'd be in any emergency, bein' born timid, with a daisy in his
mouth. So I'm a poor lone lassie now, and she gave him another
poke—this time in the thigh.

—Dont you think you ought to get back, he warned; the Tans
might come again.

—Ay, indeed, they might; a body can never know what them
fellas'll do. An' it only a little way from Christmas, too. Ah! she
said, suddenly, looking into a dream distance; it's good to be near
one of your own: th' only two Protestants in th' house, not countin'
me husband. Of the crowd, not countin' him, only two who have
th' proper way o' worshippin', an' are able to foresee th' genuine
meanin' of th' holy text.

—There's me for you, said Seán, thinking neither you nor your husband bothered about religion, one way or another.

—Then youre sadly mistaken. I cant remember a year we missed feelin' the curious chantin' glow in th' air of a Christmas mornin', an' us on our way to church. In a proper mood, an' that was often, I could see what you'd think's th' star ashine on the tip of the spire's top; an' me ears can hear th' dull plod of the three camels' feet in th' deep sand, bearin' th' three kings with th' three rich gifts from Persia, or some other place in th' wilds of a faraway world; an' all th' time an anxious man seekin' shelther for his good woman, with the valleys levelled an th' hills hidden be th' fallin' snow, dyein' her rich dark hair grey with its fallin' flakes, a sly soft carpet for her sandalled feet, an' sore they were from th' sting in its frosty tendherness; while th' tired Joseph thrudged demented behind, wondherin' if they'd find their lodgins only on the cowld, cowld ground. But God was good, an' found the shelther of a stable for the bewildhered, half-perished man, with his thin gown sodden, his toil-marked hands a hot ache, an' his poor feet blue with the bitther penetration of th' clingin' snow; an' afther Joseph had shooed th' puzzled animals to a safe an' ordherly distance, th' little fella was soon snug in a manger on top o' warm heaps of sainfoin, thyme, rosemary, an' lavender.

—Youre wrong there, said Seán, for how in such a bitther season could anyone come on spring and summer plants like those?

—I dunno, she murmured, unless God turned th' hay an' th' sthraw into th' sweet-savourin' herbs. But it's far betther not to thry to go into them things. Are you afraid to look at me, or what? she ejaculated, turning away from her dream; for Seán had turned his head away to escape the charm of the white bosom and soft thighs. As long as you dont make too free, I dont mind, though I feel a little shy in this scarce get-up.

A shoulder-band of the overall had slipped down, and she had saucily drawn an arm out of it altogether so that near half of her body to the waist was bare, and he saw a breast, rather lovely in the light of the candle, looking like a golden cup with a misty ruby in its centre. If he only had her in a shady corner of the Phœnix Park, or in a room of his own in a house where she wasnt known, the world would be well lost for a period of ecstasy. But not here.

—Your husband's a good fellow, he said, trying to keep his mind off her, and would rejoice to see you as you are now. He thinks a lot of you.

—He oughtnt, she said, sarcastically; where'd he get another like me? He means well, poor man, but honest it's pathetic when we're alone, an' he thries to get goin'. Askin' me to tell him when he's hurtin' me! She went into a soft, gay, gurgling laugh, putting a hand over her mouth to quench the merry sound of it. It's funny to talk of it here, but maddenin' when I'm with him. I'm often near worn out thryin' thryin' to coax a little flash of endeavour outa him. He does his best, but the little sting he once had 's'gone with the wind—joy go with it! She now laughed venomously and loud, making Seán fearful of someone hearing her. Wait till I tell you, she went on— you'll die laughin'! You should see Charlie when he's at the he-man business—are you sure you wont get faint, Nellie? Dont forget to say if I'm hurtin' you, dearie! One night, when he was—you know —I jerked him clean outa th' bed on to th' floor—th' bump shook th' house! D'ye know, honest t'God, he just lay stunned there. Put th' heart across me. Ever afther, d'ye know, I've had to handle him like a delicate piece of china! No; poor Charlie's style's too shy for me. Not like Jim Achree's. J'ever hear 'o his?

She slid down till she was half lying over him, and sang sedulously beside his ear:

> Jim Achree's style has a wondherful way with it,
> All th' girls' minds are in sad disarray with it;
> Whenever they venture to have a short play with it,
> Good girls want to stay with it, ever an' aye.
>
> Oh! Jimmy Achree, shure your style is your own,
> Amazin' th' way it has flourished an' grown,
> With lovely threats shakin', tense with mischief makin',
> Knockin' poor women flat in a gorgeous cyclone!

—Looka, she said, breathlessly, th' least bit o' fondlin' now, an' I'd swoon away, helpless an' benighted.

—In the midst of death we are in life, thought Seán. He tried to turn his head away so that he wouldnt be prompted by the white breast that was like a golden cup with a misty ruby in its centre; but

34

his head refused to stir. Instead, he found his hand was sliding over her fair bosom. He felt her arm pushing a way under his head till it was firmly round his neck, while the other pushed the clothes from covering him. He was lost, unless he yelled for help, and that he couldnt do.

—Youre a good young man, he heard her whispering, an' would never take advantage of a woman alone in your room in th' dead o' night, with but a loose slip between you an' a swift lie-down on a bed o' meadow-sweet. Dont sthruggle, man, or you'll upset things! Why'r you thryin' to keep me from gettin' th' clothes down? Youve far too many on you; a little cool air'll do you good. Take th' good things while theyre goin'. She whipped the clothes down with a fierce jerk, and lying beside him, pressed her mouth to his. Her big innocent eyes looked frantic now.

—G'won, she muttered, panting, be as rough as you like with me —it's what I'm longin' for for weeks! And half mad himself, now, he gripped her like a vice, and sank his fingers into her flesh.

Then they suddenly went still as death, listening; listening to the whine of a motor-engine cruising down the road outside. Then another whine followed that, and another the last, till they mingled into one shrill, threatening whine that went echoing round the walls of the old house.

—Out in strength tonight, thought Seán; more'n three of them; each of them crooning a song of death to someone. Ireland's modern, senseless Tanshee!

Suddenly the shrill whine lifted into a shrill, quavering scream, the scream fading into the throb throb of active engines as the lorries stopped outside, or very near, the house.

—They've stopped at this house, or th' next one! said Nellie, loosening her arm from around his neck, and sliding swift from the bed to the door. Who' ha' thought th' basterds would bother to come twice th' same night? Christ! It's this house theyre makin' for! And swiftly came a great hammering on the door again. Nellie frantically twisted and turned at the key, but she couldnt get the door of the room open.

—In they'll come, she squealed softly, an' I'll be exposed to th' world as a fast woman. She tugged and writhed till the slip fell from her shoulders, leaving her naked, fuming, at the door. You it was, she half shouted, turning a red and bitter face towards Seán, that lured me into this predicament, never able to let any decent woman pass without thryin' to meddle her!

Seán as eager as she was herself that she should go unseen, leaped out of bed, hurried over, and with a hard twist, turned the key. Snatching up her flowered overall, she whipped the door open, rushed out, and up the stairs, without another word. Shutting the door again, he fled back to bed, digging himself down deep into it once again, listening to hear if it was Tan or Tommy who had entered the house. The door spun open, and a torchlight shot terror into his eyes. Silently he waited for a blow or a shot, but neither came. He opened his eyes, and saw a young khaki-clad officer just inside the door, a torch in one hand, a revolver in the other. Behind him were two soldiers with rifles at the ready. The officer stared at Seán, then slowly returned the gun to a holster, and the soldiers, at this sign, stood at ease, and rested the butts of the rifles on the dirty floor.

—Get up; dress; go out to the street, said the officer, tersely; this house has to be searched room by room. Dont try to go farther than the wire cordon ringing the district: orders are to fire on any who do. He watched Seán dressing, and when he saw him clap a cap on his head, asked, Havent you an overcoat?

—A sort of a one, said Seán.

—Better than nothing; you'd better put it on—it's damned cold outside.

—Decent man, thought Seán, putting on his old coat; has an occasional thought for others. Thank God, the Tans are absent!

He went out into the dark hall, and near bumped into a Tan standing there, fingering a heavy revolver. A cold shiver trickled down his spine.

—Where are you going? he asked.

—Outside to street—officer's orders, said Seán.

—What officer? asked the Tan.

—Military officer, sir.

—Oh! Military officer, eh? Well, we give the orders here—understand?

The Raid

—Yessir, said Seán, promptly.

—Are you a Sinn Feiner? he questioned, twisting the gun in his hand.

—A Sinn Feiner? Me? No fear.

—You were one, then.

—No; never, said Seán, emphatically. Thank God, thought Seán, he didnt ask if I had ever been a Republican. The ignorant English bastard doesnt know the difference.

—Well, you're an Irishman, anyway—you cant deny that!

—No, sir, I cant deny that: I'm an Irishman, right enough.

—Well, shout To Hell with Ireland, and you can go—no mutter, but a shout the house can hear. Now!

But Seán fell silent. God damn him, if he'd do that! He knew his face was white; he felt his legs tremble; but he fell silent, with a stubborn look on his face.

—Go on, you Sinn Fein rat, shout it!

A streak of light fell on them, and Seán saw the young officer coming to them. He stopped, looked at Seán, then looked at the Tan.

—What's wrong here? he asked. Let that man go into the street.

—You mind your own damned business, snarled the Tan.

—I am minding it, said the young officer. I happen to be an Irishman, too. Have you any objection to it?

—I dont take orders from you! said the Tan, roughly.

—I'm not sorry for that, the officer said; but this man does—didnt I give you an order to go into the street? he asked, turning to Seán.

—Yessir.

—Carry it out, then, he said sharply; and Seán, turning swiftly, made a quick march through the hall, out by the door, into the street.

It was very cold, and from the timid gleams from a waning moon, Seán saw that path and road were white with a covering of rich rime frost. Groups of people were standing, huddled up against the railings of the houses, while more were oozing sleepily out of the remaining ones, shepherded into bunches by armed soldiers. The women were trying to coax warmth into their tearful and shivering children by wrapping flimsy rags round their shoulders, and tucking the little

ones into their arms. Several searchlights wandered through the
street, flashing over the groups of people, or tinselling along the walls
of the houses. At one end stood an armoured car, the lids raised,
showing the heads of several Tommies who were quietly chanting
an advice to the shivering people to pack up their troubles in their
old kit-bags. Along the road, over the calm, quiet chastity of the
white frost, slid a diamond-shaped tank, looking like a dirty yellow
crawling slug, machine-guns sticking out from slits, like ugly pro-
truding eyes staring at the cowering people.

He saw a commotion round the door of the house he lived in. He
mooched over till he was beside the steps to look over the shoulders
of a rank of soldiers. A prisoner! Who could it be? He whisperingly
asked the soldier in front of him what had happened.

—An awrsenal! whispered the soldier hoarsely. Rear of th' 'ouse
an awrsenal discovered! 'nough gelignite to blow up 'ole nighbour-
hood. A blighter there drew a gun, but was shot through hand afore
'ee could pull trigger. 'Ere's the bawstard coming!

Amid a group of soldiers with rifles at the ready, marched a thin
forlorn figure, but the lips in the pale face were tight together, and the
small head was held high. Peering closer, Seán saw that handcuffs
kept the two small hands locked together; and that from one of
them red blobs were dripping to the white frost on the path, leaving
little spots behind like crimson berries that had fallen on to snow. In
the hall, he heard the voice of Nellie shouting.

—That's me husband! he heard her shout; a good man an' a brave
one! Yous'll never shoot the life outa Ireland, yous gang o' armed
ruffians! Here, take me, too, if yous arent afraid. Keep your pecker
up, Charlie—Ireland's with you!

Seán peered closer. Good God—the prisoner was the timid, in-
significant Charlie Ballynoy who took no interest in politics! A
lorry full of soldiers swirled into the kerb. The handcuffed prisoner
was pushed and lifted into it. Standing there in the middle of the
soldiers, with the searchlight covering him with glory, he held up his
iron-locked hands from which clouts of blood still dripped.

—Up th' Republic! he shouted with the full force of his voice.

The lorry drove off, and the red specks in the rime turned brown
and lonely. Heads that had lifted, bent again, and all was quiet once

more. A bleak dawn at last began to peel the deeper darkness from the sky, and the scene crept into a ghostly glamour, brightened by the pale faces of the waiting people, the pale moon sinking deeper into a surly sky, and the rimy frost on pathway, road, and roof grew whiter. Dirty-yellow clad figures moved into the whiteness from one dark doorway to move out of it again into another blacker still, while the brown, slug-like tank crept up and down the road, charring the dainty rime with its grinding treads—the new leviathan that God could ne'er control.

GRAHAM GREENE
Convoy to West Africa

T HESE extracts from a journal kept in December and January 1941-2 if they are of any interest at all are of interest as an indication of the kind of raw material a novelist stores. He goes through life discarding far more than he retains: he may never use what he retains: but the points he notes are what he considers of interest at the moment of occurrence. The journal was not kept for publication.

9 December 1941

Breakfast in the Adelphi—the huge solid overgrown pub: the sense of comfort and security and being on dry land. Then a taxi-drive through battered streets to the dock, tearing up letters which hadn't been sealed by the censor and scattering them through the window. Empty Sabbath-like wastes with nobody about to ask the way. The difficulty of finding something as large as a ship. At last the ship—a small 5,000-ton oil-driven cargo ship, one of the newest of the Elder Dempsters, with neat bright little single-berth cabins and only twelve passengers. Three R.N.V.R. officers (one had only been twice at sea in his life as far as Hamburg): some Fleet Air Arm petty officers; an elderly American civilian called X, a great authority on Byzantine art and a vegetarian: two oilmen: an odd foreigner with very little English, a great square head and the strangest square plus-fours. About 2.30 we start. A last look at England in Mersey mist, but then the positively last appearance doesn't come off: we anchor in the Mersey. After tea boat drill—the rather boisterous occasion which used to turn up once on every voyage: this time a serious rehearsal. Nobody enjoys it much. All day two rafts are suspended on a slope each side of the ship ready to be cut loose: one hold contains rubber rafts. On the poop the anti-aircraft men in khaki and any old sweater keep watch round the Bofors gun.

After dinner one of the R.N.V.R. officers, middle-aged with a Glasgow accent, tries heartily to pull us together. We 'volunteer' for submarine and machine-gun watches.

We are making for Belfast to-morrow and the odd foreigner is a Dutchman—one collects scraps of information, just as in the old days on the first evening of a cruise. One establishes a home with the scraps. . . . The second officer has been twice blown up.

I unpack my books and then pack them up again after looking at the new covers. I talk to Sparks. He has been away from the sea for ten years in a radio business of his own. He has returned unenthusiastically to escape the army. Everybody in the ship from the captain to the kitchen hands seem new to her. They wander round finding their way about like the passengers.

Began reading *The Mask of Dimitrios*, by Eric Ambler. Visiting a stranger's flat one always looks at the bookcases. X has on board Rowse's *Tudor Cornwall, Grey Eminence*, Laurence Binyon's poems. F., the young R.N.V.R. officer who seems likely to prove my drinking companion, has brought *The Pickwick Papers*. There is a tiny library in the smoking-room but it isn't open yet.

'We'll get properly organized,' the Glasgow man says, 'to-morrow.'

To-night one will sleep safely quiet in the Mersey.

10 December

We leave after breakfast. Passengers are to do three four-hour watches during the day: two men on machine-guns above the boat deck for aircraft, and two below the bridge for submarines. The Glasgow man is head of my watch. One climbs a short vertical steel ladder into a kind of conning tower containing each a gun with steel shield. A sailor shows us how to tilt the gun and fire: he is one of the few who were in this ship last trip. Two ships were torpedoed the first night out from the Mersey, but the passengers' watches had only continued two days. The submarine watchers had watched from the bridge, but they had got so drunk the captain had refused to allow them there again. Little fear of that this time—we are a very sober, sedate company. The siren keeps on blowing—rather disturbing as one must count the blasts—seven short and a long for boat stations.

41

A cold grey day: the sea getting up: soldiers in Balaclavas by the Bofors: a black steward making water in the bilge.

Two hours watch, and half an hour as well relieving the previous watch for lunch. Then an hour on submarine watch—bitter cold especially to port. Even a bird can look like a periscope. At dinner the Chief told us that in weather like this it was easy for a submarine to follow a ship unobserved during the day above water and submerge at night for the attack. Two ships in which he had served had been torpedoed after he had left them. One hopes that his luck will hold. Never more than five days leave between voyages.

An hour with the machine-gun—a little less cold up there. The steel shields like the wings of black angels. Past the Isle of Man, and a plane in the sky, presumably one of ours. News on the wireless of the sinking by the Japs of the *Prince of Wales* and the *Repulse*.

It's odd how on submarine duty one thinks only of that danger and on machine-gun duty only of the air. Perched up above the deck one hears the wind in the wires like choral singing from inside a church.

Felt seasick at tea and lay down till dinner. In the bitter cold of the bows recited Hail Marys to distract myself. Over and over again one forgets that this is war, looking forward to the south and the warm weather, then the sense of danger comes back like nausea. I wear a vest at night, only partly for the sake of warmth. About midnight the siren woke me. I counted seven short blasts and in the hurry of getting out of bed I didn't notice the fact that there was no long blast. Wondered bemusedly what to put on first. Then the quiet made me hesitate and think. My next-door neighbour was less cautious. I saw a Fleet Air Arm uniform flash past the door, and then I saw him return slowly. We are all new boys who don't know the customs. It was only the approach to Belfast. After a day at sea the curious effect of voices shouting *outside* the ship: the odd casualness of 'Do you want a pilot?'

11 December

Lying in the lough outside Belfast.

The Fleet Air Arm warrant officers cling together: they are distinguished from officers by the extravagant cleanness of their shirts and collars: they wear gloves all day.

Convoy to West Africa

Books for a desert island—this is what I have brought with me for the Coast. Short notice prevented me getting Gibbon and *Anna Karenina*.

Short Stories of De Maupassant
The Old Testament (in the World's Classics)
The New Testament and *Acts* (in the World's Classics)
Father and Son, by Edmund Gosse
The Mask of Dimitrios, by Ambler
Wanderings in South America, by Waterton
The Knapsack, Herbert Read's anthology
Oxford Book of Seventeenth Century Verse
Selected Poems of Rilke
Selected Poems of Wordsworth
Golden Treasury
Broadway Book of English Verse
Penguin Selection of Browning
Blackwell's one-volume Shakespeare
Kindness in a Corner, by T. F. Powys
Life of Tolstoy, by Aylmer Maude
North and South, by Mrs. Gaskell
Haydon's *Autobiography*
and a number of Trollope's—*The Duke's Children, Can You Forgive Her?, Ayala's Angel, Ralph the Heir, The American Ambassador, Sir Harry Hotspur*, and *Miss Mackenzie*.

So far in spite of nausea and watches I have kept up an average of 500 words a day on 'British Dramatists'.

All day hove to in the lough. The Dutchman turns out to be a Pole born in Georgia who fought in the Russian army during the last war: a Mahomedan. He explains something with a map to the American X: the square monolithic face becomes suddenly kindly because at last he can communicate in his own language. X seems to know all languages. An elderly man with an old maid's face and feminine wrinkles and steel spectacles and an extraordinary gentleness and kindness of manner. He has a flat in London and a house in Massachusetts where he was born which belonged to his great grandfather. He also has a *pied-à-terre* in Istanbul. At six listened to the wireless in the steward's cabin. Germany's declaration of war on America. X gently and courteously pleased. 'We are allies now.'

The ship's library open. Read Hanley's *The Ocean*—an open boat story. It seemed unreal. No mention of the Cold.

Found an old acquaintance in the purser, who had been in the *David Livingstone* when I went to Liberia years go.

Books in the chief steward's cabin included a Dunsany, Silone's *Fontamara* and Mottram's *Spanish Farm*.

12 December

Into Belfast. Little white lighthouses on stilts: a buoy that seems to have a table tied to it: a sunken ship right up in the dock. Cranes like skeleton foliage in a steely winter. The flicker of green flame in the bellies of building ships. Hundreds of dockyard workers stop altogether to see one small ship come in.

Endless impatient waiting for the immigration officer to come on board. Why the anxiety to get ashore in so dull a place? It is the cruise spirit perhaps. I thought it just as well to go to Confession before the Atlantic. The hideous Catholic church difficult to find in Protestant Belfast. At the Presbytery a towsled housekeeper tried to send me away when I asked for a confession. 'This is no time for confession,' trying to shut the door in my face. The dreadful parlour hung with pious pictures as unlived in as a dentist's waiting-room, and then the quite nice young priest who called me 'son' and whose understanding was of the simplest. In the same street the pious repository selling Woodbines from under the counter to old women.

In the evening a dozen and a half Galway oysters and a pint and a half of draught Guinness at the Globe. Then back to the ship. X had lunched with the Consul-General. 'The last time I saw him,' he said gently, 'was on the military road they were building in Georgia to Tiflis.'

'Glasgow' turns out to be the drunk one traditionally has on board every West Coast boat. He had been on shore to see the dentist and he showed us two gaps where teeth had been drawn. 'When the captain heard that,' said the chief steward, 'he said "I've never heard that one before. Soap and matches is what the sailors say when they want to go ashore for a woman."'

'Glasgow' with his little hooked bird's nose and his sudden tipsy release of mental activity was like a minor prophet. You felt he was the chief character in a play like *Outward Bound*, the chorus who warns the audience that the ship is doomed. 'Well, gentlemen,' he had us all penned in the small smoking room, 'we're going to be together for five or six weeks, and there's going to be a wonderful interchange of mind. I've been looking forward to this, the wonderful discussions we'll have. We've come into this ship all thinking different things, but when we go out of that door we'll all think the same. Discussions—I don't like argument. Discussions. Political discussions. I'm not interested in what *you* think: I'm interested in what I think. We'll knit it all up together. This is a wonderful experience. It will be the most wonderful experience of my life, the deepest experience. I'll impose on you all what I think. I won't disguise it from you, gentlemen, I'm a drinker. I buried my wife last August and since then poor old Joe's had nothing to do but get drunk. A clean break. I look forward, gentlemen, to the wonderful discussions we'll have. I'll learn—it's the only thing worth doing, learning. I shan't learn a lot: I shall learn a little bit. But somebody said a book is worth reading if you only learn from one sentence. I couldn't remember these quotations if I wasn't drunk.' The unwinking gentle courtesy of X as this went on. Glasgow has certainly succeeded in transforming the dead sobriety of the ship since the first day. It is more like the old *David Livingstone*.

The chief steward gave advice. Always leave one's door hooked ajar. After leaving Belfast always sleep in trousers, shirt and pullover: you don't bother to dress properly in an emergency with the lights out. He prefers a submarine attack to a plane: usually more time to abandon ship. He was torpedoed his last trip and they had three-quarters of an hour. Only one man killed in the engine room.

The Pole argued about religion when 'Glasgow' had staggered to bed. 'I am Mussulman.' He demonstrated with glasses. 'This one is negro, this is Catholic, this is Protestant, this is Mussulman. All same God.' His objection to English draughts (at which he is beaten) as compared with Continental. 'It is not strong. No strategy.' He abandons the game in despair.

45

We leave Belfast. Again the showers of sparks from the oxy-acetylene welders and the blue and green lights of the electric welders. The open hull of an aircraft carrier lights up like a toy stage as a welder gets to work and a tiny figure can be seen against the confused background of steel—then darkness again and then again the green light and the tiny figure.

We lie all day in the lough. The captain goes off in a launch for orders. Rumour that we shall be here three days. Perhaps a dozen cargo ships smaller than ours lie around, a destroyer, a merchant cruiser with a plane on board painted blue and white, and a beautiful windy little corvette hung with bunting like a Picasso water-colour which steams round the ships in the late afternoon as though to take a look at her charges. An impression that departure is near.

At 4.30 p.m. boat drill. Distribution of small red-globed electric torches which clip on the shoulder and help one to be observed in the water.

After dinner 'Glasgow' comes into the smoking room drunk again. He had his wish and involved us all in argument by dropping the statement: 'Winston. I've got no use for him. A political adventurer. Tell me one success he's had.' I think old X was shocked—perhaps more shocked by the equanimity of the other passengers. Before 'Glasgow' arrived he had been dropping gentle and random remarks—the best restaurant in Cairo: how they make coffee in the Caucasus: a sweet scented night flower in India: sitting there in a disreputable old soft hat and a scarf twisted round the neck (the scarf I think came from Albania). 'Glasgow' began to argue hotly in favour of dictatorship against democracy, and suddenly X dropped softly, 'I have a letter Abraham Lincoln wrote to my grandfather. My grandfather was angry with him for not passing quickly an anti-slavery law. Lincoln's last sentence was——' X's voice became a soft poetic croon: '"The people must decide or how are we greater than kings?"'

The fourth engineer has skipped the ship and will presumably try to get across to Eire. He was ten pounds in the company's debt and couldn't get a drink till it was paid off. How oddly dramatic ships

Convoy to West Africa

are. My last voyage—in a German ship from Vera Cruz—the cook committed suicide rather than return home. That was in 1938. The ships around us are not part of the convoy. To-morrow morning we start for the rendezvous, but if there's a fog we may miss it and have to wait weeks for another.

14 December

A rough day between 9 and 4 and a little before tea I was sick. Unable to write. We leave the lough and join a line of about seven ships. Submarine watch 9 to 10.15: with the machine-gun 10.15 to 11.30, and then after a rather scanty lunch relieved someone at the gun from 1 to 1.30. The last watch high wind and icy sleet. Couldn't get warm afterwards. Lay down. By teatime we were in calmer water coming up by Bute towards Greenock, presumably to meet the rest of the convoy. Bright brown heather on one side and a wild sunset blazing up behind the hills on the other. Sunset reflected on the seagulls' wings. We drop anchor and wait. Manage to do a little work on 'British Dramatists'. Anyway one more night in safety and pyjamas. Happidrome is blazing out from the radio in the steward's cabin: shouts of comedians and blares of mechanical laughter. Left again at midnight. Read *Herr Witch Doctor*, by Sarah Gertrude Millin.

15 and 16 December

Rough both days. Making no more than 4 knots against a head-wind going south-west. Sick both days. During the afternoon watch on Tuesday, a plane came low over the convoy, and another ship fired a machine-gun at it. It was one of our planes, but the gunner was technically correct. Our planes are not allowed to fly directly over a convoy. No writing either day. Old X has brought a supply of Ovaltine with him and has it last thing at night.

18 December

Stormy again after one fine day. Party began in the chief steward's room at 10 a.m. and continued till I went on duty at 12.30. The second engineer played the piano, the purser tried to sing and the second steward served what he called 3d. cocktails—rum and milk—giving a dramatic recitation in a tin hat.

47

After lunch quiet reigned and old X talked gently of Henry James and his brother William, and the box he had shared with Henry and the Ranee of Sarawak at the disastrous first night of *Guy Domville*. The submarine watch has been abolished as we are on the inside of the convoy.

The chief steward tells me he is nervous at night: this is his first trip after being torpedoed and his cabin looks exactly like the previous one. The second steward, who is a little cracked, has been torpedoed three times, but the gipsy told him he wouldn't be torpedoed a fourth. X tells an anecdote of Gertrude Stein who was asked at a lecture why it was that she answered questions so clearly and wrote so obscurely. 'If Keats was asked a question would you expect him to reply with the Ode to a Grecian Urn?'

19 December

The second steward—the cracked one—was a prisoner for two years in the last war—according to him in Siberia. I don't know how this works out. He explains his paunch by it. 'I hate them,' he says, blocking the way in his white jacket, 'I'd kill a German child that high. I'd kill a German woman who was pregnant with one. If I'm alive you'll hear of me after the war in Lord Beaverbrook's papers. I might have gone into Parliament after the last war if I'd chosen. And if I die, I've left a letter for my two daughters—they'll carry on. There'll be two rebels in England if they try to let them off this time.'

'Don't talk of dying.'

'I'll never die. I live by prayer. I pray at sunrise and sunset like a Mahommedan.' (He is a Catholic.)

All the time he and the chief steward are immensely stirred and excited by the idea of Christmas.

The second waylays the passengers and tries with bulky importance to arrange a Christmas entertainment. Huge plans are discussed and disappear again: the drink gamble (everybody to put in £2 and drink as much as they like), a treasure hunt for a bottle of whisky. Crowded meetings in the steward's cabin.

To-day for an hour or two it was sunny and even warm, but now we've begun to roll again and the weather has clouded. Last night we were supposed to be about the latitude of Newcastle—ten days after going on board.

At night 'Glasgow' drunk and boring. 'I am drunk all the time. Drunk at breakfast. I've got a bottle of rum in my cabin. I'm drunk and proud of it. I hate criticism. Why shouldn't I be drunk? It feels good to be drunk and it sharpens the intellect.' The Fleet Air Arm warrant officers watch him disapprovingly, wearing gloves.

20 December

Rough again. Eleven days since we started and it's doubtful whether we are yet the latitude of Land's End.

Explosion in one ship at about 6 a.m. and a warning bell to the crew. Rumour now says we are parallel to Brest. A heavy swell, and on the last watch thick mist coming up.

21 December

Early watch with heavy mist—visibility about 100 yards and ships' sirens all blowing different tones. About 8.15 the mist rose, and there we all still were in our exact places, chugging slowly on. A destroyer dropped depth charges while we were at breakfast and later raced by towards the head of the convoy. For the first time we sat out all the morning drinking gin and vermouth. Apparently we carry a cargo of T.N.T. as well as aeroplanes. The passengers become nervously humorous on the subject. By the evening we had altered course again to the west. Shall we never go south? A notice has been posted that we will not be served meals without lifebelts which we must take everywhere. Shared a bottle of 1929 Beaune (5s.). There is a little pre-war store of wine on board. Claret at 3s. 6d. and champagne at 21s.

22 December

Colder again but about 8 we turned south and after lunch some of the convoy turned off over the south-western horizon. We missed their presence.

The gunlayer who was in the Post Office shivering in his jersey: sad brown eyes: one of the only two naval men in the crew. He complained of the impossibility of getting covers for his guns which rust in the salt damp. The Elder Dempster offices, he said, full of young women making tea: 'they all seem to have plenty of tea and sugar.' Note how on a ship all the time people seem to be tying up things with string, balanced in reckless positions.

Finished *Parents and Children*, by Compton-Burnett, disposed of Congreve in 'British Dramatists', played three games of chess with the Pole, winning one.

23 December

Drank with the chief steward. He feels very jittery at night. Hasn't yet gone to bed but lies on his couch. The cargo of depth charges and T.N.T. under his cabin.

Legend of foreign ships in convoys which deliberately show lights to help the enemy. When this happens the Commodore appoints a rendezvous, and the convoy scatters. The foreign ship finds itself arrive alone at the rendezvous: the rest of the convoy has taken a different course. For the first time in the afternoon real warm sun and blue sea. Played chess with the Pole. It is not to be avoided. If I lie down in the afternoon he pokes his shaven Mongolian head through the cabin door and says 'Check?' During the game he sings all the time to himself, 'Good. Very good. It is very good,' and tries to take back his pieces. I won one game in four.

24 December

Warmer and sunnier. Passing between the Azores in sight of land. A party again with the steward, the purser and 'Glasgow' before lunch. The steward demonstrates how to test a French letter. Keeping the watch now from deck chairs.

Started the evening with a half-bottle of champagne. Then Beaune for dinner followed by port and brandy. Then down to the stewards to help with Christmas decorations, developing into a party that only finished at 2.30 a.m. French letters blown up the size of balloons and hung over the captain's chair. The black steward Daniel stood on his hands and put his feet round his neck. The Fleet Air Arm sang 'Danny Boy', 'When Irish Eyes are Smiling', 'Widdecombe Fair' and the like. The cracked second steward became boring with over-repeated turns: we had heard so often already the poem in praise of the Merchant Service written by his daughter and recited for no apparent reason in a steel helmet. The chief steward put on a cloth cap and gave a dramatic recitation about a lamplighter. Then Cookie in his dirty white singlet and dirty white apron, thin consumptive fanatical face with long razor nose and three days' beard. He sang a magnificent anonymous ballad on the sinking of the Elder Dempster liner *Vestris* to a melancholy tune. He copied it out for me afterwards and this is how it went.

THE SINKING OF THE S.S. VESTRIS

Proudly she sailed from New York City,
Bound for a land O'er the Sea,
And on her decks the wives and husbands,
Children with hearts gay and free.

She sailed on her way o'er the deep blue Ocean,
With never a thought or a fear,
But there on the Bridge stood Captain Carey,
A Sailor for many a year.

Then came the storm that hit the *Vestris*,
Wild waves were roaring high,
And there in her side a hole was poundered,
Then they knew that death was nigh.

Great was the toll of life that was taken,
Husbands and Wives torn apart,
Many a home with loved ones missing,
Many a sad broken heart.

There on the Bridge stood Captain Carey,
Hoping his Ship he could save,
But too late he sent a message,
The *Vestris* was doomed to her grave.

Sad were the cries of Men and Women,
Mothers with babes held so tight,
Brave men who fought to save their loved ones,
Lifeboats that sank in the night.

There on the deck stood a grey-haired Captain,
Waiting for death to befall,
Yet we know that someone blundered,
He must forgive after all.

We are all adrift on life's mighty Ocean,
Where each mistake has its cost,
And we must learn from this sad story,
He who hesitates is lost.

25 December

Christmas Day started at 11 in the morning with a bottle of champagne to cure the hangover. Round-the-Empire broadcast and the King's rather lugubrious speech at lunch. Dinner with a huge menu. Hors d'œuvre, soup, fried whiting, tinned asparagus, roast turkey and chipolatas, plum pudding, grape fruit ice. It was like peace. Toasts to the King, Churchill, Roosevelt (for X), Sikorski (for the Pole), etc. Then the captain, the mate and the chief came to the smoking-room. A shy R.N.V.R. officer tried to play hymns (the only tunes he knew), but the atmosphere by that time was not propitious. Played Sing, Say or Pay. Broke up traditionally at midnight with Auld Lang Syne, and afterwards I settled down to chess with the Pole. One was less homesick than one had expected. Presumably that was the drink. Woke up at about 5 in the morning with an explosion: I thought that one of the convoy had caught it, but it must have been the clap of the wind as we changed course.

26 December

Nothing to record but a slight somnolence. Even the convoy seemed a bit jaded. More rusty than ever and no bunting.

27 December

The chief steward depressed. On his last voyage he was torpedoed just about here—nine days from Freetown. They lost seven ships in three nights—his ship was the last to go. One had forgotten there is such a thing as a straits in the Atlantic, but between Dakar and Freetown the coast juts out to meet the Brazilian bulge, and that

Atlantic channel is the happy hunting ground for submarines. Naturally every sailor is convinced that the submarines are using the port of Dakar whatever the politicians say.

It is warmer and sunnier. Reading Huxley's *Grey Eminence* with unexpected pleasure.

Third boat drill this evening. Afterwards few people seemed to be about the deck though the evening was balmy. I don't know whether the tension is in my own mind alone, or among all the passengers.

28 December

My daughter's birthday. Drank champagne in her honour before lunch and split two bottles of claret at night. Party in chief steward's cabin afterwards. I feel now as if I'm just coming out from under an anæsthetic, and I feel scared of the loneliness I shall feel when I leave the ship. Have given up drinking gin—it's too depressing.

29 December

The heat is really being turned on now. Went very slow all day—presumably to keep a rendezvous. Nightmare at night of the traditional kind—being trapped in darkness.

30 December

The commodore's ship breaks down and one escort ship remains behind with her. Rumour says we are about opposite Dakar.

Very hot in the afternoon. Read on deck. Agatha Christie's *Evil under the Sun* and Rilke. It was like a lazy day on a peacetime cruise. Over and over again one began to think as though it were peace and this a holiday, and then one would remember that an explosion might come at any minute. Party before lunch and before dinner in the steward's cabin. The usual West Coast tales are starting up like plants in the heat. How one remembers them from eight years back. The doctor who cuts a tumour off a black girl's breast and tosses it to her waiting relatives. 'Here's a dash.' The black crew are partly paid in rice—so many tobacco tins a day. They insist on the tobacco tin as a measure, not realizing that it only needs a little pressure by the thumb on the bottom of the tin to reduce their ration by a tiny amount on each tin.

53

The flushed constipated Fleet Air Arm warrant officer mooning around the deck with a mournful overcharged air but still wearing gloves. 'Sometimes I've been 17 days,' he says.

31 December

Apparently at 10 last night excitement was caused by the sight of either an island or a ship blazing with lights on the horizon. Light in our blacked-out progress is like something from Jules Verne. It turns out to have been a Spanish or Portuguese liner—the first out-of-door lights we have seen since leaving land.

The commodore's ship overtakes us soon after breakfast, and then the first sign of land, the coast appears—not a seabird but a Sunderland flying boat taking a look round for submarines. We feel very cheerful when we see it, as though up to now we had been lost on the empty sea.

Last night a nightmare again. A friend accidentally draws a breadknife across his throat and cuts it. He lifts up the flap of flesh to see how serious it is. Taking him to hospital I see a woman in a car knock down a small boy of my son's age at the kerb and she then walks on him accidentally. The skin is wrinkled up exposing the red raw apple cheek.

The convoy changes direction sharply and for a moment it looks as though we were going on alone. A very lonely feeling.

New Year's Eve drunk party. The cook brings in his jazz band, playing with ladles and cooking pots. Daniel the black steward dances in the passage and twists his legs round his neck. The steward falls down in the galley during a wrestling match and cuts his head open. Fish and chip supper. Broke up at 2.30 a.m.

1 January

The Pole discusses with gleaming eye the advantage of having three wives. 'One wife, she rule. Three, I am king.'

2 January

Seaplane with us all day. The convoy divides. Some ships with railway engines on the decks make for the Cape. Eleven of us are left with escorts.

A very hot night brings back the subject of polygamy. Somebody asks the Pole, 'How would you manage with your three wives on a night like this?'

'Ah, you think European passion. *Passion Orientale* not like that. There is grass, fountain. Big bed in the garden.'

Apparently about 11 p.m. a submarine was detected 60 miles off. Another rumour is that four days ago we were followed for some time.

3 January

Another large convoy of big ships hull down ahead of us—perhaps transports.

Very hot. About 10 a.m. in the mist and heat the hills behind Freetown. Before noon we had entered the boom. The great bay crowded with shipping. The strange bubble-like mountains, the yellow beaches, the absurd Anglican cathedral built of laterite bricks in the shape of a Norman church. It felt odd and poetic and encouraging coming back after so many years, a shape imposing itself on life again after chaos. It was like seeing a place you've dreamed of. Even the sweet hot smell from the land—is it the starved greenery and the red soil, the bougainvillea, the smoke from the huts in Kru town, or the fires in the bush clearing the ground for planting?—was strangely familiar. It will always be to me the smell of Africa, and Africa will always be the Africa of the Victorian atlas, the blank unexplored continent the shape of the human heart.

GEOFFREY MATTHEWS

Five Poems

DIVING

With pulse and beauty like a caught bird trembling,
Plumes soft-allayed, this water lies. The bathers,
Who stripped to catch the rainbow of its wing,
The vivid secret, that goes out with murder,
Vindictively surround the idle border.
Outrage might waste it all, so no one bothers.

The round sun twinkles on the sill of water
Like a hot coin. In apricot unease,
The watchers wait, and cannot speak or stir.
Two legs like bars of shaped and breathing gold
Sway doubtfully: a girl stares, half-beguiled,
Yet dare not plunge into her lover's eyes.

But someone starts, stands up, breaks suddenly loose;
He grasps, he springs. Ah, this will sack, destroy.
The soft wings open like convolvulus
Stabbed by a bee's abrupt invited lance,
And triumph, gathering up the secret silence,
Shouts through a silver megaphone of spray.

SONNET FOR PHYLLIS

You weep for some renowned and simple thing:
Plain looks, or too much teasing on a day
Torn by the smile of someone who's away.
Your tears are clear of all self-questioning.

My moods drain from a more bewildered spring:
I weep when prophets groan for words to say,
Or when fanfares of gallant mouths display
One more magnificently naked king.

I'm too acquainted with the dark demand
That drives my thoughts to bruise, as fire from stone,
Sentence against sentence, bone on bone,
Myself more blind than you can understand.
So, dear, our distance sets us hand in hand,
To grieve together that we grieve alone.

THE FAIRIES CAME

Groping, lurching,
Trudging, running,
They stole into the town,
Under the glinting cinders
Of the electric standards
Sunning yet more brown
Their urchin faces brown.

The traffic-light
Climbed up to red,
Soundless on rubber paws
The buses prowled and purred,
Crimson as ladybirds;
All were in bed indoors
But the night-fighter crews

And the factory-shifts.
No sirens whimpered,
No howl from the dogs,

When they crept into the town
With pads of starlings' down
On nimble withered legs,
With spindrift on their clogs.

Christopher lay awake,
Half gleeful, half in fright.
Only a salt-filled jar
Saved him: they lugged the grains
Numbering with angry pains
Bright cataracts, hour by hour,
Cake, boulder, spar.

Lazily Orion rolled over,
And Sirius yawned,
Green eye, white tooth, red tongue.
The salt-jar was upset,
A robin's clarinet
Scattered the dawn with song.
Christopher lay alone.

AWAY

Rain drops forever here,
But this was rarer than rain,
More salt and saying more
Than rain ever expressed.
The sky stood without stain
High abroad over your breast,
Yet the rain dropped and ran.

It was a falling tear
That suddenly made plain
Your love for him somewhere
More than I ever guessed—

Your love that dropped and ran
Over his risk, over his rest,
Far from this other man.

TO A YOUNG GIRL

Firelight over your throat
Firelight about your hair
Across your face the firelight
Treacherously pure.
With the same pure pretence
A soldier laughs to war,
And I read in this radiance
The fear you must endure.

Shameless virginity
Shines like the innocence
Of a defiled city,
Like the white countenance
Of the moon in the marsh-pool.
For an equal peace you must
Outgrow the innocent fool,
Be cheated into trust.

Life springs of mud and air—
Wing, petal, bone—
The black-hearted storms are
Cloud, cloud alone.
So flower of you must survive
The thaw-flood, the unclean
Silt, as these cinders give
Pureness, possessing none.

Drag, dear, from drunken songs
The inextricable chord,

Geoffrey Matthews

From these chimneys of tongues
Inhale the smoking word,
And let the coal's lips kiss
Aureoles in your hair,
Else have you no pureness,
However chaste you are.

E. J. SCOVELL

Two Poems

THE FIRE IN THE GRATE

The fire with hollow note
Like a cluck, purring, or a dove's
Calling in deep caves of throat
Or caverned water, moves

As confidently in its sphere
Self-occupied, as though its wanderings were bound,
Like a bee's or a child's on ground,
By its own nature and its little power.

The tired close their eyes and hear
How it makes a living peace and sucks away care
By its quick sentient creature's voice and way,
Like the child busy with his life in play,
Who gives breath also, fanning the heart's air.

A BABY'S HEAD

The lamp shines on his innocent wild head again.
Only for a moment are you both flowers and men,
Your souls like souls of flowers wholly immanent;
Your soul a texture and your love a scent.

In fifty years if you have beauty it will be
Words written on your face, abstract as history.
The light will call you foreign with its sharp and changed
Glancing, among earth's aspects call you strange.

E. J. Scovell

Now even the captive light in a close-sheltered room,
Claiming you as its kind, pours round your head in bloom,
So melting where it flows that the strong, armour-browed
Skull seems as pervious as a cloud;

Or seems a field of corn by the wind liquified,
Streaming over the arches of a round hill-side.
Contours and skin make tender the rims of light and shadow,
The pale and darker gold of the upland meadow.

Only for a moment your cavernous human brow
Will dwell in the world of sense as naturally as now,
Beautiful with no meaning, but that it calls to those
Who by nature love you, for their love.

ANTHONY WEST

The Precious Myth

I REMEMBER as a child, at the age when one has read the *Wonder Book of Railways*, going on a summer excursion in Cornwall. There was scalded cream and strawberry jam and crockery with mottoes written on it; one ate sitting on benches at fixed tables in summer-houses in the garden, and after one went to the museum shed. In a large tin-roofed affair, something larger than an army hut that was placed across a pre-Roman graveyard, I remember peering down through a glass cover into the open graves at the brown bones that had been there for perhaps 2,500 years.

It seemed then that I was looking at things as remote as might be, at the signs of a life as unimaginable as that of a fish. I had learned of Cæsar and Alexander, but I had not then lost anyone kin or friend near to the heart to give me a sense of community with the dead. The bones at the bottom of these Cornish peepshow boxes had nothing to do with Cornish teas, so far as I could imagine, and it was not conceivable that they could have cherished any cause that might have been mine. I think it was Pepys's stone that gave me the sense —the probably untrue anecdote that when his coffin was opened all his flesh and heart were dust, but that there remained there his bones and the stone which killed him. I cannot say why, but this story for some reason brought me through the barriers of costume and oddity of phrase for the first time, and brought me face to face with a long-dead person as such and not as an historical fact. Now that history is taught as we teach it, now that there has been discovered an historical sense and a feeling for periods, it is only too easy to think of historical characters grappling with problems of their time and not ours. But the deeper one fishes into history the less dead the people get, and the less historical their problems, both private and public. Chinese poems that, even if they cannot be dated with precision, are more than 2,000 years old deal with the sort of feelings one knows.

A woman walking up a hillside, washed out by the heat, irritated by the idiot chirruping of the crickets, and longing for her husband to come back from the war, is one's own private knowledge. China has very little recorded history, and there has been little mulling over past events there. But ideas have always been recorded and discussed by later generations regardless of their time, as if we treated St. Augustine's ideas by the light of to-day and thought of him as a contemporary. Our antiquarian approach keeps St. Augustine in his historic place, a visit to his brain is an excursion to an historic site, and the visitor peers down into the tomb at something remote and preserved. The Chinese classics have remained so alive and so much part of contemporary thinking that the time-chained Western scholar is afflicted by a sense of the improper when faced with them. If they were as old as all that they ought to be dead, is roughly the reaction, and much sinological scholarship has been devoted to flitter-witted denigration based on text dating. X claims to be 3,000 years old, the earliest known text is 1,600 years old, and contains characters that only came into use in the preceding hundred and fifty years. It cannot therefore be as old as the Chinese pretend, and we will therefore not bother about it because there is something dubious about it. The Historic approach is a method of murdering traditions, and of ensuring the death of a traditional culture. The legacy becomes an anachronism, and reference to the past becomes a self-conscious affair of Art Workers' Guilds, 'classical studies', and the like. Dead as mutton. Singularly inane ideas about progress come to fill the vacuum: *a newer brighter sort of man is grappling with problems his ancestors never had to face.*

The mess is certainly bigger, but there is nothing much new in the presence of a horde of stinking tartars on the Elbe. They have been to Paris before now. If there is anything extraordinary about the situation, it is that it should conform so closely to the historic patterns; if one could not read and confirm one's belief that man was able to reason, one might well come to conceive in him some such instinct as moves the lemmings into the sea. The loblolly crew of modern chieftains with their backgrounds of bank-robbery and artistic aspirations, with the roots of their power in the factories and their satellite slums, may seem different from the furred and jewelled heroes of the past because their propaganda and their speeches rattle in our heads to fill us with illusions. It may seem as if a conflict of ideas about Liberty, Democracy, and so on, has brought the Russian British and American Armies together on the Elbe. But the rapacity of the German military caste personified by Hitler was in fact responsible. And at the beginning of the last century the Russians, British and Prussians went to Paris too—for all manner of reasons that seemed real enough at the time. Almost everything it is fashionable to say about Germany now was fashionable as the thing to say about France then, and indeed for some time after. (Sir Charles Dilke, who had been brought up to detest militarism and dictatorship, went to work for the Red Cross in the war of 1870-1—on the Prussian side of the lines, of course. He changed sides when he saw what the Prussians were like, but his arguments remained unchanged.) I find it difficult, myself, to care much about the label on the bottle when the red or white draught inside is the same poison brewed from Cæsar's laurel crown. It is in the nature of things, if one learns anything at all from history, that whatever the form of the state sooner or later an individual within it will have his dream of power and conquest and organize his ruffians to make the dream reality. The process is one of the great literary themes, a matter of the greatest importance to humanity, and is likely to remain so until this planet is colder. But I rather fancy it only remains a great theme while it remains a study of the leader and his circle of *aides* and opponents, and that it fades into a matter of journalism when it is treated as a matter of the impact of a propaganda on a particular pattern of state. That treatment is all right as part of a course in a leadership school, where petty tyrants are trained, but it certainly is not the concern of the artist. His concern is with the splendid diversity and complexity of human behaviour. I cannot think of any great writer or poet who did not diminish his stature when he wrote of current affairs, or did anything but waste his talent when he took his material from yesterday's and to-day's newspaper.

This has been said before often enough, but it always needs saying. Every generation produces new rationalizations to seduce the artist—explanations of the wholly changed and special circumstances which make it important for him to turn aside from his real work to produce political reach-me-downs: loyal addresses to the King, or Lord Protector, such stuff as Tennyson's 'Form, Form, Riflemen, Form!' I do not mean the simple attacks on the integrity of the 'where are our war poets' order from those who hate the arts, but those which come from people who are apparently on the side of the angels: the sillier admirers of France and the brisker adherents of the liberal cause.

When France went under in 1940 the whole nation went under, and as De Gaulle explained the other day she was the only European country in which the legal source of law and authority fell into the hands of the Germans. The whole of French life fell under the shadow, and the only writers who achieved publication were either those acceptable to the Germans, or those considered worthy of support by the resistance presses. The resistance literature is, politically speaking, a fine manifestation of France's powers of endurance and recovery, but it is very doubtful stuff as literature. The admirers of France, who stop nothing short of idolatry, wriggle on their bellies in self-abasement before it, crying that it is the only considerable work that has been produced in the past five years. But when one reads such poems as *Les Yeux d'Elsa*, or the much touted *Silence de la Mer* one recognizes very moderate talent. Few of the other available French writings reach a higher level, and most of them bear in them more evidence of the weariness, strain and boredom of defeat and occupation, than of any vivid rebirth. So far as their writers deal with ideas, they deal with them in the fashion of very weary or very neurotic people—circling the same point endlessly and constantly returning to it with an air of making a vital discovery. Their admirers rank them in a peculiar fashion, X is very good, he did dangerous work for the Resistance, Y is not quite so good, he *did* nothing and only wrote for the clandestine press, D is mediocre—he was published in the Vichy-controlled papers and later in Algiers . . . and as for B, B is quite hopeless, you would never know from his writing there had been a war at all or that Fascism existed. The standard is that of news-value, the man most involved in current events is the best writer; it is called being close to reality. The argument is that there is greater virtue in the French writing to-day than in the English writing of to-day, because it is in closer contact with reality. From this it is argued that the French tradition must be more alive than the English, and that the only hope for an English writer is to get blood in his veins by becoming a client of the French literary movements. As a warning one can but read *The Unquiet Grave* in which an English writer tosses his tradition overboard in favour of a few French aphorists and the gossip of the Magny dinners: it fully illustrates the truth that there can be no profitable exchange between cultures if one approaches the other on its knees, and with a begging bowl in its hands. The best the client culture can produce in such circumstances is such figures as Anarcharsis Klootz or Palinurus. Profitable cultural exchanges are only to be made as if between equals, fully aware of each other's own virtues and defects. Just now France is sick and weak, and her writers are, under the pressure of intolerable events, producing evanescent work. The merit of a literature, certainly, has nothing to do with the military successes or failure of the national state from which it comes—our success, and the French defeat, are irrelevant. But defeat has its atmosphere, and in it the French are not doing their best work. So far from being in closer contact with reality than we are, they are trapped in the cage of their own special case, and, while they wrestle with all manner of complex feelings of shame and humiliation, they are unlikely to make contributions of any general European value for some time. If it comes to any question of a blood transfusion we will be the donors.

The other party that rebukes us for living in a sterile dreamland is concerned with the same question, although they are wholly indifferent to the virtues of the French or any other culture. They claim that by a series of happy historic accidents England has been isolated from the main current of European affairs, and that while she has been wrapt in a dream of material prosperity, terrible new things have risen out of the ground; Fascism, Communism, the terrible mindless, rightless, proletariat. Awake, awake, they cry—in a variety of accents—you are out of touch with reality! So Mr. Koestler in *The Yogi and The Commissar* says, and so say they all. Most of them, like Mr. Koestler, are fugitives, overwhelmed by the defeat of the forces of law and order abroad, who have found sanctuary here. They do not think to wonder why there is sanctuary to be found here, like owls in a barn, they think the thing part of the natural order. It never apparently occurs to them to consider that the thing has been maintained and kept in repair. Their heads are full of historic rubbish that prevents their seeing the continuity of anything, or the existence of anything real. This is the historic period of the struggle between the proletariat and the forces of Monopoly Capitalism, that is quite a new thing, a new sort of reality, and your old traditional stuff cannot be relevant. This is the argument:

'The whole body of ideas had undergone a radical transformation: Relativity and Quantum mechanics, Hormonology and Psychoanalysis, Leninism and Behaviourism, Aviation and Wireless, Expressionism and Surrealism—a completely new universe had taken shape in the library; and the dazzling light it radiated drove the intelligentsia half crazy by its contrast to the anachronistic, dusty-musty traditions still governing everyday conduct and beliefs. What an historical opportunity for debunking and rebuilding; but where were the allies to carry it out?'

There is no suggestion that the ideas could stand on their intrinsic merit, by absolute standards of validity.

'An intelligentsia deprived of the prop of an alliance with an ascending class must turn against itself and develop that hothouse atmosphere, that climate of intellectual masturbation and incest, which characterized it during the last decade.'

If this means anything, it would appear to mean that *might is right*, and that it is futile to express ideas that do not appeal to the big battalions. This is a dusty-musty old heresy that our fusty old forefathers drove out a long time ago, without the help of the latest thing in physics or psychology. But of course if you do not read what they have to say, you can have no way of finding that out. Here is Mr. Koestler's advice to the common reader:

'Read for pleasure, man, and don't bother about Peguy or *Finnegan's Wake*. Go to the public library or the bookstall, open a book at random, browse, read a page, and you will see whether you want to read it or not. Never force yourself to read a book—it is a wasted effort. That book is right for you which needs just the amount of concentration on your part to make you turn the radio off. Read fiction only if it excites you; all great works of fiction, even *Pilgrim's Progress* (that's good—that *even*) are exciting reading for a certain type of reader at a certain period of his life. If the right book falls into your hands at the right time, you won't be able to put it down. At any other time it is wasted on you. And the same goes for essays, history, philosophy. If you don't feel that it has a direct bearing on your own personal interests, worries, and problems—put it away.'

This is how the common reader is to come to grips with reality, as his fancy bids him. One cannot think very highly of the method. Mr. Koestler recognizes that from time to time it is necessary to guide people, and to bring them up against things their fancy bids them turn from. Mr. Koestler feels very bitterly about those who consider that stories of Nazi atrocities have no 'direct bearing on their own personal interests, worries, and problems. . . .' Assuming that the common reader is such a person, Mr. Koestler writes—'you are the neurotics who totter about in a screened phantasy world because you lack the faculty to face the facts. Were it not so, this war would have been avoided, and those murdered within sight of your daydreaming eyes would still be alive.' The recommended guiding technique is not much better than the reading technique.

'I know one who used to tour this country addressing meetings, at an average of ten a week. He is a well-known London publisher. Before each meeting he used to lock himself up in a room, close his eyes, and imagine in detail for twenty minutes that he was one of the people in Poland who were killed. One day he tried to feel what it was like to be suffocated by chloride gas in a death train; the other he had to dig his grave with two hundred others and then face a machine-gun, which, of course, is rather unprecise and capricious in its aiming. Then he walked out to the platform and talked. He kept going for a full year before he collapsed with a nervous break-down. . . . I think one should imitate this example.'

I do not, and I should think most English people would agree that this is not the way to come to terms with reality. I think English people would prefer to hear someone talk about atrocities who had spent the last twenty minutes before he spoke checking what he had to say against the evidence he had for saying it, and in weeding out what he found to be imagined rather than known. The English do not believe that one comes on the truth of things by sitting in locked rooms with shut eyes, one comes to terms with reality by keeping one's eyes open in the world of everyday. The secret of the English attitude is contained in the lines of John Clare on Cowper that say 'he made the English village classic ground'.

The thing lies in the adoption of the Roman mythology and Roman law. Between 1500 and 1800 the main flow of English life went into a wedding of the knowledge of the Renaissance with the native habit of mind. A morality was devised based on an image of Roman virtues that may never have existed but which were all the same as real as anything can be. Archæology has shown that the Roman Republic was not as the sixteenth and seventeenth centuries imagined it, but the literature of integrity that sprang from the delusion has a magnificent reality that cannot now be set aside. It remains the mainspring of our being. The chief element in the pattern is the logically absurd and yogi-like conception of a whole no greater than its smallest part. The state is no greater in the eyes of the law than any one of its individual members: it is only for very brief periods and in very special cases that the plea of expediency or public utility can stand against the claims of an individual in the English courts. There every trick by which the rights of an individual can be filched away has been tried, and the classical drama of the conflict between the hero and the tyrant played out in the terms of humdrum disputes between humble people and petty authorities. The law and its magnificent principles are alive, and in continuous development. The past, in the form of precedent, is constantly admitted in argument, and the lessons of the past are not thrown away because they were learned in the past. Maine, Dicey, Hobbes are alive and hundreds of long-dead judges with them; we do not peer obscurely at them through the glass lid of a tomb. We can throw it all away, because it is not smart, modish and French, and is ordinary and humdrum. Or we can throw it away because the novelties of our time—*Aviation and Wireless*—inform us that we live in a new world whose inhabitants have been dwarfed by some enchantment of the *zeitgeist*. But if we throw away these things, accept the legend that the past is dead, and abandon the myth that the least of our villages is inhabited by people of the same stature as the most dignified and virtuous of the gigantic figures in the classics, by virtue of their integrity, why then, the past soon will be dead to us and integrity be held cheap. When it is, it will not be long before the spirit dies, and this country ceases to be a place of refuge for those overwhelmed by defeat and social breakdown in countries where the spirit never lived.

GEOFFREY GRIGSON

William Barnes
1800-1886

RECOLLECTIONS we have of William Barnes are mainly of him as a middle-aged, old or dying man. Many of them are in the *Life* written by his daughter, Lucy Baxter,—a book, so few were those who admired Barnes, which sold only 267 copies. William Allingham, Locker Lampson, Coventry Patmore, above all, and later on Edmund Gosse and Thomas Hardy all knew him; and his poems were read and felt and criticized by Patmore's friend, Gerard Hopkins.

Gosse and Hardy went to see him not long before his death: 'We found him in bed in his study, his face turned to the window, where the light came streaming in through flowering plants, his brown books on all sides of him save one, the wall behind him being hung with old green tapestry. He had a scarlet bedgown on, a kind of soft biretta of dark red wool on his head, from which his long white hair escaped on to the pillow; his grey beard, grown very long, upon his breast; his complexion, which you recollect ['you' is Coventry Patmore] as richly bronzed, has become blanched by keeping indoors, and is now waxily white where it is not waxily pink; the blue eyes, half shut, restless under languid lids . . . I wish I could paint for you the strange effect of this old, old man, lying in cardinal scarlet in his white bed . . .'[1]

Then, in the autumn, on October 11th, 1886, there shot a flash from the sun on Barnes's coffin to Thomas Hardy watching his funeral (the funeral of the man who taught him the forms of poetry):

[1] 'An English Classic: William Barnes', by Coventry Patmore, *Fortnightly Review*, Nov. 1886. Palgrave also describes him, a year before his death, his 'finely cut face', his 'hands fine like a girl's', adding 'Titian or Tintoret had no nobler, no more high-born looking sitter among the doges of Venice.' From his diary, in *Francis Turner Palgrave*, by Gwenllian Palgrave, 1899, p. 185.

Thus a farewell to me he signalled on his grave-way
As with a wave of his hand [2]

Gosse's description of Barnes, in scarlet, against white, shows him
on his death-bed in one of those clear contrasts of colour which
inform Barnes's poems from the very first up to the end. But before I
discuss the way he saw, the way he felt, and the way he wrote—and
there is a disciplinary good to be had from Barnes as well as a great
pleasure—I would like to swing back from his documented decline
to the little documented and less explored years in which he was
formed.

[ii]

' . . . I, the son of John and Grace Barnes, was born at Rush-hay,
a farmling at Bagber in the Parish of Sturminster Newton in the Vale
of Blackmore'—and from there on, it is true, we know the skeleton
of his life—a Dame school, a period in the offices of a Sturminster
and a Dorchester lawyer, learning of Latin and Greek and Italian,
early poems, running a school of his own at Mere, study of French
and Persian, marriage to a girl of considerable beauty and good
sense, wood-engraving—'I had from a love of Art, tried my graver
on wood, quickened moreover by Bewick's works, and it was a day-
dream of my youth that I might follow Art as my way of life'—the
shift to another school at Dorchester where he was 'so lucky, as to
have . . . a friend who was a good Oriental scholar, Col. Besant,
theretofore of the native Bengal Infantry, and author of the Persian
and Urdu Letterwriter, with whom for some years I read a little
Hindustani or Persian once almost every week.' He kept his diary in
Italian, and early on he visited Wales, explored Welsh poetry, and
prosody, long in advance of Hopkins, 'For the sake of British History
and the old Bardic school of poetry, I have felt it well worth while to
learn something of Welsh, for it seems to me that for a man to study
the early British history of our land without Welsh is, as it were, to
dig the earth with a sharp stick, instead of a spade, and I have been

[2] 'The Last Signal: A Memory of William Barnes' in *Collected Poems*, 1923,
p. 444.

so lucky as to have Welsh friends who could read Welsh to me.'[3] He had a liking for archæology. He had a turn for mechanical invention, and instrument making, and mathematics, and helped Major-General Shrapnel with some of his mathematical calculations for artillery. He was a musician, singing, playing several instruments, and composing; in fact, through all his pursuits, as in his poetry, goes a passion for form and order and reason. There is an excellent formality about his wood engravings, and all through his life he felt the desire for visual order within a frame. When he was 21, he went so far in his wish to be a professional engraver and artist that approaches were made for him to Rudolph Ackermann in London, but the replies of Ackermann and the engraver Edward Scriven were discouraging.[4] He remained an amateur, and a picture collector, owning work by Richard Wilson, Etty, Bewick, John Baverstock Knight, Westall, Danby, and others.

[iii]

In all his early life—and it would not be easy to calculate how much of a handicap this was—Barnes had no friend or acquaintance of his own stature. He knew, and was helped by older men with some scholarship and ability, but he had no contact at all with any other considerable poet until he reached early middle-age. He was not aggressive, and beyond the approach to Ackermann, never seems to have had a thought of coming nearer to London than Mere, or of introducing himself to any other writer. He liked Dorset and Wiltshire, he liked scything, he liked his wife, his children and his pursuits. ' " Mr. Barnes", his wife would say, "you are burying your talents in this poor out-of-the-way place." ' He had a 'marked shyness of demeanour, an awkwardness in his gait and mien, and a certain amount of indifference to his personal appearance'. He was 'morbidly

[3] All these quotations are from a copy of Barnes's MS., 'Notes on the Life of William Barnes', in possession of the Barnes family. There is some doubt as to whether Barnes was born in 1800 or 1801, though he was christened early in 1801. Thomas Hardy believed it to have been in 1800.
[4] *The late Rev. William Barnes as Engraver*, Vere L. Oliver, F.S.A., Dorset Natural History and Antiquarian Field Club Proceedings, 1925.

modest'. And 'so uniformly mild were his manners and language that he was often suspected of being deficient in determination and spirit; a suspicion which in reality had no very solid justification; but Barnes was such a decided advocate of peace at any price that he would never, except when driven by sheer necessity, enter any arena as a probable disputant'. He kept good discipline in his school, never used the cane, and always wore (in the class-room) 'a long, light-blue, rough-faced, flannel-textured dressing-gown' (somewhere, if it still exists, there is a painting of Barnes as a young man in his dressing-gown). In his twenties, he was an odd, prematurely bald-headed scholar and schoolmaster.

These notes about young Barnes were written by one of his pupils,[5] who added that he was 'nearly isolated' socially, and was looked down upon in Mere, and in Dorchester as well. He had his few friends; but whether 'nearly isolated' is an exaggeration or not, it is certain that all his richest years of creation were passed in a loneliness of spirit and intellect. Barnes, like his neighbours, was unaware of the comparative standing of his own genius, and the world was unaware of it until Coventry Patmore began to review him and praise him when he was nearly 60. And then the world quickly returned to its old indifference.

'He is of no school but that of nature', wrote Patmore, which is true, so long as you do not interpret it to mean that he was a naïve, or unlearned writer. 'Mr. Barnes, in his poems, is nothing but a poet. He does not there protest against anything in religion, politics, or the arrangements of society; nor has he the advantage of being able to demand the admiration of the sympathizing public on the score that he is a chimney-sweep, or a rat-catcher, and has never learned to read.' [6] But for all his meticulous, highly professional knowledge of writing, and his rare gift of sustaining his sensibility and skill, all through life, Barnes was so fulfilled (except in a worldly sense: he had plenty of troubles before he settled down into being a parson) that I doubt if he ever quite looked upon himself as a 'poet' in our conscious European way. He was much more like a plant, which

[5] C. J. Wallis, 'Early Manhood of William Barnes the Dorset Poet', in the *Gentle-man's Magazine*, July, 1888.

[6] 'William Barnes, the Dorsetshire Poet', in *Macmillan's Magazine*, vol. VI, 1862.

does not exist for its flowers.[7] Such a lack of vanity and ambition coupled with so much expert skill may be unique. If he had moved among men of letters, he might have gained much, but he might equally have stained the clear run of his talent. Landor might have companioned him well, and invigorated him, but who else? He was narrowed by Dorset, but Dorset, for all its indifference, kept him safe, like Clare in his asylum.

[iv]

His first book was *Poetical Pieces*, printed for him in Dorchester in 1820—ten poems in ordinary English. He was then twenty years old, and there is nothing much to mark in these conventional album verses but their neatness, and the fact that he began to write in normal English, and for many years continued to do so. *Orra: A Lapland Tale*, Dorchester-printed in 1822, is worth more. It stands to his later writing like *Gebir* to the rest of Landor, or *Midnight* to Crabbe, or *A Vision of The Mermaids* to the rest of Hopkins, and it came partly out of his reading of Joseph Acerbi's *Travels Through Sweden, Finland, and Lapland to the North Cape*, a travel book published twenty years before, and partly from eighteenth-century visions of the frozen sea. The title-page text comes from Dryden's version of the Georgics:

> There as they say perpetual night is found
> In silence brooding on th' unhappy ground.

And the subject is Orra's search for her lover, a night she spends in a frozen cave, where her boat breaks away, so that the answer (undescribed) must be death. Barnes's unending love of clear, contrasting colour is now put down for the first time:

> Her bosom seemed, beneath her long black hair,
> Like snowy hills beneath the clouds of night—

---

[7] 'W. Barnes left no list of his poems, and rarely talked of them . . . he seems to have written when the inspiration was upon him, and, having written, he was satisfied.' His son, Rev. W. Miles Barnes, in the introduction to *Poems in the Dorset Dialect*, 1906, p. 2.

William Barnes

As graceful as the silvery cloud
    That glides upon the summer air—

And softly now her snowy eyelids close,
    Weighed down by slumber, o'er bright blue eyes—

There are three seedlings which develop in his later poetry. In *A Vision of the Mermaids* Hopkins's way of making a detailed jewellery out of his observation already shows itself lusciously and thick. In Barnes's *Orra*, you see already how carefully he is going to select, and how sparsely, and so how brightly, he is going to use colours for emotion.

Out of its order—because it is almost as little known—it will be as well to look inside the last of his early books in ordinary English, *Poems Partly of Rural Life*, published in 1846, in London. The sonnets, and probably many of the other poems in this book, were written much earlier—most of the sonnets in 1830 (when he also wrote sonnets in Italian). Barnes's poems never develop an emotional, or rather a psychological, subtlety. When—as often—they are exceedingly sure and moving, simple, elemental feelings are made to pull at our hearts by an intricate subtlety of rhythm and pattern. That subtlety he had not made perfect by 1830, so that the simplicity of statement stands out a bit too much. Yet I do not see why so classical and serene a poem as his fifth sonnet, *Leaves,* should remain obscure:

Leaves of the summer, lovely summer's pride,
    Sweet is the shade below your silent tree,
    Whether in waving copses, where ye hide
    My roamings, or in fields that let me see
The open sky; and whether ye may be
Around the low-stemm'd oak, robust and wide;
Or taper ash upon the mountain side;
    Or lowland elm; your shade is sweet to me.

Whether ye wave above the early flow'rs
    In lively green; or whether, rustling sere,
    Ye fly on playful winds, around my feet,
In dying autumn; lovely are your bow'rs,
    Ye dying children of the year;
    Holy the silence of your calm retreat.

And other poems to be remarked in this book are *A Winter Night,
Rustic Childhood, The Lane,* and *Burncombe Hollow.* Two stanzas
from *Rustic Childhood* will show Barnes's eye for light and for
objects. Many nineteenth-century poets observed exquisitely, but not
many could order this observation so well as Barnes, and space it
out with such an infallible effect:

> . . . Or in the grassy drove by ranks
> Of white-stemm'd ashes, or by banks
> Of narrow lanes, in-winding round
> The hedgy sides of shelving ground;
> Where low-shot light struck in to end
> Again at some cool-shaded bend,
> Where we might see through darkleav'd boughs
> The evening light on green hill-brows.
> > I knew you young, and love you now,
> > O shining grass, and shady bough.
>
> Or on the hillock where I lay
> At rest on some bright holyday;
> When short noon-shadows lay below
> The thorn in blossom white as snow;
> And warm air bent the glist'ning tops
> Or bushes in the lowland copse,
> Before the blue hills swelling high
> And far against the southern sky.
> > I knew you young, and love you now,
> > O shining grass, and shady bough.

The same qualities, not yet finally intensified and refined, you can
read in 'The Lane':

> I love the narrow lane's dark bows,
> When summer glows or winter blows;
> Or when the hedge-born primrose hides
> Its head upon the drybanksides
> By ribby-rinded maple shoots,
> Or round the dark-stemm'd hazel's roots;

Where weather-beaten ivy winds
Unwith'ring o'er the elm's brown rinds
And where the ashes white bough whips
The whistling air with coal-black tips;
And where the grassy ground, beside
The gravel-washing brook, lies wide . . .
And wither'd leaves, too wet to ride
The winds, line ev'ry ditches side . . .

I find very little forced or awkward about 'The Lane', and I have normalized the italic letters of the original, which Barnes put in to show how the poem was written on the alliterative principles of Old English poetry—again an anticipation by many years of Hopkins's concern with Old English. (Barnes had much else to import into the nineteenth century, out of the wide reaches of his scholarship and his curiosity.)

[v]

Barnes's poems in normal English up to, and after this 1846 volume, are more numerous and more accomplished than is realized, but in the Dorset dialect he certainly did come to the top of his classical perfection. Thomas Hardy has quoted from Barnes's statement that he wrote in dialect because he could not help it: 'To write in what some may deem a fast out-wearing speech form, may seem as idle as writing one's name in the snow of a spring day. I cannot help it. It is my mother tongue, and is to my mind the only true speech of the life that I draw.' [8] That always struck me as rather a puzzling statement. It is true that, having spoken in dialect as a child, for some time he probably kept a Dorset accent (as Coleridge kept something of a Devonshire accent). As a man, he could no doubt slip from English into Dorset English (he preached his sermons in Dorset); but his first promptings were to write poems in plain English, which he did until he was 34, and continued to do, at intervals, all through his life. And after 1867, for his last nineteen years, he

---

[8] Preface to *Select Poems of William Barnes*, 1908, p. viii. For the full statement see preface to *Poems of Rural Life in the Dorset Dialect, Third Collection*, 1862, p. iii.

reverted to English and wrote only one poem in dialect.[9] In other words he could perfectly well help it, and often did. Had Barnes made a statement which was obviously untrue? In his fragment of his own life he wrote a little differently: 'As to my Dorset Poems and others, I wrote them so to say, as if I could not well help it, the writing of them was not work but like the playing of music, the refreshment of the mind from care or irksomeness'.[10]

And others—that is to say, it was a general statement about all his poems, and perhaps a deliberate qualifying of his earlier statement that he could not help it—as if he felt that, if nearly true, it was not quite true enough.

Writing in dialect began as a preference, a choice which Barnes made out of his philological delvings. His daughter confirms that in her *Life* of William Barnes and says 'when he began, it was as much the spirit of the philologist as the poet which moved him'. And she quotes his statement that 'the Dorset dialect is a broad and bold shape of the English language, as the Doric was of the Greek. It is rich in humour, strong in raillery and hyperbole; and altogether as fit a vehicle of rustic feeling and thought, as the Doric is found in the *Idyllia* of Theocritus'[11]; and elsewhere, several years after his first Dorset poems were written, but several years before the first book of them came out, he affirmed that Dorset dialect was 'purer and more regular than that which has been adopted as the national speech'.[12] So, far from being a spontaneous act, this choice of dialect was a learned perversity, which he was able to carry through, since dialect had been his first speech, without the defects of being perverse. Once he began, he found he could do it by nature. Then, no doubt, he could not help continuing.

What I mean will be clarified by thinking of Doughty, who set out to revitalize English by reviving, with an early dictionary always alongside his writing hand, the dead, unspoken English of the sixteenth century. Doughty is unreadable, Barnes is a delight. Barnes is

---

[9] Introduction by Rev. W. Miles Barnes, to *Poems in the Dorset Dialect,* 1906.
[10] 'Notes on the Life of William Barnes', by himself. MS. transcript in possession of the Barnes family.
[11] *Life,* p. 84.
[12] *Gentleman's Magazine,* January 1840, p. 31.

genuine, Doughty a monster, and perverse, with all the defects of perversity.

And as a prolegomenon to the Dorset poems it is worth referring also to Hopkins's letters. Hopkins had already admired Barnes for a good many years when Coventry Patmore sent him three volumes in 1885, and he had some sharp words with Bridges (who admired Doughty) over Bridges' 'contemptuous opinion' of Barnes—'the supposed emotions of peasants'. 'I hold your contemptuous opinion an unhappy mistake: he is a perfect artist and of a most spontaneous inspiration; it is as if Dorset life and Dorset landscape had taken flesh and tongue in the man'; [13] and writing earlier to Bridges, he makes a comparison, the rightness of which I will not argue about, between Barnes and Robert Burns. Burns, he says, does not translate: take away the Scotchness and something ordinary remains, but Barnes does translate, and without a great loss.[14] And that at least is true: a lack of knowledge of the euphony of Dorset dialect does not, to my ear, make it impossible to enjoy Barnes's poems clearly and intensely. There are two lines I keep among the furniture of memory, and keep in this form:

> The cuckoo over white-waved seas
> Do come to sing in thy green trees.

Barnes wrote:

> The gookoo over white-weäv'd seas
> Do come to zing in thy green trees.

The translation I make, more or less without meaning to, is much nearer Barnes's writing than, shall I say, Barnes's, or anyone else's reading of the Idyls of Theocritus was ever near to the original sound of Theocritus; and though I have no suspicion that Barnes ever wrote any of his Dorset poems first in ordinary English—in the English he habitually used in his reading, in his letters, and, I suppose, in his thoughts, the English versions that he did make of some of the Dorset poems are no less lively and authentic. The English

[13] *The Letters of Gerard Manley Hopkins to Robert Bridges,* ed. C. C. Abbott, 1935, p. 221. The date of the letter is Sept. 1st, 1885.
[14] *Ibid.,* p. 87, August 14th, 1879.

Geoffrey Grigson

version of *The Mother's Dream,* for instance, is not less good than the
Dorset original.[15]

[vi]

There is a remark in Llewellyn Powys's letters that Barnes never
writes about the sea. That is nearly, if not quite, true of all his poems
except *Orra,* and the superb image of the cuckoo. He had no taste
for the sea, one of many facts which mark him off from other poets
and painters and writers of his time—Darley, Tennyson, Swinburne,
Patmore, Courbet, Melville, Emily Brontë, for example. And there
is a deeper explanation for it than a land-locked childhood, and
Barnes's intense cultivation of his inland, rural imagery. He had no
use for the swell and turbulence and endless width of the sea—for
its lack of form. He is not a poet for expansive mystery, or for
crossing the bar, for the infinite in any way.[16] He does not feel lost,
or overwhelmed, or bound to fight against a universal ocean. He
accepts, and does not interrogate, the universe. And his form, and
his observation, are two things I want to explain. However narrow
Barnes may have been, form and observation are qualities in his verse
that we can profit by. He was not a fragmentary poet, or a Samuel
Palmer with eight or nine years of lyrical vision and explosion.
Lyrics such as *White an' Blue,* with its airy vitality and youthfulness,
were written when Barnes was nearly 70 years old. And often it is
not easy, so much are his poems conceived or carried out as a unit,
to isolate a stanza or an image for admiration. Coventry Patmore well
remarked 'often there is not a single line worth remembering in what
is, nevertheless, upon the whole a very memorable poem'.[17] The

[15] The Dorset original of 'The Mother's Dream' is in *Poems in the Dorset Dialect,*
1906. The Rev. W. Miles Barnes explains in the introduction that many of the poems
in *Poems of Rural Life in Common English* (1868) were translations from the Dorset.

[16] Tennyson—it is typical of the nineteenth century—writes of death as crossing
the bar and putting out to sea. The eighteenth-century attitude is to sail calmly or
contemplate storm from the quiet of the harbour, e.g. Matthew Green:

> I make (may heav'n propitious send
> Such wind and weather to the end)
> Neither becalm'd, nor over-blown,
> Life's voyage to the world unknown.
> (*The Spleen*)

[17] 'William Barnes, the Dorsetshire Poet', *Macmillan's Magazine,* vol. vi, 1862, p. 156.

poems are rhythmically united, and tied together still more tightly by refrains. When I was putting together my anthology *The Romantics* —this will illustrate the unity I am talking of—I ended Barnes's poem *The Sky A-clearèn* at a point where I could bring out the pictorial exquisiteness of the third stanza—one of his colour-contrasts:

> The drevèn scud that auvercast
> The zummer sky is all a-past,
> An' softer âir, a-blowèn droo
> The quiv'ren boughs, da shiake the vew
> Laste râin draps off the leaves lik' dew;
>   An' piaviers now a-gettèn dry,
>   Da steam below the zunny sky
>   That's now so vast a-clearèn.
>
> The shiades that wer a-lost below
> The starmy cloud, agen da show
> Ther mockèn shiapes below the light;
> An' house-walls be a-lookèn white,
> An' vo'ke da stir oonce muore in zight,
>   An' busy birds upon the wing
>   Da whiver roun' the boughs an' zing,
>   To zee the sky a-clearèn.
>
> Below the hill's an ash; below
> The ash, white elder-flow'rs da blow;
> Below the elder is a bed
> O' robinhoods o' blushin' red;
> An' there, wi' nunches all a-spread,
>   The hây-miakers, wi' each a cup
>   O' drink, da smile to zee hold up
>   The râin, an' sky a-clearèn . . .

It was just possible to do it—to make the mutilation, and let it stand —but I felt the poem, like that, seemed to bleed. Its form, like a statue with an arm broken above the elbow, foretold the rest. The rest, it is true, is touched—this is Barnes's Victorian vice—with a weak sentiment, even if the remaining stanzas are demanded by the broken pattern:

> ... Mid blushèn maïdens wi' their zong
> Still draw their white-stemm'd reäkes among
> The long-back'd weäles an' new meäde pooks,
> By brown-stemm'd trees an' cloty brooks;
> But have noo call to spweil their looks
>   By work, that God could never meäke
>   Their weaker han's to underteäke,
>   Though skies mid be a-cleärèn.

> 'Tis wrong vor women's han's to clips
> The zull an' reap-hook, speädes an' whips;
> An men abroad, should leäve, by right,
> Their bit o' vier up at night
>   An' hang upon the hedge to dry
>   Their snow-white linen, when the sky
>   In winter is a-clearèn.

But what mutilation would be possible at all in a later poem such as *My Love's Guardian Angel*, where the refrain is worked up to the emotional weight of its last use?

> As in the cool-aïr'd road I come by,
>   —in the night,
> Under the moon-climb'd height o' the sky,
>   —in the night,
> There by the lime's broad lim's I did stäy,
> While in the aïr dark sheädes were at pläy
> Up on the windor-glass, that did keep
> Lew vrom the wind my true-love asleep,
>   —in the night.

> While in the grey-wall'd height o' the tow'r,
>   —in the night,
> Sounded the midnight bell wi' the hour,
>   —in the night,
> There come a bright-heaïr'd angel that shed
> Light vrom her white robe's zilvery thread,

William Barnes

Wi' her vore-vinger held up to meäke
Silence around lest sleepers mid weäke,
—in the night.

'Oh! then,' I whisper'd, 'do I behold
—in the night,
Linda, my true-love, here in the cwold,
—in the night?'
'No', she did answer, 'you do misteäke:
She is asleep, 'tis I be aweäke,
I be her angel brightly a-drest
Watchèn her slumber while she do rest,
—in the night.'

Zee how the clear win's, brisk in the bough,
—in the night,
While they do pass, don't smite on her brow,
—in the night;
Zee how the cloud-sheädes naïseless do zweep
Over the house-top where she's asleep.
You, too, goo on, though times mid be near,
When you, wi' me, mid speäk to her ear
—in the night.

[vii]

Barnes's Italian journals I have not been able to see, but he seldom
put down any more detail about the poems he was engaged on than
a laconic 'scrivendo versi' or 'versi scritti', [18] so it would not be
possible from them to date either their evolution or his complicated
experiments in form. *Poems of Rural Life in the Dorset Dialect*, his
third book of poems, was published in 1844, when he was already
in his forties. Much of the contents must be earlier than that: he had
written his first dialect poem, 'The 'Lotments', I think, ten years
before when he was recovering from an illness.[19] And here I may

[18] *Poems in the Dorset Dialect*, 1906. Introduction, p. 3.
[19] '1834 I wrote the first of my *Poems of Rural Life in the Dorset Dialect* . . . The first
Dorset Idyl was written in my room when I was uphalening from a sickness, an ailing
of the liver.' MS. Scrapbook in Dorchester Museum.

give the names of all his later collections. Few libraries have his poems complete. *Orra* is not in the British Museum. The recent *Cambridge Bibliography of English Literature* doubts if there is a copy, though two exist, as well as the manuscript, in the Museum at Dorchester. After the first Dorset collection of 1844 and the English poems of 1846, came in 1859 *Hwomely Rhymes*; in 1863 *Poems in the Dorset Dialect; Third Collection;* in 1868 *Poems of Rural Life in Common English;* in 1870 *A Selection from Unpublished Poems,* published by Winterbourne Monkton school; and in 1906, posthumously, *Poems in the Dorset Dialect,* printed by the *Dorset County Chronicle.* Several of his best poems are in this last rare pamphlet, which the British Museum lacks, as it lacks *Orra* and the pamphlet of 1870.

Through all these books, all these poems, he steadily keeps up his sheer skill, with much variation in form. Hardy noticed that 'on some occasions he would allow art to overpower spontaneity, and to cripple inspiration' [20]; but he allows that rarely enough, and his art is so fine and certain that he seldom seems monotonous through mannered repetition, or overworking, of successful effects. If I read Clare's poems, so deficient was Clare in this cultivated strength of Barnes, I find myself overfed with the visionary substance of poetry, which has simply been put down in the readiest, easiest and most obvious jog-trot form. Barnes was less completely *in* the world of nature than Clare. He does not achieve Clare's absolute hits,—he is not a seer—but he does not come down to Clare's dribble of absolute misses.

Form to him was fitness: he wrote several things about it, and he explored as well the origin and simplest nature of poetry. 'Matters most interesting to me are those belonging to man, in his life of body mind and soul, so in his speech, manners, laws and works.' [21] As for man, 'the natural man is unfallen man, as he was finished by the hand of God, when He saw all that He had made to be very good'.[22] And whatever fallen man may be, 'the beautiful in nature is the

[20] *Select Poems of William Barnes,* 1908. Preface, p. ix.
[21] Transcript of MS. 'Notes on the Life of William Barnes', by himself, in possession of the Barnes family.
[22] Review: 'Patmore's Poems', in *Fraser's Magazine,* July, 1863, p. 130.

unmarred result of God's first creative or forming will . . . the beautiful in art is the result of an unmistaken working in man in accordance with the beautiful in nature'.[23] He maintained 'there is no high aim but the beautiful. Follow nature: work to her truth'.[24] But 'the beautiful is also the good by reason of a fitness or harmony which it possesses'.[25] He admired 'the beauty and truth of colour and action in the Dutch school; and'—since he is anything but Dutch—'the harmony, tone, and effect of colour, even with bad drawing, and, in some cases, it may be with a want of depth, in a work of Turner'.[26] In all the beautiful things of a landscape, he discovered fitness— 'fitness of water to irrigate growth, and to run for all lips to the sea; fitness of land to take and send onward the stream; fitness of strength to weight, as of the stem to the head of a tree; fitness of elasticity to force, as that of the poplar, and the bough whose very name is bending, and the bullrush and grass to the wind; fitness of protection to life, as in the armed holly and thorn, and the bush, or ditch-guarded epilobium; and a harmony of the whole with the good of man'.[27]

Harmony was a favourite word, and harmonic proportion a favourite topic, with Barnes. He wanted harmonic proportion in churches—'that too little understood and wonderfully neglected principle of harmony in form as well as in sound'[28] ought to be applied, so he maintained, to the relative heights of the tower, the nave and the chancel. He framed his pictures and bound his books in harmonic proportion. He held that poetry must keep in with the fitness of nature and must conform to the nature of speech and the natural cause of poetry among men. 'Speech was shapen of the breath-sounds of speakers, for the ear of hearers, and not from speech-tokens (letters) in books',[29] and discovering what he could about the origins of poetry from books of travel and philology and his own study of European and Oriental literature, he believed that poetry did not spring from cultivation or refinement, but from elemental neces-

[23] 'Thoughts on Beauty and Art', *Macmillan's Magazine*, vol. IV, May–Oct. 1861, p. 126.
[24] *Ibid.*, p. 126.   [25] *Ibid.*, p. 128.   [26] *Ibid.*, p. 137.
[27] *Ibid.*, p. 133.
[28] Letter on harmonic proportion as applied to churches in *Gentleman's Magazine*, December, 1843.
[29] From the 'Fore-say' in *An Outline of English Speech-Craft*, 1878.

sity: 'there has never been a full-shaped tongue that has sounded from the lips of generations of any tribe without the voice of song; and . . . to a bookless and unwriting people verse is rather a need than a joy'.[30] It is curious to find him down in his Dorset isolation writing that 'the measures of song . . . may themselves be measured, not only by the steps of the dramatic dance, but by the steps of a march, or by the strokes of oars, as in the Tonga songs of the kind called Towálo or paddle songs, which Mariner says are never accompanied with instrumental music, but which are short songs sung in canoes while paddling, the strokes of the paddles being coincident with the cadence of the tune'. [31]

In English poetry, his own practice was based on the Enlightenment; and no doubt he owed that salutary basis, in part, to being out of the swim, to being brought up in a countryside where the eighteenth century was still alive in the nineteenth; and to associating early with old-fashioned men for whom the Augustans were more important, still, than Wordsworth, or Keats, or Shelley. Such is the viable advantage of not always being modern, or up to date. He was little touched with an Elizabethan or a Miltonic romanticism, much as he studied the structure and prosody of Milton and the Elizabethans. Spontaneity, singing because you must, 'like the playing of music, the refreshment of the mind from care or irksomeness'—yes. But he read Dryden and Pope, and he quoted Mrs. Cooper on Waller's poetry, that Waller 'rode the Pegasus of wit with the curb of good manners'. [32] It would be interesting to know when he first read and absorbed the Earl of Mulgrave's *Essay Upon Poetry*, with its emphatic praise of Homer and its emphasis on 'exact *Propriety* of Words and Thought' in the writing of songs:

> *Expression* easie, and the *Fancy* high,
> Yet *that* not seem to *creep,* nor *this* to *fly*;
> No Words transpir'd, but in such *order* all,
> As, tho' by Care, may seem by Chance to *fall.*

[30] 'The Old Bardic Poetry', *Macmillan's Magazine*, vol. XVI, 1867, p. 306.

[31] 'On the Credibility of Old Song, History and Tradition', *Fraser's Magazine*, September, 1863.

[32] 'Plagiarism and Coincidence', *Macmillan's Magazine,* vol. XV, November, 1886, p. 77.

William Barnes

Mulgrave, said Barnes, 'writes to fancy or genius

> . . . I am fain
> To check thy course, and use the needful rein.

Without *judgement,* fancy is but mad', he quoted, and went on, 'A Welsh bardic canon says: the three qualifications of poetry are endowment of *genius, judgement* from experience, and *happiness of mind.'* [33] Paraphrasing Mulgrave, he liked lines which are written 'with a skill that conceals skill', that 'keep all the strait rules of verse, yet flow as freely as if they were wholly untied'. Then, 'we cannot but feel that kind of pleasure which is afforded by the easy doing of a high feat, besides that which is afforded by good writing'. [34]

After all that, neither the complexity of his lyric dodges and formalities, nor his care (how different from much in Tennyson) to pick over his observation and select from it, and never or seldom to overcrowd, continue to be surprising, however rare they are in other men's poetry between 1830 and 1870.

To analyse Barnes's skill exactly, one would need some degree of his own knowledge of Italian, of Persian (Petrarch and Sa'di were his favourites) and of Welsh, and other languages as well. On his eighteenth-century basis of 'exact propriety of word and thought' he heightened his verse in every way he could, by setting himself tasks of every kind. There are clues to this heightening, and to his mind, in the elaborate exemplification of rhyme in his *Philological Grammar* (1854), a book which he 'formed from a comparison of more than sixty languages'. He sympathizes with all rhyming tasks which can be alloyed into the structure of a poem. 'A poet may impose upon himself any task,—as that he will introduce some forechosen word into every distich or line, or exclude it from his poem; or that every line shall end with a noun; or that his poem shall take a chosen form to the sight; or he may bind himself to work out any unusual fancy.' He mentions George Herbert's poems in the form of wings or an altar, reproves Addison for calling Milton's matching of words of the same root 'poor and trifling', as in

---

[33] *Ibid.,* p. 77.
[34] 'The Old Bardic Poetry', *Macmillan's Magazine,* vol. XVI, 1867, p. 307.

That brought into this world a world of woe
Which tempted our attempt.

'However poor and trifling this figure might have seemed to Addison, it is sometimes very striking, as shown in the spontaneous language of mental emotion', and he gives other examples of this root-matching, 'called by the Persians . . . derivation', from Virgil, Sophocles, Crabbe, Tennyson, Cowper, Coleridge, George Herbert, Shakespeare and other Elizabethans. Other poets of his age had taken from Elizabethans only an attitude, or fairy nothings (compare much of Darley or Hood), or insubstantial horrors. Barnes looked at the way they wrote, their word-repetitions, their collocation of two words alike in sound, unlike in meaning, their acrostics, their elaborate alliterations, and so on, which are paralleled by the elaborations and conventions of the Persian mediæval poetry he so much enjoyed. The Persian poets and the Elizabethan lyric writers (and, for that matter the English poets of the Enlightenment whom Barnes learned from first of all) concerned themselves more with virtuosity of language than with originality of ideas. Beside the Augustan uniformity of common sense and a commonly held stock of knowledge, one could place the statement of the Arab historian, Ibn Khaldún, that 'the Art of Discourse, whether in verse or prose, lies only in words, not in ideas . . . ideas are common to all, and are at the disposal of every understanding, to employ as it will, needing no art'.[35] That certainly was how Barnes thought of poetry, elaborate in art, simple in ideas, and straightforward in effect. And he transfers much of the elaboration that he discusses to his own verse —for example, from Eastern poetry the 'kind of word rhyming, or word-matching' called *adorning*, 'in which every word of a line is answered by another of the same measure and rhyme in the other line of the distich':

> As trees be bright
> Wi' bees in flight.[36]

The Persians, he says, use an ornamental punning or 'full-match-

---

[35] Quoted by E. G. Browne: *A Literary History of Persia*, vol. II, 1906, p. 85.
[36] This and the few subsequent quotations are from Barnes's *Philological Grammar* (1854).

ing . . .' a full likeness in sound, of words which differ in meaning. He used it in *The Wold Wall*:

> Ah! well-a-dae! O wall adieu.

He used the peculiar parallelism of Hebrew poetry—the principle of 'Tell it not in Gath, publish it not in the streets of Askalon'—in *Melhill Feast*, for example:

> The road she had come by then was soon
> The one of my paths that best I knew,
> By glittering gossamer and dew,
> *Evening by evening, moon by moon*—

or in the uncollected *Troubles of the Day*:

> As there, along the elmy hedge, I go
> By banksides white with parsley—parsley-bloom.

Welsh and Irish poetry were sources for him. For instance, in Irish poetry 'there is a kind of under-rhyme, or rhyme called *union*, which is the under-rhyming or rhyming of the last word or breath-sound in one line, with one in the middle of the following one'. Here it is in *Times o' Year*:

> Here did swäy the eltrot *flow'rs*
> When the *hours* o' night wer vew,
> An' the zun, wi' eärly *beams*
> Brighten'd *streams*, an' dried the dew . . .

But his most pronounced Celtic borrowing is the *cynghanedd*, the Welsh repetition of consonantal sounds in the two parts of a line, divided by a cæsura, which is better known in English through its use by Gerard Hopkins. The familiar instance comes as a refrain in the poem so celebrated through its musical setting, *My Orcha'd in Linden Lea*, in which the apple tree

> Do leän down low in Linden Lea,

where the *cynghanedd* consonants are DLNDNL/NLNDNL; but there are plenty more, such as 'In our abode in Arby Wood', or 'An' love to roost, where they can live at rest'.

Hopkins was made a bit uneasy about this particular borrowing. Barnes he wrote 'comes, like Homer and all poets of native epic, provided with epithets, images, and so on which seem to have been tested and digested for a long while in their native air and to have a *keeping* which nothing else could give; but in fact they are rather all of his own finding and first throwing off'.[37] This he thought 'very high praise' and he found his rhythms 'charming and characteristic', as they are, certainly. But his use of *cynghanedd* he did not think successful. 'To tell the truth, I think I could do that better' and he added that it was 'an artificial thing and not much in his line'.[38] I believe Hopkins was half-true, and half-wrong in not realizing how much Barnes's line was at once conscious and unconscious art—half-true, because although Barnes's most perfect poems are sometimes elaborate tasks, they are usually ones influenced by his borrowings from world prosody, but not embodying them pure and direct.

Barnes's soul was not lit by sulphur, he did not, like Melville, measure himself against fate or walk on the sea-bottom, 'left bare by faith's receding wave', or wrestle with God, or hang, as Hopkins hung, desperately, on the dreadful cliffs of the mind; he may, as Hopkins agreed with Bridges in saying, have 'lacked fire' (though that is not always so, in my judgment), but he *knew* and felt as much about the function in human life, the origins, nature, and adornment, of lyrical poetry, and its form, as any poet who has written in English. To paraphrase a valuable remark of Auden's, he disciplined himself and proved the power of his creative impulses by accepting the limitations of form. He created a system of poetry for his own use.

[viii]

And Barnes knew also about the interest of poetry. Form and interest, structure and selective observation—in these, in the lack of them, have been most apparent the weakness of English poetry (and painting too), in the last hundred years. Barnes, Hopkins, Hardy (though his forms, in spite of his study of Barnes, have an intricate

[37] In *Further Letters of Gerard Manley Hopkins,* ed. C. C. Abbott, 1938. Letter to Patmore, October 6th, 1886.
[38] *Ibid.*

tight roughness like a clump of brambles), Auden, though not I think Yeats, and not Eliot, in spite of their degrees of stature, have been strong where others have been weak in both of these qualities. Observation, not always well selected, and seldom well alloyed and organized in form, has been common enough. But by itself the similarity of the shape of poems on the pages of books shows at one look the monotonous lack of skill in form, and lack of concern for it, which have been so common. In the matter of interest, in selective observation, it may be that we are catching up; it may be that talented English writers of verse go on being deficient now mainly in any passion for the structure of verse (in these, in structure and interest, may I say that those admirers of each other, Miss Sitwell, who chatters like four knitting needles about vowels and consonants and the colour and physique of sound, and Mr. Stephen Spender, are still in the infant's class?). But, whatever the advance, it may be just as well to finish on Barnes's epithets, images, and substance.

I have quoted Barnes's view of nature, though not completely: man has fallen, and nature as well is not unmarred, but 'the beautiful in nature'—that is 'the unmarred result of God's first creative or forming will' and 'the beautiful in art is the unmistaken working of man' in accordance with this unmarred result, which is good also by its fitness or harmony. The fallen working to the unfallen.[39] 'Look for pleasure', Barnes wrote, 'at the line of beauty, and other curves of charming grace in the wind-blown stems of grass, and bowing barley or wheat; in the water-shaken bulrush, in the leaves of plants, and in the petals of flowers; in the outlines of birds, and even their feathers and eggs; in the flowing lines of the greyhound, the horse and cat, and other animals; in the shell of the mollusc, and in the wings and markings of insects; in the swell of the downy cheek, the rounded chin, the flowing bendings of the pole and back, and the outswelling and inwinding lines from the head to the leg of woman stepping onward in the pride of youthful grace; and tell us whether nature does not show us graceful curves enough to win us from ugliness, even in a porringer.'[40] And 'fitness' made him an enemy of veneers and shams: 'does nature make you a handsome tree or flower near

[39] 'Thoughts on Beauty and Art', *Macmillan's Magazine*, vol. IV, 1861, p. 126.
[40] *Ibid.*, p. 128.

your town, and slight her work in the wold? or light up your water
for a crowd-sought park, and not for the wanderers in the wilds? No.
Nature and true art are faithful. . . . We have churches with a fine,
high-wrought street end, and brick walls behind, out of man's sight
(poor Pugin's eyesore!), as if the builders worked not for good, but
for man; and so a low aim has wrought a low work of art. Of such
a sham some writer speaks somewhat in the following strain,—for I
quote from memory:

> They built the front, upon my word,
> As fine as any abbey:
> But thinking they might cheat the Lord,
> They made the back part shabby.' [41]

Nature must therefore be sifted for the authentic, for the beautiful
in nature; and the heavy grain of this sifting, its force, is concentrated
into Barnes's epithets—'green-treed':

> As evenèn aïr, in green-treed spring,
> Do sheäke the new-sprung pa'sley bed—

or 'sweet-breath'd':

> An' sweet-breath'd children's hangèn heads
> Be laid wi' kisses, on their beds—

or 'dim-roaded' night, or 'blue-hill'd' as an epithet for the world, or
'sky-back'd', for the flight of clouds, and many more—epithets which
are impressed with the force of experience. He told Palgrave that 'he
had taken Homer, and him only, as his model in aiming at the one
proper epithet in describing'.[42] And this sifting gives his epithets a
serenity and wide truth that one misses in the particular detail of
much Pre-raphælite description, from Tennyson to the passionate
observation of Hopkins. Read, or broadcast to an audience who
have not the texts in front of them and do not know them, Dyer's
eighteenth-century *Grongar Hill* and Tennyson's over-embroidered
Progress of Spring (an early poem, it is true), and one poem is
fuddling, the other comes to the audience clear through the sim-

[41] 'Thoughts on Beauty and Art', *Macmillan's Magazine,* vol. IV, 1861, p. 136.
[42] *Francis Turner Palgrave,* by Gwenllian Palgrave, 1899, p. 185.

plicity and sparingness of its effects. Barnes's poems, are, for effects, half-way between the two; but riding his Pegasus on the rein, he would never go so far from the wide truth as Tennyson peering unfamiliarly into the inside of a horse-chestnut flower for an image:

> a but less vivid hue
> Than of that islet in the chestnut-bloom
> Flamed in his cheek—

Barnes holds the rein at some such limit as 'where the black-spotted bean-bloom is out' or 'thatch-brow'd windows'.

He keeps in with this restraint in preferring the quickly-taken truth of descriptions of states of light, states of air, and states of colour— sometimes all three in one. For instance in *My Love's Guardian Angel*, which I have quoted:

> As in the cool-aïr'd road I come by,
> —in the night . . .

in

> High over head the white-rimm'd clouds went on,
> Wi' woone a-comèn up, vor woone a-gone;
> An' feäir they floated in their sky-back'd flight,
> But still they never meäde a sound to me—

or

> I'm out when snow's a-lyèn white
> In keen-aïr'd vields that I do pass,
> An' moonbeams, vrom above, do smite
> On ice an' sleeper's window-glass—

or in three stanzas from *In the Spring*:

> . . .O grey-leafy pinks o' the geärden,
> Now bear her sweet blossoms;
> Now deck wi' a rwose bud, O briar,
> Her head in the Spring.

> O light-rollèn wind, blow me hither
> The vaïce ov her talkèn,
> O bring vrom her veet the light doust
> She do tread in the Spring.

O zun, meäke the gil' cups all glitter
In goold all around her,
An' meäke o' the deäisys' white flowers
A bed in the Spring . . .

But Barnes's use of colour is often, as I have said, the setting of one colour sharp against another one, a visual antithesis, like two halves of a line in Pope balanced against each other. Long after he had begun this, he began to look deliberately for its counterpart and warrant in nature, making a list of 'the contacts of sundry pairs of colours on natural bodies', such as white and black in the bean blossom, yellow and orange in toadflax or the brimstone butterfly. 'Nature is very sparing of showy contrasts of warm and cold colours. Red and blue are very rare, and of yellow and blue the cases are but few; and black and blue are found in lepidoptera more often than white and blue are seen in our Flora and Fauna.' [43]

Blue and white, all the same, was the coupling he most often repeated, though frequently he set yellow against black:

> There near the wheatrick's yellow back,
> That shone like gold before the sky,
> Some rooks with wings of glossy black
> Came on down wheeling from on high
> And lightly pitched upon their feet
> Among the stubble of the wheat—

White sometimes against red (I have quoted one example—elder flowers against red campion):

> Oh! the cherry-tree blossom'd all white
> And again with its cherries was red—

Or white against green as in the cuckoo lines or *Zummer Thoughts in Winter Time*:

> When white sleev'd mowers' whetted bleädes
> Rung sh'ill along the green-bough'd gleädes.

[43] 'Thoughts on Beauty and Art', *Macmillan's Magazine*, vol. IV, 1861, p. 132.

But blue and white began with *Orra* (and even before that in a poem in his first book of 1820):

> And softly now her snowy eyelids close,
> Weighed down by slumber, o'er her bright blue eyes,
> As bound beneath the cold and wintry snows,
> The azure wave of ocean frozen lies—

and they were observed together again and again, in his wife, in skies, in butterflies, in flowers against sky or reflected sky. Examples are in *White an' Blue*, where the colours are the substance of the poem, in *The Water Crowfoot*:

> Thy beds o' snow-white buds do gleam
> So feäir upon the sky-blue stream

—in *Zummer Stream*:

> There by the path, in grass knee-high,
> Wer buttervlies in giddy flight,
> All white above the deäsies white,
> Or blue below the deep blue sky

—in *Not Sing at Night* (a poem not reprinted since its appearance in the Poet's Corner which Barnes inhabited so often in the *Dorset County Chronicle*):

> Or where below the clear blue sky
> The snow white linen hung to dry,

And blue and white well express the mathematics, the clear, the serene, and the harmonious in Barnes's make. Blue and white are the serenity of nature—the nature, said Barnes, which 'is the best school of art', adding 'and of schools of art among men those are best that are nature's best interpreters'.[44]

[ix]

We have too much of a habit now of reflecting our discontent with an author's political convictions, or his political indifference, or

[44] 'Thoughts on Beauty and Art', *Macmillan's Magazine*, vol. IV, 1861, p. 132.

his inconsistency, back on to all of his work, as though the issues of the sadness of our time were immeasurably greater than ever before in the human race. We forget that there are still for each of us what we must regard as constant transcending verities, that what appears to be 'reaction' may be much more vitalizing than the thirty-shilling suit of modernity or *avantegarde*, or immediate politics, that being a trimmer need not imply a lack of inward truth, whether the trimmers are Dryden, or Turgenev, or a good many living European authors who have touches of Munich about them. Barnes may, in a very good sense, be a minor poet; but not in the sense that his writing is a mess of words occasionally lit by a sparkle of pure intuition. And I may have suggested, wrongly, if you recall the quotation from Patmore, that Barnes was indifferent to the times, or separated from them entirely. As far as not being indifferent possesses value, that was not so. The anxious bewilderment between faith and science scarcely reached him, and scarcely ripples in his poetry. I can only recall one open reference to it in his poem, *The Happy Daes When I Wer Young*:

> Vrom where wer all this venom brought
> To kill our hope an' fâint our thought?
> Clear Brook! they water coodden bring
> Sich venom vrom thy rocky spring—

—the venom being 'what's a-tā'k'd about By many now,—that to despise The lā's o' God an' man is wise'; and he affirmed in another poem

> My peace is rest, my faïth is hope
> An' freedom's my unbounded scope.

'That is a subject connected with politics, not with poetry', he said to his son when he reminded him of a request that he should write a Dorset recruiting poem. 'That is a subject connected with politics, not with poetry. I have never written any of my poems but one with a drift. I write pictures which I see in my mind'. [45] The one poem, the early Dorset Eclogue, *The Times*, with its fable of the pig and the crow, he had written against the Chartists. He felt

[45] *Life of William Barnes*, p. 323.

that the Chartists would unsettle the Dorset labourer without remedying his condition; and, with his views of God, nature, man, harmony and fitness, what did disturb him, deeply, was the unfitness he saw in the social development of the nineteenth century, and in the consequent decay of freedom; the unfitness which caused him to write the curious amalgam of wisdom and simplicity he called *Views of Labour and Gold* (1859), in which he was concerned 'to show the possible effect of the increase of great working-capitals and monopolies on the labourer's freedom or welfare'. Two extracts will give its tenor:

'The kindness which is done by capital when it affords employment to people from whom, by a monopoly, it has taken their little business, is such as one might do to a cock by adorning his head with a plume made of feathers pulled out of his own tail.'

'It is more healthy to rack one's mind in effectual devices to win a skilful end, than to work as a machine without a free aim or thought; and so, as a Hindoo poet says, to be like a smith's bellows, breathing without life'.

But Barnes's social views, simply consistent with his views of the world, of life and art, are only a stroke in the drawing of a full portrait of Barnes. They are less important than the wavy, mazy, slow, river-like rhythm of his poem *The Clote* (clote is the yellow water-lily):

> O zummer clote, when the brook's a-slidèn
> So slow an' smooth down his zedgy bed,
> Upon thy brode leaves so siafe a-ridèn
> The water's top wi' thy yoller head,
> By black-rin'd allers,
> An' weedy shallers,
> Thee then dost float, goolden zummer clote.

—less important than the rhythm with which he patterned his life and his impulses to describe and sing. There are poems which are slightly embarrassing, in which Barnes tails—I hesitate to describe it so—into a provincialism of sentiment; but his tailings are more innocent and slighter than the monstrous wallowing falls into the same weakness—not confined to Dorset—of some of Barnes's greatest coevals.[46] And even his weakest poems are strengthened by their pattern and dexterity. In the narrow sense, there are not art-and-society reasons for urging that Barnes should be read, urging that he should have the status given to him ungrudgingly by Patmore, Hopkins, and Thomas Hardy. He may—and I think he did—give to English writing more than has ever been suggested or allowed. Hardy he very much influenced, and Hardy's rhetoric and pattern were the first to strike the authentic note in Auden's life: 'He was both my Keats and my Carl Sandburg'[47]—the note and the Contemporary Scene. And how much effect did he have on Gerard Hopkins, who read Barnes when he was an undergraduate, complimented him by critical admiration, and put some of his poems to music? Both Hopkins and Barnes were after a revitalized language for poetry. Were Barnes's poems—to name only a little thing—the seeds of Hopkins's own concern for Welsh and for Anglo-Saxon? Is it entirely a coincidence of period and a consequence of identical aims that 'or as a short-stand-night-watch quick foreflown' and 'which at early morn with blowing-green-blithe bloom'[48] are not lines by Hopkins, but translations from Old Friesian by Barnes? Or that both invented their own critical terms rather than take them ready-made and devitalized from philologists and prosody? Or was Barnes not the instigator of much which has come down through Hardy and through Hopkins as well?

Yet these questions are only, again, the more trivial baits to reading him—to reading one of the few nineteenth-century poets who 'conceived of art, like life, as being a self-discipline rather than a self-expression'. Barnes, if he were more read, could become one of the healthy, if lesser, antidotes to the Romantic disease. He is not a rustic aberration; and it is to me one of the signs of the uninquisitive

---

[46] There is nothing metaphysical about Barnes; and the Persian poet he appears to have liked best, Sa'dí, was also the least metaphysical, or mystical, of the great Persians, the most 'homely', and the one most abundantly translated into English between 1850 and the eighties; though he also admired Háfiz. Barnes greatly liked *The Angel in the House*; but I doubt if Patmore's *Unknown Eros* (which he read) would have spoken much to him.

[47] 'A Literary Transference', *Southern Review*, vol. VI, No. 1, Summer, 1940, p. 80.

[48] *Early England and the Saxon English*, 1869, p. 173.

untasteful scholarship and spiritual laziness of scholars and publishers in England that there is no complete, critical edition of Barnes, and that no one has ever brushed together, for example, his fragments of translation and the many English poems not included in his three English collections.

Certainly Thomas Hardy's *Selected Poems of William Barnes* (it is still in print) did Barnes a service; but it neither served him, nor does it serve us, with our present change of need, by any means adequately.

Just as Barnes kept in Dorset during his life, so he has been kept there ever since. The point is to deliver him—to extract him from his rather snobbishly affixed integument of mud; to exhibit his mind's cool-aired quality.

RHYS DAVIES

A Drop of Dew

William Price of Llantrisant

B Y the middle of the nineteenth century it had become plain that
few of the valleys of the Welsh county of Glamorgan would
remain tranquil for much longer. The coal and iron which
were to transform the district into what the visiting and horrified
Carlyle described as a 'vision of Hell' were being discovered everywhere under the feet of surprised farmers and rustic landowners (one
of these had leased all the fabulously rich minerals under his land
for a term of 99 years for £30 per annum and six horse-loads of coal
per week). To house the streams of workpeople trekking towards
this new cornucopia, blocks of dwellings were built in quick, ruthless uniformity; dismally grey 'towns' appeared, public-houses and
Nonconformist chapels breaking the monotony of those rows stretching from belching pits and ripped fields of iron ore. The 'sooty nose
of King Coal,' as a contemporary Welsh poet mourned, was indeed
being thrust inquisitively into these green hollows.

It seemed to another local man, closely watching these developments, that the race of people—mostly from other parts of Wales—
possessing the valleys was in danger of developing wrongly. If the
workers were not completely demoralized by this new industrial age
(their ill-organized but furious strikes for better pay and conditions
kept a rough idealism glowing in their hearts), at least they might
rapidly lose their old racial integrity and their heritage of myth,
legend, poetic gaiety and personal liberty. This watchful man was
Dr. William Price, who, born in 1800, saw the century through to
1893. His astonishing life of rebellion, both physical and visionary,
and his obstinate retrogression to what he deemed the true 'pagan'
mode of living best suited to man, made him into a celebrity who
was derided, feared, clapped into jail, exiled, and also sought as a

miraculous healer of bodily ailments and a seer who could bring
back into the spirit an old half-forgotten poetry.

At the junction of two of the busiest of the valleys, the Rhondda
and the Merthyr, stood Pontypridd, an old market town overlooked
by a Rocking Stone which tradition connected with the Druids.
There on moon-lit evenings while the grim chapels below preached
their puritan doctrine to congregations groaning in a sense of original
sin, and while the pits and ironworks clanged in the new era, Dr.
Price, fantastically dressed in a green and blue costume and chanting
a 'Song of the Primitive Bard to the Moon', performed rites which he
declared were druidic. A few disciples clustered around the authori-
tative and impressive doctor, who held a crescent-topped staff, but
the crowd was sometimes inclined to mockery. Yet those who were
of the old tribe perhaps found their blood oddly stirred in racial
memories. For this—so the local old bards claimed—was the place of
the solemn Grey Cairns with their urns of bones, and dark pools
where the ancient priests planted the water-lily whose stem sym-
bolized the umbilical cord, this was the monolith where the dim
ecclesiastical poets gathered for worship of the druidic goddess
Cariadwen, Queen of Heaven and mother of Gwen, the bardic
Venus.

The performance on a twilit common liberated only one part of
Dr. Price's protest against a drab creed and a commercial morality.
More serious offences were to be practised and both legal and human
forces attempt a curtailment of his rebellions. Meanwhile he walked
the Pontypridd streets and visited the industrious valleys wearing his
everyday dress—a white tunic covering a scarlet and gold waistcoat,
trousers of green and scarlet stripes, and a head-dress ('a symbol of
healing', he declared) in the odd shape of a complete fox-skin, the
brush dangling down his back. Sometimes he was accompanied by
two of his 'free-love' children, the boy wearing a miniature replica of
his father's costume.

People derided this flamboyance, but no one could mock at his
fame as a very successful physician and surgeon, just as the ill-paid
miners could not complain of his habit of giving them his services
free of charge; usually he extracted payment (high) only from the
rich. He also was known to assist, professionally, materially and

spiritually, outcast girls condemned by the chapels—but in this what could be expected of a man who preached such dangerous theories about love and marriage and, moreover, used to roam the hilltops stark naked, declaring the sun a healing power?

Son of an ordained priest and Master of Arts, William Price was reared in a neighbouring district and in a home where only Welsh was spoken. He attended a school at Machen and then lived for five years with a Caerphilly doctor as a kind of apprentice. At home this priest's son had already troubled the neighbourhood by his nudity on a hillside in full view of the village. From Caerphilly he went to London, and the Royal College of Surgeons found that this very hard-working and penurious student passed all the examinations within twelve months. He qualified in 1821 and after further experience as an assistant in London returned to Wales and established a practice near Pontypridd.

Within a few years he earned an excellent reputation as a surgeon. And in spite of his socialistic preachings and behaviour he secured a friend, firm and influential, in Francis Crawshay; Dr. Price had been hastily called to this iron king's mansion and saved the life of Mrs. Crawshay by performing the Cæsarean operation. Later, Crawshay, in his turn, saved the doctor from a pursuing creditor by concealing him for some months in the mansion—after the doctor, nailed into a wooden chest, had been smuggled out of his new residence (a couple of towers he had built) past waiting officers of the law.

Not content with this fame as a surgeon, he began to announce: 'Man is greater than God, for man created God in his own image.' And: 'The chapel preachers never lead the people except at funerals. They are always on the side of the rich and are merely concerned in seeing that the people believe in the divine origin of landlords and masters.' And other pronouncements infuriating to the strong hierarchy of ministers and deacons, who began retaliating by spreading it about that the heathen Dr. Price had disinterred the body of his father and cut off the head for some baleful rite. The body had certainly been exhumed, but only that he could conduct a post-mortem to settle a law case in which it was claimed that his father suffered from mental illness.

This affair had led to the first of Dr. Price's many appearances in the courts. His second was in connection with a claim to the Ruperra estate, which, he declared, had originally belonged to the Druids and had been bequeathed to his father by its factual owner. In the 725 folios, now in the Public Record Office, which he deposited in support of this claim, he based his contention on the 'authority vested in the primitive bard to govern the world'. It is reported that 'nothing came of the matter'. But his appearances in court were always spectacular and he was allowed to give long eloquent speeches. Once he sued a bailiff for the sum of tenpence. Indicted for perjury at another time, dressed in a smock of fine linen and a shawl of royal tartan plaid, he refused to be sworn on the Bible because it contained a map, and then challenged the jury. 'As my brain has been ploughed and harrowed,' he cried, 'for the last five months, and sown by the conspirators with the seeds of villany and malice, I beg you to listen to me patiently and with all the indulgence you can afford, while I, an innocent victim of persecution, mow down their harvest of perjury.' Then later, 'Cannot her Majesty, as the Mighty Huntress, in her day, before the Lord, go out like the Sun to find beasts of prey enough for her bloodhounds without hunting them to sacrifice the liberty and life of an innocent man upon her criminal altars with the bloody hands of her priesthood? What! Does the equivalent Queen of Great Britain, the mistress of the civilized world, in her day, fear the light of the Sun living in a drop of dew and identified in the name of William Price?' Yet, always conducting his own case, he showed a legal knowledge that, despite his denunciations of the law and lawyers, was greatly respected in the courts. In another case he took with him to court his infant daughter Iarlles and constantly referred to her as his 'learned counsel'. Everybody looked forward to a Price law case.

Already, in those ever-growing valleys pressed into dark slavery, he was establishing the beginnings of a fireside treasury of tales. But his most remarkable activity was much later. During these earlier years, a man of lordly manner and handsome, generously-bearded face (in a daguerreotype taken of him he is carrying a lighted torch, a sickle and a sword thrust into a flowing waist-sash), he strode the valleys in his brilliant garb and spread in cottage, public-house, on common and by a printed pamphlet or two, beliefs and opinions flatly contradictory to accepted notions—at the same time often rescuing a limb from amputation here, and there curing a disease abandoned as hopeless by another doctor. 'This unscientific, money-making and superstitious profession!' he called his medical brethren. He declared that doctors should pay the expenses of people they had allowed to fall ill, adding, 'We are suffering under the curse of the past mistakes of our profession. We have been educating the public into the false belief that poisonous drugs can give health. This belief has become such a deep-rooted superstition, that those of us who know better and who would like to adopt more rational methods, can only do so at the risk of losing our practice and reputation. The average doctor is at his best but a devoted bigot to this damnable teaching which we call the medical art, and which alone in this age of science, has made no perceptible progress since the days of its earliest teachers. Some call it recognized science, but I call it recognized ignorance!'

He never lost his contempt of medicines and pills. He was a vegetarian and zealously spread this gospel. But he performed a locally famous operation by grafting a piece of bone from a calf's leg on to a miner's limb crushed in a pit. His one table extravagance was champagne. This he drank as often as means permitted.

During the many strikes and agitations which were giving the valleys an added notoriety he did not hold his tongue. To the Coal Kings he thundered: 'You are the Welsh Pharaohs who think you can suck the life-blood of the colliers for ever. You have grown fat and prosperous; you own the big houses; you wear the finest clothes; your children are healthy and happy; yet you do not work. How then have you got these things by idleness? Let me tell you. You have been stealing the balance of the low wages you have been paying them! Take heed, you men whose bodies and souls are bloated by the life-blood of the poor, take heed before it is too late. Remember that the oppression of the Pharaohs of Egypt did not last for ever, and neither will the oppression of the blood-sucking Pharaohs of Wales.'

And to the men: 'There are two worlds. Not heaven and earth, but the world of the mansion and the world of the cottage, the world of the master and the world of the slave; the world of the exploiter and the world of the exploited; and between these two worlds there has begun a relentless and a grim struggle. And remember that there can never be peace in society until the world of the master and the exploiter is abolished. Then, and only then, will the toilers come into their own and all men shall enjoy the fruits of their labour.'

Extraordinary words in such closed self-contained districts as these haggard valleys, in the middle of the nineteenth century. They must have contributed a share towards making this race of workers so conscious of its power that later the South Wales area became one of the world's brave battlefields for industrial reform.

Before these outbursts, in 1839, Dr. Price had vanished for some time. After the Chartist rising of that year he was obliged to hide in Paris. He had been a supporter of the movement and when, on the rejection by Parliament of the Charter petition, it was decided that in the ensuing insurrection the South Wales contingent should march on Newport and seize the town, Price was appointed leader of the Pontypridd section. He gave a two-hour speech at a secret meeting of the armed men among the hills—'Let all cowards go their way, for they have no part to play in this great struggle. Men of the valleys, remember that the principle behind Chartism is the principle which acknowledges the right of every man who toils to the fruits of his labour. . . . Every man here to-night must be unafraid to speak his mind, and unafraid to act according to his conscience. I am with you all the way—I, Doctor William Price.' The attack on Newport was an abject failure; the authorities had gained knowledge of it, and in the historic battle outside the Westgate Hotel many Chartists were killed by a detachment of soldiers.

A warrant out for his arrest and all the ports watched, Dr. Price lay low for a few days—and then had the satisfaction of being helped to board a ship at Cardiff by Police Inspector Stockdale who was on duty with the warrants for Price and others in his pocket. The person the Inspector so kindly helped on board was a tall handsome lady, who appeared to be a little unwell. Dr. Price had sacrificed his fine beard. Eventually he reached Paris. There he was befriended by a rich compatriot, became acquainted with Heine, another exile, and practised as a doctor. In the Louvre he excitedly discovered a precious stone inscribed with mysterious hieroglyphs which he alone of all mankind could decipher. Twenty centuries ago, he announced, it had been ordained that this 'Druid's stone' would be discovered by himself and thereby convey to him regal power and the authority of the old religion; after close study, the hieroglyphs had given up their secret to him. This agile intellectual exercise achieved, he next involved himself in a scandal and a quarrel with Captain Phelps, the rich Welshman who had befriended him. Phelps had found that his daughter's absences from home were not always spent with Dr. Price in the Louvre. The doctor was teaching the principles of sun-worship to this beautiful and intelligent sixteen-year-old girl; the naked couple, during summer afternoons, were seen gambolling and caressing in a pastoral retreat outside the city. But Price only stayed in Paris until it was safe to return to Wales. And Pontypridd, on the whole, was glad to see him back.

It was not long before he was engaged in a new series of litigations, mostly over property and his desire to build a 'palace' near the traditional burial-place of Druids. He actually began work—illegally —on this building, but was ejected by that Lady Llanover who still kept a bardic harpist on her domestic staff. The towers which were to serve as entrance to the domain are still to be seen outside Pontypridd, two round fortress-like erections coated in white stucco flanking what was to be an imposing gateway; they are a graceful contrast to the adjacent dreariness of modern dwellings. It was while he was beseiged in these towers that his daughters nailed him into a chest and had it safely carried out.

Later he settled at Llantrisant, and with the last of his loves, Gwenllian Llewelyn, a woman much younger than himself. With his handsome presence, dominant character, romantic costumes and theories, he attracted women; they were also deliciously alarmed by him and his views on marriage. 'I have found it unnecessary to enter into any legal marriage, because I do not, as an evolved being, require any law or religious ceremony to compel me to love the woman I have chosen as my mate. The artificial thunder of the Church and the State on marriage cannot frighten me to live with any woman under compulsion. No law made by god or man can compel a man or a woman to love each other, but it can and does compel them to live with each other, which is quite another thing.' He believed that lovers should enter into a probationary period of union, and that a marriage should be freely dissolved by mutual consent, the community only intervening to safeguard 'that which is of vital interest to it, the children'. He was never legally married; his several children did not seem incommoded by this. One of his daughters he styled 'The Countess of Glamorgan'.

After a few more adventures, including another flight to Paris to escape a debt, he moved finally into Ty'r Clettwr, the cottage he had taken at Llantrisant, a hillside village beyond Pontypridd which from below has the aspect of a medieval walled town in Provence and still remains almost untouched by the sooty nose of King Coal. As well as Gwenllian Llewelyn he had with him some of his children. And it was here, some years later, that he performed the act which was to rouse to full fury the latent hostility always felt for him, but which also was to bring him wide fame and posthumous canonization by the future Cremation Society.

Among his other unacceptable, hygienic and anti-chapel preachings he had always advocated cremation. He had already cremated dead animals. But no one was prepared for the dreadful act he now perpetrated on a Sunday morning, at the very time when the Llantrisant chapel was conducting a Christian service. The date was January 13th, 1884.

Five months before (Price was then 83) another son had been born to him. He named him Iesu Grist (which is Welsh for Jesus Christ). But this most loved son, whom he announced would restore the full splendour of the druidic kingdom to the world, died. On the Sunday following the death he carried the body, wrapped in linen, to a high field above Llantrisant which he owned. A cask of paraffin had already been conveyed there. He lit a wide ring of fire about this altar, placed the body on the cask, and set a torch to the oil. He remained chanting within the circle of fire.

Meanwhile news of his blasphemous intention had spread. By the time the chapel had emptied other villagers were speeding up to the field, some armed with sticks and cudgels. The police had also been informed. Two constables hurried up, arriving in time to prevent the unmoved doctor from being assaulted, if not lynched; they had to draw their batons. One constable, cape over head, dashed to the cask and snatched out the half-burned body. Price was arrested and taken to Pontypridd police station—for his own safety, the police later contended. The whole district was set by the ears.

Dr. Price, released after one night's detention, remained calm. At an inquest on the body the coroner found himself unable to grant permission to the police to bury it; Dr. Price was claiming ownership. And also refusing to promise not to attempt this 'cremation' again. ('I am not asking you to return to me the body of my child, I am demanding it.') The body was returned to him and, ignoring the dangerous anger he had roused—he was denounced from pulpits all over Wales—he carried the cremation through some weeks later at the same spot. He was not molested; it was known that a legal prosecution was being instituted. But shortly afterwards a mob attacked his cottage with stones, calling on the old heretic to face them. The doctor was not at home. But Gwenllian Llewelyn appeared holding a pistol in each hand and threatening to shoot. She broke up the mob.

He was indicted at the next Cardiff assizes, before Mr. Justice Stephens, for cremating the dead body of his child. Dressed in a snowy linen robe and his famous coloured shawl he spoke with his customary eloquence and legal knowledge. The case became famous throughout the world. The judge pronounced that cremation of the dead was not illegal provided that it was carried out in such a manner as not to constitute a public nuisance at common law. After his acquittal, Price instituted proceedings against the Pontypridd Police for false imprisonment and was awarded damages. He also caused a commemoration medal of the cremation to be struck, and sold three thousand of these at threepence each. And shoals of letters arrived at Ty'r Clettwr in praise of the epic act on Caerlan Field. For the first time in Christian Britain cremation had received legal sanction.

For the rest of his life he unabatedly expressed his various beliefs; he tried, without success, to raise funds to build an ornate crematorium; and local hostility became mingled with a grudging realization that a great if peculiar man was resident at Llantrisant. There was one event which could not but rouse universal respect and admiration. At the age of 90, this vegetarian once more—and for the last time—became a father. The boy was again named Iesu Grist. (Dr. Price's views on Jesus Christ are not recorded, but he appears to have traced some relation of Christianity to Druidism.) He lived until he was 93. Up to a week before his death he still received patients, who now came in great numbers from all over Wales. His last living act was to drink a glass of champagne. But Dr. Price was not done with splendours yet.

He had left detailed instructions for the disposal of his body. 'No sorrowing and no black clothes', and his memorial was to be a painted sixty-foot pole crowned with a crescent moon. He had already designed and supervised the construction of his coffin, and such instructions as the amount of coal to be used and the manner of lighting the pyre were explicit. All his wishes were observed. And he would not have been offended by the vast crowds of spectators that assembled, together with hordes of his old enemies the police, on the morning of January 31st, 1893.

Attired in his splendid clothes and fox-skin head-dress he lay in a muslin-draped iron coffin. It was carried out of Ty'r Clettwr on a bier, and borne to Caerlan Field followed by his gaily-clad children, Gwenllian Llewelyn, and a few friends. Hundreds of admission tickets to the field had been issued. But the excited crowds had begun to assemble from all the valleys since 4 a.m. and they pressed in horrified fascination towards the field.

Up there a hasty structure of masonry, packed with shavings, wood and paraffin-soaked coal, had been built. It contained a kind of open oven. Three tons of coal and one of wood lay nearby. Policemen were forced to help the bearers carry the coffin up the slope and place it in this pioneering crematorium. Two friends of the doctor's applied torches. After witnessing the first flames curling round the coffin the family returned to Ty'r Clettwr. Stokers remained to feed a rapidly mounting fire. The iron coffin lay in the oven for eight hours; it became red hot and flames could be seen issuing from the holes Dr. Price had designed in its sides. It was withdrawn with long iron hooks and found to be shattered. But, when cool, what remained was carried back, escorted by police, to Ty'r Clettwr and laid in the parlour (it seems for the collection of possible ashes). The crowds, twenty thousand strong, had broken into the field; they had to be beaten back by the police so that the stokers could do their work.

For some years afterwards the tall crescent-topped pole towered up familiarly in this still noisily developing district. But gradually the celebrated doctor, his extraordinary and commanding figure visible no more, became almost forgotten except in local anecdotes which varied from amused appreciation to anger—and which sometimes had that awe of the mystical and the things to do with enchantment and poetry that is so pronounced an element of his race. An element that has even survived the extreme industrialism of the particular locality where Price had fought throughout his life.

Dr. Price had contributed his share towards preserving that valuable element. It may be that he did not work very consciously to preserve it, and many of his exploits make him seem merely a flamboyant exhibitor of his own vigorous sense of drama, an actor *manqué,* an egocentric character determined to become public property. In a memoir an otherwise sympathetic friend called him 'shady'. He certainly had no sense of financial responsibility and appeared to think that he could help himself to any piece of land which he decided was hallowed by druidic associations. He also laid claim to knowledge of ancient lore that no one could disprove since there was no consulting authority left on earth. And except in legal archives which contain his rhetorical deposits laced with a cabalistic kind of poetry he has left no written records of his philosophy and opinions to be judged. He was a man who expressed his natural poetry by vocal and physical action. But it is because of the poetry he stood for, in a time and place that sadly required it, that (his exploits apart) he is interesting and of some importance.

With his exceptional talents as a doctor he could have earned position and fortune in some more luxurious place than those valleys filled with an oppressed people whose 'degraded condition', a Royal Commissioner reported in 1847, 'I regard as entirely the fault of their employers, who give them far less tendance and care than they bestow on their cattle'. But Price chose to stay among his people and, throughout his life, to lift to his lips an old battle-horn. He was a descendant of the warrior-bards who were always at the side of those nimble Welsh kings and leaders incensed by the attempts of invaders to obliterate the ancient heritage of this small race. Instead of foreign soldiers he had coalowners and iron-masters to grapple with—more subtle invaders. His task was to ensure that these did not utterly possess the spirit of his people.

His many speeches to the miners and iron-workers were devoid of that mystic poetry that convoluted his druidic utterances; they were shrewd, full of common sense, contained an ability to perceive the future, and they glowed. He went up and down the blackening valleys scattering fiery particles; and also salt on the tails of the industrial kings. But this was not all. He was a member of a race that is moon-struck. That has never quite forgotten the primitive magic of natural forces. That loves unbridled songs, and rhythms, drama. Before the Reformation members of the true race had danced and told their flower-tinted tales in an imaginative awareness of the sensuous world. Later there was the nonconformist blight, which nevertheless in its first vigour canalized the old poetry into displays of magnificent oratory and into splendid lyrical hymns, only to become a grey obliterating nineteenth-century cloud frowning over a confused people.

Dr. Price saw this and endeavoured to invoke the moon's magical touch again. He saw that a fatter wage-packet was not enough; the ethos of his people required a more durable preservative.

W. J. TURNER

The Theme of Love

Love has been the theme of all the ages
Of every poet, painter, musician, philosopher
Also the scientist whose thermo-dynamics
Expresses the futility of a world without love.
Love winds up clocks, gives lustre to ceramics
Burnishes the peacock, digs in dull earth yellow ochre
Finds a subtle companion for that dark colour bistre
And a like pearl-bedfellow for the turtle dove.

Love is a discovery, central, irrefutable
Not to be seen from fore-mast or mizzen-mast
A crystal island by all circumnavigable
Missed by many mariners in lust's wave transparenter
Though of the same substance yet in some manner different
Essence more exquisite—as the pearl of the oyster
Sweeter than the fragrance of the dew-wet-briar
Burning in the sun on a summer morning.

Yet Love is terrible, ruthless, a destroyer,
Being an absolute, Eternity's moment
With the heart still beating though Time left standing
Vanishes. So vanishes every particular
To unite in a blinding diamond whiteness
Self-abnegation as complete as adamant
Foundation unshakeable laid for future generation
By caprice Cupid-gesture reckless as the wind.

Cupid himself, limbs than-down-tenderer,
A boy carved in marble, rosy his thighs
Of foam now solider than cradled Cytherea
Invulnerable to suasion, to violence or sighs

The Theme of Love

Born of wild gentleness, of Zephyr and Boreas
Flint-tipped his arrow, so soft his hand
Ignores who invoke him but with side-glance startling
Strikes deep in the dumb heart his smiling command.

The world is peopled with lust's lawful offspring
Minions of passion's untroubled delight
But Love is a wanderer, fiercer, discreeter
Seeking the quiet, the rare, never-plumbed one
Mirroring the self in the self's other ego
The lovely the unapproachable, the worshipped worshipper
Who divines in the temple a nameless altar
Where the fleeting god may lingering loiter

May even turn and stay to be ravished
'Tis only a sunbeam gleaned from dark winter
Heart to heart flashing like bells of snowdrop
Flowers of deep meaning in the silence singing
Whose footfalls are gods or angels vanishing
Each indecipherable with its own soul-signature
Bodies of pure white and coral perfection
Linked as in song earth's darkness to enter.

Growing older we say this is all illusion
Not once or twice only has Love a life stricken
With menace to others and to all well-being
But like a clear sky after sunset the heart
Finds not a trace of that dream-like lightening
Invisible all the wrecks lit with devastation
Vanished to the bottom of a now peaceful ocean—
The Moon tranquil, in the full heart no confusion.

NIKOLAUS PEVSNER

The Architecture of Mannerism

E NGLAND distrusts generalizations. The tendency is to treat each case on its own merit and leave the perfection of codes of law to more logical and less practical nations. The extent to which this attitude influences political, social and legal matters is familiar. Less familiar is the connection of this weakness or strength of character with the proverbial vagueness of English philosophical terminology.

Taking research into art and architecture as an example, there is plenty of antiquarian and archæological work going on, but little that reaches broader conclusions as to the characteristic style of a man or a nation or an age—to say nothing of those still broader conclusions which allow for the carving out of æsthetic theories with their appropriate terminology.

The word style in fact is hardly yet accepted in the sense in which the French, the Italians, the Germans, the Americans use it. To the man in the street its foreground meaning is still that which comes up from associations with 'stylish', doing something 'in style', and so on. 'He writes a good style' is nearer to the philosophical meaning of the term. For it is certainly at least one of the legitimate uses of 'style' to denote the personal mode of expression of an author and an artist, and if you write of Wordsworth's as against Keats's style or Rembrandt's as against Rubens's you are philosophically precise and yet not likely to be misunderstood even in England.

But when it comes to introducing such terms as Baroque, nobody can be sure whether it will be taken by the English reading public as a synonym of fantastic or—in the deeper sense—as the final essence distilled out of all the individual qualities of all the leading personalities of one particular age. Hobbes's and Spinoza's philosophy, Bernini's and Rembrandt's art, Richelieu's and Cromwell's statecraft have certain fundamentals in common, and on these we can establish a Baroque style of exact meaning.

England has been characteristically slow in accepting this working hypothesis. Continental art history began to investigate the opposed principles of Renaissance and Baroque art in the eighties of last century, chiefly in Switzerland (Wölfflin 1888), Germany (Schmarsow 1897) and Austria (Riegl, before 1905). The final summing up was Wölfflin's famous *Grundbegriffe,* which came out in 1915 and was translated into (bad) English in 1932. But you can still find in the subject catalogues of important libraries under *Artists, Renaissance*: Raphael, Rembrandt, Reynolds, Rubens.

Now, if fixed terms for styles of ages are there to keep a host of data in reasonable order, then there is obviously no point in using such words as Renaissance, Baroque and so on, unless their very job is to keep Raphael, Rembrandt, Rubens and Reynolds apart. Surely the first step in tidying up the vast number of works of art and architecture produced in the West between the fifteenth and the eighteenth centuries is to separate what expresses Renaissance spirit from what is Baroque, to separate, that is to say, the static from the dynamic, the compact from the expansive, the finite from the infinite, the ideal from the over-real or over-expressive.

However, this juxtaposition which, thanks to the relative popularity of Wölfflin's book, can be taken as known to readers of these pages, if not to the general public, is historically inadequate. Wölfflin chose his examples to illustrate the Baroque almost exclusively—and very wisely—from the seventeenth century. And, as he says himself that after 1520 hardly any work of pure Renaissance character was produced, what happened between 1520 and the end of the sixteenth century? Where do Parmigiano, Tintoretto, Greco belong? The Renaissance believes in the beauty and vigour of the human body; the Baroque does; but these three painters and their contemporaries don't. The Renaissance believes in the proud independence of the human personality and the solidity of matter. The Baroque does; but Parmigiano, Tintoretto, and Greco evidently work towards a contraction of all that is material, in order to achieve an exquisite and decadent elegance or a supreme spiritualization. Neither of these goals is Renaissance, neither is Baroque. And as

117

our eyes learnt to see these specific qualities of sixteenth-century art and our minds (thanks to contemporary developments) widened to understand them, a new term had to be coined to label them. Mannerism had for a long time been used to designate certain schools of painting and sculpture in Italy, carrying on the manner of late Raphael, Michelangelo, Correggio and other Renaissance artists, and an Italianizing school in the Netherlands; so the word could easily be widened out to be applicable to the whole style of Italian and perhaps European painting and sculpture of the later sixteenth century. In this new sense Mannerism was first used and its extent and character defined between 1920 and 1925. (Dvořák 1920, Pinder *c.* 1924, W. Friedlaender 1925, Pevsner 1925.) Since then it has become accepted on the Continent and in America. Younger scholars use it in as precise and familiar a way as Renaissance and Baroque.

However, analyses and definitions have proved easier concerning pictures and works of sculpture than concerning buildings. Hardly anything to my knowledge has yet been published in this country about Mannerist architecture, although such books as Anthony Blunt's *Mansart* presuppose familiarity with the term and its architectural implications. So what I propose doing here is to look closely at ten or twelve buildings of the sixteenth century, to prove the incompatibility of their formal and emotional character with that of works both of the Renaissance and the Baroque, and then point to certain characteristic events in contemporary thought and feeling to show the same spirit at work in history and architecture.

Bramante, born in 1444, that is eight years before Leonardo da Vinci, stands at the beginning of the High Renaissance. He died in 1514, just before it came to an end. In his old age he designed the Casa Caprini in Rome which Raphael completed for himself in 1517 (fig. 1). It has since been altered out of recognition. It is a building of five bays and two floors, a comfortable human size, easily manageable by the surveying eye and easily comprehensible to the mind. The ground-floor is rusticated as a base for the main floor, the *piano nobile*, above. This has coupled columns to frame the windows and the generous wall spaces on their sides and above. All the windows have identical balustrades below and pediments above. An entablature and cornice terminate the facade. A minimum of motifs is used, but with a maximum of care for proportion and detail. Ground-floor and upper floor are of exactly the same height. The proportion of the windows between top of balustrade and foot of pediment is repeated by the proportion of the bays between the columns. No ornament appears anywhere. The Doric columns are unfluted, the metopæ undecorated. The effect is of a noble perfection and grave harmony.

Bramante's style inspired a whole group of younger architects in Rome. Raphael, born in 1483, is the most notable of them. To his generation belong Serlio, born in 1475, Peruzzi born in 1481, and Sammicheli born in 1484. Others were young enough to start as Raphael's assistants. The most important of these is Giulio Romano (1499–1546).

The group was dispersed by the Sack of Rome in 1527, which took Sammicheli to Verona, while Giulio Romano had gone to Mantua already a few years before. These two were the first to take the innovations of the Roman High Renaissance to the North of Italy. However, in their works the Renaissance seems to have lost its serenity and most of its balance.

About 1530 Sammicheli designed three palaces at Verona, the Palazzi Canossa, Pompei and Bevilacqua. The first two show him a faithful follower of his master, the third (fig. 2) is surprisingly original. Here is just as in the case of the Casa Caprini a building of two storeys with a rusticated ground-floor and a first floor with columns to separate the window bays. The entrance was intended to be central so that we have to add in our minds four more bays on the left to the ones actually built. The fenestration of the *piano nobile* is a little more complicated than in the Casa Caprini, but the triumphal arch motif of the openings: low—tall—low or *a—b—a*, is in its perfect symmetry and its pyramidal composition not alien to the Renaissance (Alberti's S. Andrea in Mantua, Bramante's Belvedere Court in the Vatican, etc.). So if the façade of the Palazzo Bevilacqua were simply a five-times-repeated *a—b—a—b—a—b—a —b—a—b—a*, there would be nothing new or embarrassing in it. Nor are a decorated frieze or some figures in the spandrels of the windows ornaments to which the Renaissance, especially in Northern Italy, would necessarily object. It is the details which confuse one as soon as they are studied.

The bays of the ground-floor are not all of the same width. Narrower and broader spaces alternate, but the difference is not marked enough to make one feel certain of its meaning, particularly as all the windows have the same dimensions. The composition of the first floor is even more intricate. The first, the third and the (missing) fifth main windows have columns with spiral fluting, the second and the (missing) fourth straight-fluted columns. That is logical enough, but the pediments above the small windows do not tally with this rhythm at all. If we call the triangular ones α and the segmental ones β we would, over the whole projected extension of the front, get a rhythm looking like this: (from right to missing left) α—β—β—α—α—β. That means that above the central entrance the triumphal arch is rudely thrown out of symmetry. It has two symmetrical spiral columns, but one α and one β pediment. You may say that the little pediments are an afterthought of Sammicheli's to achieve superficial symmetry, when he knew that the palace was not going to be carried on to the left. But even if that is so, no Renaissance architect would have tolerated the presence of two alternatively exclusive rhythms in the finished front. They jar painfully once they have been noticed, and they are not even the only motif of such obstinate illogicality. Another is the uncomfortable balancing of the α and β pediments, especially the segmental β ones, on the round-headed windows.

Victorian ostentatiousness of decoration has made us insensitive to the subtler values of architectural expression. Modern architects suffer from this lack of visual discrimination in the general public. Criticism suffers from it too; this is my excuse for what may be considered unnecessarily close analyses.

How necessary they really are is proved by the fact that Giulio Romano's most famous building at Mantua, the Palazzo del Té, a spacious ducal villa built between 1526 and 1534, appears in textbooks as a characteristic example of the Renaissance style. At a first glance it may well look like that. Yet, is the entrance side (fig. 3) really placid and as happily spaced as a Bramante design would be?

There are again two storeys, separated by a flat band with a sharply incised key pattern, the ideal Greek solution to the representation of movement in a static ensemble. However, the band is cut up by giant pilasters. Are the two storeys then two, as the band says, or one, as the pilasters say? This lack of clarity would have been intolerable to a pure Renaissance artist. Moreover, pilasters lose their *raison d'être* if they are not spaced regularly, but Giulio breaks that regularity in the very centre of his composition to house his three entrances. And he does worse at the corners. To stress these by a coupling of pilasters was in no way against Renaissance feeling. But the two outside pilasters stand closely together, while the two inner ones are separated by niches—a horrid heresy. Then, there is the rustication. The main windows and the doors have imitation-rusticated surrounds of a jagged restless pattern, and those of the doors jut out into and across the horizontal band.

Now all this is not just haphazardly insensitive. It obviously is the expression of a new will, a deliberate attack on the Renaissance ideal of the isolation and balance of all parts, and, what is more, an attack launched surreptitiously by an artist who all the time takes every care to preserve the *dehors* of classical correctness, a care which has indeed deceived observers of several centuries.

Dissonance is even shriller in the façades towards the inner court (fig. 4). Here attached columns (the plain and sober Doric columns of Bramante) replace the pilasters. The rhythm of openings is the simple triumphal arch rhythm (*a—b—a*) of the Renaissance. But why do the pediments lack bases? Why, if rustication is used, should it occur only in odd places? And why, to take the most scandalous breach of etiquette, should every third triglyph be dropped down so as to hang into the zone of the upper windows? It looks as though the building were on the point of collapsing, and that is exactly the impression the architect wished to give: precarious instability instead of the repose of the Golden Age. Evidently, to Giulio and his generation that repose had become unbearable. Restlessness and discomfort appeared as positive values. This is also the reason why the high finish achieved by the Renaissance is placed side by side with rude blocks of unhewn stone, and their incongruous proximity is relished. Nature in the raw becomes for the first time a motif of art.

This interpretation of Giulio's rustication is not a modern subtlety. Already in 1537 Serlio wrote about it that it seems 'partly a work of nature and partly a work of the artist.'

Rustication in palace architecture was, it is true, by no means an innovation of the sixteenth century. But when the Early Renaissance uses it, say in Michelozzo's Medici Palace in Florence, it appears as a solid and powerful basis to the noble building of man. Nowhere does it endanger the superiority of the human achievement. In the courtyard of the Palazzo del Té nature breaks into the architect's artificial world, spoiling it and reminding us irritatingly of our own helplessness. How panic-stricken Giulio must sometimes have felt in the presence of nature, is proved by the most famous of his wall-paintings inside the Palazzo del Té, the Hall of the Giants, with walls showing on all sides colossal, brutish giants tumbling down on us amid crashing boulders. Nor can this nightmare of instability, this memento of the untrustworthiness of the material world, be set aside as a mere sign of one artist's deranged mind. It adorned one of the main rooms of the Duke's *maison de plaisance* and was apparently widely admired. The distaste of Renaissance perfection must have spread far.

The question has often been asked what made Michelangelo in his *Day* and *Night*, his *Dawn* and *Evening*, and in several of his reliefs keep areas of unworked stone standing. The answer is, I think, that he wanted to give the impression of his figures only just emerging into life, under his exertion, out of a stony, sub-human pre-existence. To shape the image of man entirely liberated from these dark forces must often have seemed a sacrilege to the youngest and again the old Michelangelo. Hence also his many unfinished works.

Again, a different aspect of this new attitude to nature is the Mannerist liking for the grotto. Here such architects as Buontalenti and Palissy employ the highest skill in achieving an elaborate likeness of nature left to herself. There is in this, as well as in Palissy's trick of using casts from lizards, beetles and plants to decorate his bowls and dishes, a good deal of naïve pride, of course, but it should not be forgotten that such verbal imitation of nature, coming as it did, immediately after the great power of idealization which the Renaissance had achieved, is also an admission of defeat and a sign of distrust of human achievement.

The Architecture of Mannerism

To return to Giulio Romano, it must, after the analysis of the Palazzo del Té, be of special interest to see how he expresses himself in a building in which he was entirely free from the wishes of any patron: his own house, built in 1544 (fig. 5). Now here he appears at his most formal, evidently determined to prove what was at the time by no means yet accepted: that the artist could be the best-mannered of courtiers. We can be sure that he wished to avoid solecisms, yet the design is full of them, according to Renaissance standards. The course between ground-floor and upper floor is pushed up into some sort of fragmentary pediment of the central door; the arch of the door is pressed down into a Tudor shape, and the band which runs along the ground-floor on the level of the imposts of the door arch is broken up into unconnected bits. Or are we to believe that the rusticated frames of the windows conceal the band? This is hardly possible, as any indication of three-dimensionality is absent. All is as flat as paper, and the *piano nobile* windows which one would expect to project with their pediments, are even slightly recessed instead. A most eloquent detail is the decorated bands round the windows. Their ornament seems at first crisp, cool and structurally sound, until it is seen that they run right on into the pediment zone, without any cæsura where structural logic would have placed one. The pediments thus cease to be pediments proper. Their weight is reduced. Nor are the windows shaped strong enough to support weight. This deliberate weakness of the windows makes it impossible for them too to revolt in the sense of the Baroque against the tightness of the arched panels in which they are set.

This denial of expressing strength to carry as well as weight of load is one of the most significant innovations of Mannerist architecture. The Romanesque style had mighty massive walls, the Gothic style shafts soaring-up unimpededly, the Renaissance a balance of upright and horizontal. Now the wall ceases altogether to be mass, just as a figure by Parmigiano, Tintoretto or Greco ceases to be body. Nor is the Mannerist wall a system of active forces, just as there are no convincing active forces in Parmigiano, Tintoretto and Greco. But the result of this is by no means immobility, either in painting or in building, owing to the insistence of the Mannerist on discordant motifs and contradictory directions everywhere.

Nikolaus Pevsner

Peruzzi's Palazzo Massimi alle Colonne in Rome (1535) is also a popular textbook illustration of pure Renaissance. To this the Wölfflin generation has objected that the design of the front is against Renaissance principles, because the excessive weight of the three upper storeys presses down the entrance loggia (fig. 6). Against Renaissance principles the building certainly is, but pressure I fail to see. On the contrary, the curious thing about the façade is its seeming paperiness. It is slightly curved, and that alone gives it something of the appearance of a mere screen. The two rows of top windows have, instead of the substantial pediments of the Renaissance, excessively delicate and flat ornamented surrounds, strap-work of the kind which a little later became so popular in the North. The gradation of parts which the Renaissance had evolved is given up as well. The same smooth pattern of the ashlar stone goes from bottom to top, and the second- and third-floor windows are of identical size. Peruzzi, who had, in the Villa Farnesina twenty-five years before, shown a perfect command of High Renaissance harmonies, has here abandoned them for unstable relations in the flat.

It may need some study to see the Palazzo Massimi in this new light. In Michelangelo's architectural experiments of the twenties no effort is required to see how revolutionary they are. The Laurenziana Library and its ante-room were designed in 1524. The library itself lies fifteen steps above the ante-room, but the ante-room reaches up higher still than the library. This excessive verticalism is yet further emphasized by the many closely set verticals of dark grey marble, streaking the white walls (fig. 7). The result is a feeling of discomfort which grows worse, when one begins to examine the structural elements in detail. The system is Bramante's approved alternation of window bays (the windows are blind) and coupled Doric columns. But Michelangelo hated Bramante's happy ease; we know that. And so he does all he can to drive out the smooth beauty of his system. His columns, instead of standing out in front of the wall, as all columns had done ever since the first columns were designed, keep farther back than the panels in which the windows are placed. Moreover, they are tightly caged without any of the freedom of development which is their due. They do not support anything either, and they appear to rest precariously on slender brackets. In fact the brackets, themselves encased on left and right, stand farther forward than the columns. So the accepted connection between brackets and columns is broken, just as the accepted connection is broken between columns and bays. No critic has ever, to my knowledge, overlooked these incongruities. But their interpretation has varied a great deal. Burckhardt, the champion of the Renaissance, has called them 'evidently a joke of the great master', while Schmarsow, engrossed in his new conception of the Baroque, wrote: 'These subdued, encased columns . . . symbolize passionate impetuosity of thought breaking forth and struggling to find an appropriate language.' Now this, to my mind, is untrue. I cannot see in the Laurenziana, anything impetuous, any violence, any struggle. Struggle can only arise between forces, and there are no forces in this architecture. Look at the delicate bands of the panels between the brackets, or the lines round the frail-looking niches above the main window-zone, or the blind windows themselves, with their square, fluted little brackets below, too weak to carry anything, their tapering and partly fluted pilasters and their capitals retracted where one would expect them to swell out.

Once all this has been observed, it will be patent that, while the columns are indeed painfully incarcerated, they do not revolt. If they did, and if the wall really pressed against them, then one would be justified in speaking of Baroque. Michelangelo's *Slaves* struggle, and they stand indeed at the beginning of a development which the seventeenth-century Baroque was to continue. But Michelangelo's architecture knows no gigantic exertions. It is paralysed, frozen, as it were, and held by iron discipline in a stiff pose of forced constraint, so accomplished that it even succeeds in appearing elegant: human freedom and human power suppressed, all swelling beauty of the flesh ascetically starved off—a perfect setting for the self-denying etiquette of sixteenth-century society.

The contrast between Michelangelo's architecture and sculpture cannot here be discussed. It is enough to state that Michelangelo (as Raphael, as Correggio) held in his hands the seeds of both Mannerism and Baroque, enough to point to one place where the interaction of the two styles of the future, that of the immediate and that of the later future, becomes most alarmingly evident. The

Medici Chapel (fig. 8) was designed between 1521 and 1534. The tombs of the two Dukes are well enough known. Their composition was to start from violently moving figures of river gods on the floor, lead up to *Day* and *Night*, and *Dawn* and *Evening*, and find its achievement in the sombre, brooding figures of the Dukes —expressive, it has been proved, of Plato's Vita Activa and Vita Contemplativa. Now this idea of an 'excelsior' through struggle to repose is wholly Baroque; what Mannerism contributes is only the lack of a final triumph. For neither is Giuliano active nor Lorenzo contemplative. Bernini would have given the one Duke wildly reaching-out gestures of triumph, the other an appearance of sensual self-abandon. Such outpourings of feeling Michelangelo never knew. And so he keeps his architecture as frigid, that is as self-consciously precious, as that of the Laurenziana. Detailed analysis of the niches above the low doors is not necessary. The various layers in depth should be observed, the angular excrescences inside pilasters and pediment, the elaborate over-precision of the garlands, and such illogical motifs as the sunk panels of the pilasters and the unmoulded block sticking out at the foot of the niche.

But architecture is not all a matter of walls and wall patterns. It is primarily organized space, and of space hardly anything has so far been said. Now it is, of course, much harder to write of space than of walls; for walls can be photographed and space cannot. To experience space it must be wandered through or at least wandered through with one's eyes. It is a process that takes time and could only be re-evoked by film.

Yet it is easy enough to say that no Renaissance architect would have exaggerated height at the expense of width and depth to the extent that Michelangelo does in the Laurenziana. Standing in the anteroom one feels at the bottom of the well or the shaft of a mine. There is lack of balance in this from the Renaissance point of view, and from the Baroque point of view lack of that final solution which a wide-windowed dome with paintings of open skies and glories of saints or kings would give. Schmarsow says that this very solution lies in the change-over from the narrow anteroom into the 'simple clarity, repose and satisfaction' of the library proper. This again I cannot see. To me the library is excessively long as against its height and certainly as constrained and precious in its details as the anteroom (brackets of the windows, balusters of the blank windows above). So Michelangelo instead of creating a Baroque overflow of dammed forces out into infinite space, keeps his room as rigidly confined as any artist of the Renaissance, but breaks the harmonious proportions and interrelations which dominate Renaissance rooms. In, say, Brunelleschi's Pazzi Chapel a beautifully balanced anteroom is followed by a beautifully balanced main room. in the Laurenziana we are thrown from a room like the shaft of a mine into a room like a tunnel.

This tendency to excess within rigid boundaries is one of the characteristics of Mannerist space. It is well enough known in painting, for instance in Correggio's late Madonnas, or Tintoretto's Last Suppers with the figure of Christ at the far, far end. The most moving of all examples is Tintoretto's painting of the Finding of the Body of St. Mark (Brera, Milan, *c.* 1565). Nowhere else is Mannerist space so irresistible. In architecture this magic suction effect is introduced into Giulio Romano's extremely severe Cathedral at Mantua with its tunnel vault and monotonous columns. But its most familiar and easily acceptable example is no doubt Vasari's Uffizi (Fig. 9). Vasari is the Mannerist *par excellence* of the generation following Giulio's. He lived from 1511 to 1574. He founded the first Academy of Art, a typically Mannerist conception with its connotations of dry rule and social dignity, and wrote the first book on the history of art, his *Vite* of 1555. This again is characteristic of Mannerist mentality: the self-conscious comparison of a late to-day with a long-past youth and a recent Golden Age. The Uffizi Palace was begun in 1560 to house Grand Ducal offices. It consists of two tall wings along a long and narrow courtyard. The formal elements by now need no special mention: lack of a clear gradation of storeys, uniformity coupled with heretical detail, long, elegant and fragile brackets below double pilasters which are no pilasters at all, and so on. What must be emphasized is the finishing accent of the composition towards the river Arno. Here a loggia open in a spacious Venetian window on the ground floor and originally also in a colonnade on the upper floor replaces the solid wall. This is a favourite Mannerist way of linking room with room, a way in which both a clear Renaissance separation of units and a free Baroque flow through the whole and beyond are avoided. Thus, Palladio's two Venetian churches terminate in the east, not in closed apses, but in arcades—straight in S. Giorgio Maggiore (1565), semi-circular in the Redentore (1577)—behind which back-rooms of indistinguishable dimensions appear. And thus Vasari, together with Vignola (1507–73) designed the Villa Giulia, the country *casino* of Pope Julius III (1550–5) as a sequence of buildings with loggias towards semi-circular courts and with vistas across from the entrance through the first loggia towards the second, through it towards the third, and through that into a walled back-garden.

For the garden of the sixteenth century is still walled in. It may have long and varied vistas, as you also find them at the Villa Este in Tivoli or at Caprarola, but they do not stretch out into infinity as in the Baroque garden at Versailles. Neither do the favourite low loggias on the ground floors of Mannerist buildings indicate infinity —that is, a dark, unsurveyable background of space, as a Rembrandt background. Back walls are too near. The continuity of the façade is broken by such loggias—that is what the Renaissance would have disliked—but the layer of opened-up space is shallow and clearly confined in depth. We have found such loggias at the Palazzo Massimi and the Uffizi. Giulio Romano screens the whole garden front of the Palazzo del Té with them, Palladio all sides of the Basilica at Vicenza. Paladio's Palazzo Chierigati is the most perfect example of this screen technique in palace architecture. It appears again in the addition by Pirro Ligorio (1493–1580) on top of the Belvedere exedra at the Vatican in the early sixties and also in the same architect's Casino of Pius IV, just behind the Vatican (fig. 10). This was completed in 1561. A main block is separated from a loggia by an oval court with low walls and two side entrances. The oval, though a favourite spatial element of the Baroque, also owes its introduction into architecture to Mannerism. Oval staircases, elongated in a typically Mannerist way from Bramante's circular staircase in the Vatican, appear in Serlio and Palladio; and Vignola designed an oval dome over the little church of S. Andrea (1554) close to the Villa of Julius and a completely oval church plan for S. Anna dei Palafrenieri shortly before his death. These rooms

RENAISSANCE

CASA CAPRINI, ROME, BY BRAMANTE

MANNERISM

PALAZZO BEVILACQUA, VERONA, BY SAMMICHELI

PLATE I

PALAZZO DEL TÉ, MANTUA

BY GIULIO ROMANO

PLATE II

GIULIO ROMANO'S OWN HOUSE, MANTUA

PALAZZO MASSIMI ALLE COLONNE, ROME

BY PERUZZI

PLATE III

ANTE-ROOM OF THE LAURENZIANA LIBRARY, FLORENCE
BY MICHELANGELO

PLATE IV

DETAIL FROM THE MEDICI CHAPEL, FLORENCE
BY MICHELANGELO

PLATE V

THE UFFIZI, FLORENCE, BY VASARI

CASINO OF PIUS IV, ROME, BY PIRRO LIGORIO

PLATE VI

MANNERISM
COLLEGIO ROMANO, ROME
BY AMMANATI

BAROQUE
PALAZZO DI MONTECITORIO, ROME
BY BERNINI AND CARLO FONTANA

PLATE VII

BAROQUE

SS. VINCENZO E ANASTASIO, ROME

BY M. LUNGLI

MANNERISM

IL GESÙ, ROME, BY VIGNOLA

PLATE VIII

have nothing yet of the surging and ebbing, ever-varying flow of such oval Baroque buildings as Bernini's S. Andrea al Quirinale and Borromini's S. Agnese. They are not static as centrally planned Renaissance churches might be; but movement is hemmed in, and the preference for oval as against circle may even be due more to the greater elegance of a long-drawn-out curve than to the spatial qualities of the oval.

The loggia behind the oval court of Ligorio's Casino of Pius is open on the ground floor between its four plain Doric columns in order to achieve a contrast of framed vista and wall. However, the wall again seems to have no solidity; it is only a screen just strong enough to act as a background for innumerable ornamental motifs and scenic reliefs displayed in a confusingly intricate manner: over-crowding but no mêlée. The walls of Mannerist rooms are like that too, with crisp stucco work and elegant figures and with inextricably complicated painted actions and allegories. Under their barrel vaults one feels as though inside a jewel chest (*Studiolo* in the Palazzo Vecchio at Florence of 1570, Gallery in the Palazzo Spada in Rome of 1556–60).

But preciosity is only one side of Mannerism. The style in painting would be incomplete without Parmigiano, but also without Tintoretto and Greco and late Michelangelo. For Michelangelo in his last works of sculpture and drawing displays none of the Baroque tendencies of his earlier life. There are no violent actions, no gigantic conflicts in the few Crucifixions and Pietàs of the fifties and sixties, the years in which Michelangelo almost exclusively concentrated on architecture, the work on St. Peter's, the Capitol, the Farnese Palace and so on. Of the candour and depth of his religious feelings we know from his sonnets. What is less known is that, when the Jesuits decided to build a large church in Rome, he offered to design and supervise the work without any fee.

He died before the Gesù was begun. But as the Jesuits were the most powerful religious force of the sixteenth century, it is worth looking at the emotional qualities of their architecture in Rome. Most people's expectations will probably be disappointed. For somehow the idea has struck root that Jesuit architecture must be in the most flamboyant Baroque fashion, and that this is what one should expect from the Counter-Reformation. Both notions are wrong. Of the real character of the Counter-Reformation more will be said later, of the character of early Jesuit architecture no better examples can be found than the Gesù on the one hand and the Collegio Romano on the other. Both buildings certainly represent Mannerist tendencies and not tendencies of the Baroque. To prove this, the last two of my analyses may be comparisons of the Collegio Romano and the Gesù with a palace and a church of the Baroque in Rome.

The Collegio Romano (fig. 11) was built by the Jesuits as their University in 1583. The architect was Ammanati (1511–92). The Palazzo di Montecitorio (fig. 12), the pre-war Houses of Parliament of the Kingdom of Italy, was begun by Bernini in 1650 for the Ludovisi family, continued for the Pamfili and then completed as the seat of the Papal Law Courts at the end of the seventeenth century by Gibbs's Roman master, Carlo Fontana. The Collegio Romano is evidently Mannerist in style, and on this uncommonly large scale the style appears particularly uncomfortable. When one stands in front of the building itself and tries to take in its excessive length of twenty bays and excessive height of six storeys and demi-storeys, the total lack of a predominant accent in spite of the stiffest formality otherwise, is most disquieting. The lantern looks as if it were meant as a climax, but it is not, because it is isolated by a balustrade from the rest of the building. Now Bernini—and he was, it should not be forgotten, a restrained architect, as Baroque architects go (though by no means a restrained sculptor and decorator)—leads his composition consistently up to the lantern. The two wings slope back symmetrically in two breaks, pushing forward the seven central bays. These are further distinguished by giant pilasters on the right and left. The treble entrance comes forward beyond the line of the centre bays, and the attic above the main cornice, seven times broken, emphasizes the centre once more, lifting up the top cornice above the clock and finally surging into the crowning ornament of the lantern. The *piano nobile* is given its due with an almost Renaissance dignity. In fact we know from the history of painting that the founders of the Baroque discovered more to inspire them in the High Renaissance than in Mannerism. Carvaggio's connections with the

The Architecture of Mannerism

Raphael of the Transfiguration and the Carraccis's with the Raphael of the Farnesina Gallery prove that sufficiently. The art of the first painters of the Baroque is in many ways a grander, less dignified and more melodramatic version of Raphael's last style. Similarly, Bernini's palace is a development of the Palazzo Farnese and of Michelangelo motifs in a more massive, less nobly proportioned and more expansive way.

The Mannerist on the other hand takes care to avoid the impression of weighty masses. He proportions carefully, but with the aim of hurting, rather than pleasing, the eye. And he is certainly far from expansive or melodramatic. The outstanding quality of Ammanati's façade is austerity. Nearly all the windows are to an irritating degree identical. Each storey has the same mezzanine windows above. There is monotony instead of gradation, no crescendo, no climax upward. Nor is there a climax in width. Instead of a central accent, a painfully small, though exquisitely detailed, niche appears in the middle of the middle part. The two symmetrical portals are typically Mannerist in the sense now familiar, with sunk panels in the fragmentary pilasters, square fluted brackets, and everything else to make them look emaciated and of stiff deportment. The large sunk panels of the walls, repeated everywhere, also seem to drain off the substance of the building. They look like plywood with top layers cut back to reveal layers below.

If this frigid, ascetic building is the Jesuit University, what was the Jesuit church in Rome intended to look like when Vignola designed it (fig. 13)? The foundation stone was laid in 1568. Vignola died before the building was complete. The façade, as well as the upper parts of the interior, are not by him, but by della Porta (who also finished the dome of St. Peter's). According to Vignola's idea the interior was to be dominated by a vast, probably dark, tunnel vault with Mannerist decoration instead of the present painted Baroque glories. The main inner cornice runs through unbroken. It would have driven the visitor eastward into the crossing under the light-shedding dome with a power equal to that of mediæval basilicas or of Vasari's Uffizi.

The façade, according to Vignola's intentions, has always been regarded as one of the foundation pieces of the Baroque; and it is indeed more energetically pulled together than contemporary works by other architects. There is consistent development from the flat side bays via the slightly projecting middle bays to the centre where columns replace the pilasters. This gradation like the crescendo of Vignola's interior from nave to lofty domed crossing (a type incidentally created as early as 1470 by Alberti), has been repeated and intensified by innumerable Baroque architects. But directly one goes for a comparison to a mature Baroque church in Rome, such as the younger Martino Lunghi's SS. Vincenzo e Anastasio of 1650 (fig. 14), Vignola's Mannerism prevails everywhere. The difference does not only lie in the Baroque's richer orchestration, with all columns and no pilasters. At least as significant is the way in which the columns elbow each other. Vignola has only two breaks in the lower entablature and one in the upper, Lunghi has four and four. He doubles the lower central pediment and trebles the top one. He holds the top storey on the sides by mighty caryatids, where Vignola uses flat, drily profiled side-pieces. But caryatids were popular with Mannerist architects, too. We have seen them in the Casino of Pius. Other famous examples are in Michelangelo's tomb of Julius II and in the sunk fountain of the Villa Giulia in Rome. The Gesù façade has them twice, and again only as an ornament without strength. As this one motif, so the whole façade: in the Baroque a turbulent struggle and a triumphant end, in Mannerism an intricate and conflicting pattern, and no solution anywhere. The final proof of Vignola's Mannerism may easily escape notice unless expressly pointed out. His ground-floor seems to have a logical composition which may be noted thus: a—b—a, A—B—A, a—b—a. According to both principles, Renaissance and Baroque, one would expect the top storey to provide a crowning A—B—A. In fact, Vignola composes it of a—A—B—A—a. How then should 'a' be understood? as part of a—b—a or as part of a—A—B—A—a? The resulting disturbance is what the architect wants, just as Sammicheli wanted it in the Bevilacqua Palace and Michelangelo in the Laurenziana.

How can this self-conscious dissenting, frustrated style be accounted for? What made such opposed characters as Michelangelo and Giulio Romano evolve it and the Popes and the Jesuits welcome it?

It is said that in 1513 when Leo X, the first Medici Pope, heard that he had been elected, he exclaimed: 'God hath given us the Papacy; now let us enjoy it.' Just over fifty years later Pius V was elected. The Vatican under him, we hear from contemporary letters, was like a monastery. Silence was kept at table, and only twice a week was meat served. Leo's interest was hunting and the theatre, Pius had been Grand-Inquisitor before he succeeded to the Papacy.

Leo is as characteristic of the High Renaissance as Pius of Mannerism. The end of the Golden Age in art came before or about 1520, with late Raphael and with Pontormo and Rosso. In thought and feeling the break was made in the same years. The Sack of Rome in 1527 is only a convenient reminder of deep inner changes. Groups of men began to assemble, bent on stricter Christian observance. The first of them, the Sodality of Divine Love, was founded in 1518; then new communities and orders quickly followed each other: the Camaldolensians of Monte Corona abandoned their mother house because of its laxity in 1522, the Theatin Order dates from 1524, the Angelican Sisters and the Guastallines date from 1530, the Somasca from 1532, the Barnabites from 1533. The Capuchins separated from the Franciscans in 1535. In the same year the Ursulines were founded; in 1540 came the brothers of the Misericord and, most powerful of all, the Jesuits.

Ignatius of Loyola was born in 1493. His early life was a soldier's. While recovering from wounds received in battle, he conceived the idea of a new militant saintliness. So he retired to Manresa and there prepared himself for his mission with fast and flagellation. Visions haunted him which he tried to overcome. Suppression of human frailty by ever-watchful self-discipline was the hard-gained outcome of his studies—a cold enthusiasm which finds its ultimate form in the *Exercitia Spiritualia* and the system of strict obedience governing early Jesuit organization. Ignatius is only one of many new saints of the sixteenth century. St. Teresa is another (1515–82), and Bernini's Baroque interpretation of her excessively sensitive character should not blind us to her immense organizational talents. Then there are St. Francis Borgia (1510–72), St. Philip Neri (1515–94) a character oddly blended of jollity and mysticism, and St. Charles Borromeo (1538–84) the charitable, miracle-working, ascetic Archbishop of

Milan who, we hear, wore chains under his Cardinal's clothing. In a recent article in *La Civiltà Cattolica* twenty-five saints are quoted who died between 1530 and 1600.

Saints and saintliness are exceptional at all ages. But life had changed for everybody in these seventy years. The Inquisition was re-introduced in 1542, censorship of books in 1543. The wars of religion ravaged Germany since the twenties. The struggles of old and new creeds, and then of Anglican and Non-Conformist are one —if not the only—main issue of English sixteenth-century history. In the Netherlands, Protestants fought the Duke of Alba's terror, and in France the conflict led up to the Night of St. Bartholomew.

This period of religious primacy was over in France when Henry IV decided for himself that 'Paris was worth a Mass' and returned for purely political reasons into the fold of the Roman Church; it was already over in England during Elizabeth's judicious and magnificently worldly reign, and in Italy when the Jesuits Toledo and Bellarmin agreed to accept cardinalates, when the political ideas of independent Venice (Sarpi) defeated the claims of the Pope, and when Paul V (1605–21) adopted the fashion of the little van Dyck beard which had been created by Henry IV. There is a portrait bust of Paul V by Bernini, and it is enough to compare it with the paintings we have of the Popes of the sixteenth century (for instance, Titian's Paul III), to see the difference in character and ambition between the two ages. It is like comparing the Shakespeare of the Sonnets with the Shakespeare of Lear, or Hillyard's with van Dyck's portraits of English noblemen.

Not that 'conceitism' ended when the Baroque replaced Mannerism. Many indeed were the innovations of the sixteenth century that lived on through the seventeenth. Such popular Baroque motifs as oval ground plans, broken pediments, twisted columns are of Mannerist origin. Their emotional context, of course, alters their message, just as new dynamic and sensuous qualities distinguish sixteenth- from seventeenth-century mystic poets and courtly poets.

On the other hand, genuine Baroque ideas, first conceived in the world-open days of the Renaissance, kept alive and grew during Mannerism, in spite of its return to medieval mentality. Faith in the autonomy of human thought and the independence of science underlie the precarious and often secret work of such philosophers and scientists as Cardan, Telesio, Sozzini and Bruno. Without them there would be no Galileo, no Spinoza, no Grotius—just as without Vignola's Gesù the favourite scheme of Baroque church architecture would not exist.

After allowance has been made for what connects Mannerism and Baroque—partly by means of a survival of sixteenth-century conceptions into the seventeenth, partly by pioneer work of the sixteenth century towards the seventeenth—it can now safely be said that Mannerism remains a clearly circumscribed style with characteristics as opposed to those of the Baroque as they are to those of the Renaissance. They can be summarized as follows.

Mannerism is a cheerless style, aloof and austere where it wants to show dignity, precious where it wants to be playful. It lacks the robustness of the Baroque as well as the serenity of the Renaissance. Mannerism has no faith in mankind and no faith in matter. It scorns that bodily beauty in which Renaissance art had excelled and sets against it figures of excessively elongated proportions, sometimes overgraceful, sometimes ascetic. Accordingly it scorns proportions in architecture which are satisfactory to our senses because of their harmony with human proportions. It exaggerates one direction in spatial compositions, as well as in wall compositions, and either breaks symmetry deliberately or over-emphasizes it until it becomes monotony. Moreover, where symmetry is broken, this is not done in the Baroque way to show man conquering matter and subduing it to his will. There is nothing so active in Mannerism. The painter distorts figures to force them into imposed frozen patterns, and the architect designs with seemingly thin materials, which never look strong enough to associate with them the carrying force of the human body, nor ever look massive enough to associate with them the weight of matter pressing down under the force of gravitation. So the Renaissance problem of balance between weighing and carrying and the Baroque problem of a contrast between the two, leading before our eyes to a final victory of one of them, is replaced by an uneasy neutrality rife with potential disturbance everywhere.

Now this is precisely what one must expect from the period which created and developed Mannerism. The great initial impact was the Reformation. It ended the innocence of the Middle Ages in the North and the—very different—innocence of the Renaissance in Italy. It gained for Europe the modern world, a world of science and individualism, but a split world. The Baroque tried valiantly once more to recover singlemindedness—in Italy by means of a self-confident religious enthusiasm, in the North by means of a science with universal claims. Mannerism could not see either of these possible solutions yet. It is a period of tormenting doubt, and rigorous enforcement of no longer self-understood dogma. What individualism had been developed by the Renaissance was to be crushed, and yet could not be crushed. So Mannerist art is full of contradictions: rigid formality and deliberate disturbance, bareness and over-decoration, Greco and Parmigiano, return to mediæval mysticism and the appearance of pornography (Giulio Romano, Aretino). For pornography is a sign of sensuousness with a bad conscience, and Mannerism is the first Western style of the troubled conscience.

Remembering once more now the wars of religion, the prosecution of heretics, Spanish etiquette and the Jesuits, the return of the Inquisition and the intricacies of the sonneteers—all this seems consistent. But one warning must be added in conclusion. This essay is a gross over-simplification. Plenty of important men and events have not been mentioned at all or only inadequately. Take, for instance, the most influential of all Italian sixteenth-century architects: Palladio. His case in the history of style, just as that of his Venetian contemporary Veronese, is far too complicated to be as much as outlined here. Renaissance elements are stronger in both of them than in most others of their generation. Of the typically Mannerist disturbances they know little, and their formality avoids the rigid and austere.

But the very fact that Palladio's influence was much more one of the printed page than of the real building is significant. Mannerism is the age of architectural treatises—an innovation, it is true, of the Renaissance (Alberti). Serlio lives almost exclusively in his *Libri d'Architettura*, and Vignola was to the architect and virtuoso of the North the author of the *Regole,* and not of the Gesù. The theory of the Five Orders, revived from Antiquity, was now made into a fetish. So Vasari's Academy was bound to appear, and his book on the history of art. Not to do more than enumerate these facts in so casual a way, amounts to a serious omission. Equally serious is the omission of Mannerist work outside Italy, not so much that of Italians abroad as original transalpine work in styles seemingly quite different from Italian Mannerism. That Rosso, Primaticcio and Niccolò dell'Abbate worked at Fontainebleau for Francis I is familiar. Their decoration is amongst the English perhaps the most widely known example of Mannerism. Goujon also belongs to the Mannerists without doubt, and the style of Lescot, Delorme and the other French-born architects of the mid-sixteenth century can hardly be analysed under any other term. Again, the Escorial, Philip II's palace-monastery, is evidently a monument of the purest Mannerism, forbidding from outside and frigid and intricate in its interior decoration; but it is essentially Italian in style and, as far as painting goes, the work of Italians: Tibaldi, Cambiaso, Zuccari, Carducci.

So it seems that, concerning the architecture of France and Spain, the application of the term Mannerism affords no problems. But when it comes to the Elizabethan style in England and to its parallels and examples in the Netherlands and Germany, are we still justified in speaking of Mannerism? Wollaton or Hardwick or Hatfield obviously are not Renaissance. Nor are they English Baroque, if St. Paul's and Blenheim are Baroque. Strapwork ornament, in its lifelessness, intricacy and stiff preciosity, is typically Mannerist. But the buoyancy and the sturdy strength of Elizabethan building are wholly absent in Italy, and wholly in harmony with the age of Drake and Ralegh.

However, one should not expect criteria of style always to be applicable to different countries without national modifications. French Romanticism is different from English Romanticism and from German. Yet all three are romantic. Similarly Wren is Baroque, but English Baroque, and the Perpendicular style is Late Gothic, but English Late Gothic. Maybe we shall have to learn the same lesson in the case of Mannerism if we wish for a full understanding of Elizabethan architecture.

Nikolaus Pevsner

FURTHER READING

In English there is still very little: Anthony Blunt's *Artistic Theories in Italy, 1450–1600*, O.U.P., 1940, and some articles in American magazines, especially the *Art Bulletin*. Nothing has as yet appeared on the whole problem of Mannerism or of Mannerist architecture. MANNERISM IN GENERAL: M. Dvořák: 'Greco und der Manierismus' (1920), in *Kunstgeschichte als Geistesgeschichte*, Munich, 1924. W. Friedlaender: 'Die Entstehung des antiklassischen Stiles . . . um 1520', *Repertorium für Kunstwissenschaft*, 1925. N. Pevsner: 'Manierismus und Gegenreformation', *Repertorium für Kunstwissenschaft*, 1925. E. Panofsky: *Idea*, Leipzig, 1924. W. Pinder: 'Zur Physiognomik des Manierismus', in *Die Wissenschaft am Scheidewege*, Leipzig, 1932. N. Pevsner: *Die talienische Malerei vom Ende der Renaissance bis zum ausgehenden Rokoko* (*Handbuch der Kunstwissenschaft*), Neubabelsberg, 1926–8. MANNERISM IN ARCHITECTURE: E. Gombrich on Giulio Romano, in *Jahrbuch der kunsthistorischen Sammlungen in Wien*, 1935 and 1936. R. Wittkower on Michelangelo's Laurenziana, in *Art Bulletin*, 1934. J. Coolidge on Vignola and the Villa Giulia, in *Marsyas*, 1942, and *Art Bulletin*, 1943. Also E. Panofsky in *Staedel Jahrbuch*, 1930, and E. Michalski in *Zeitschrift für Kunstgeschichte*, 1933. A brief summing up is H. Hoffmann: *Hochrenaissance—Manierismus—Frühbarock*, Zürich, 1938.

OWEN BARFIELD

The Psalms of David

I N common with many of my generation, I grew up with an
aversion from the Old Testament. Later on, I came to envy, for
literary and historical reasons, that close acquaintance with the
Bible which was forced on our fathers in *their* youth and which
remained with them as a cultural endowment long after so many of
them had felt the emotional reaction which I had inherited or
acquired. But I still disliked the people portrayed in the Old Testament, their whole attitude to life, their everlasting preoccupation with
sin, their perpetual backslidings and the abject, cringing way in
which they confessed them. Sometimes, it seemed, they had a very
low opinion of themselves (an opinion in which I fully concurred):

> *But as for me, I am a worm, and no man: a very scorn of men and the
> outcast of the people* . . .
> *For I will confess my wickedness: and be sorry for my sin.*

At other times they evinced a revolting self-righteousness:

> *I have hated the congregation of the wicked: and will not sit among the
> ungodly*
> *I will wash my hands in innocency, O Lord: and so will I go to thine
> altar.*

Their religion seemed to me a loveless and a joyless affair or, when
any joy did break in, it was of a kind which I could not easily
approve, much less share:

> *Behold, how good and joyful a thing it is: brethren, to dwell in unity!*
> *It is like the precious ointment upon the head, that ran down unto the
> beard: even unto Aaron's beard, and went down to the skirts of his clothing.*

This is not my idea of a good and joyful thing at all. But, worse
than this, through it all ran the central theme of obedience and dis-

obedience, rewards and punishments. Cruel and violent, alike to their enemies and to the offenders in their own ranks, and that not only by nature but by the express commands of their Deity, the only sin of which they seemed to be really ashamed was disobedience, the only virtue they recognized (and even this they spoiled by claiming rewards for it) obedience; obedience, not to the dictates of conscience, mark you, not to the words of a beloved Lord, but to their stern and even vengeful Jehovah. And this is not my idea of religion at all.

With all this I contrasted the frank and free atmosphere in which, for example, the Greeks lived their lives and out of which they created their art and their literature with its calm dignity and its saving grace of humour. They well understood the distinction between modesty and self-abasement. *They* were not mawkishly preoccupied with sin like the Jews, but knew how to clothe the theme of human guilt in the dignified vestments of tragedy.

One day however (I can still recall the time and place) a friend pointed out to me that the Jews were historically remarkable precisely because they were the *only* people in whose consciousness the naked sense of right and wrong was so powerful a reality that it took precedence of all else. I began very slowly and painfully to readjust my ideas. I began, in fact, to try and give to the Jews of the Old Testament the benefit of that historical imagination which I had applied so liberally elsewhere but for some reason had withheld from them. By historical imagination I mean the habit of mind which endeavours to approach a past epoch by seeing the world through its eyes instead of by seeing *it* through the eyes of the twentieth century and which, in assessing the contribution of that epoch to the history of human consciousness, carefully refrains from judging it by later standards—especially if the creation of those standards is part of the very contribution to be assessed.

Nowadays, we approach the Old Testament, if at all, through the New Testament. Our mental picture of a pious Jew is that of the lowest type of Pharisee as Jesus found him, our emotional reaction to the Law itself is coloured through and through by the reaction of St. Paul after his vision on the way to Damascus. The first task of historical imagination is to peel all this away. I at any rate had criticized the religion of the Old Testament as something too external, not truly of the heart, but enforced from without. Now I endeavoured to appreciate that it was largely because the Jewish nation had lived and struggled that I or anyone else was in a position to make such a criticism at all. Moral choice, responsibility, freedom —whence do we get our absolute conviction of these things? Not from Nature:

> Ah, child, she cries, that strife divine,
> Whence was it? for it is not mine!

Not from any of the heathen nations. In a pagan world of myth and imagery and idolatry, where in the sentient body and sentient soul Nature in living pictures was herself active as human impulse, the Jews alone were forbidden to make graven images. It was their whole historical task to introduce into human consciousness the very inwardness which I had pertly accused them of lacking! I had, as it happens, already accepted this from the writings of Rudolf Steiner as a fact, but it had remained for me what I will call an historical *cliché*, a proposition which I could support with a few isolated quotations and which I believed because it fitted into the general scheme of things. I had never *experienced* it outside idea, as one experiences Shakespeare or springtime or breakfast. I now wished to do so and among other lines of approach I read and re-read the Psalms.

The Psalms are the Old Testament in epitome. Of three or four of them (the 78th for instance) this is true in the most literal sense, inasmuch as they consist of brief *résumés* of the history of the Israelites; but it is true in a much deeper sense of the whole body; for the Psalms express in spirit both the Law and the Prophets. Contrast with the well-known 23rd Psalm (*The Lord is my Shepherd*), or the magnificent hymn of praise and ode to Nature, which is Psalm 104, the 119th Psalm (really a group of Psalms, one for each letter of the Hebrew alphabet). For instance:

> *I hate them that imagine evil things: but thy law do I love.*
> *Thou art my defence and shield: and my trust is in thy word.*
> *Away from me, ye wicked: I will keep the commandments of my God.*
> *O stablish me according to thy word, that I may live: and let me not be*
> *disappointed of my hope.*

Hold thou me up, and I shall be safe: yea, my delight shall be ever in thy statutes.

Thou hast trodden down all them that depart from thy statutes: for they imagine but deceit.

Thou puttest away all the ungodly of the earth like dross: therefore I love thy testimonies.

My flesh trembleth for fear of thee: and I am afraid of thy judgments.

I think that most of us feel that, while we can admire and love the 'prophetic' element in the Psalms, the Law is a very different matter. Why such enthusiasm about it? The prophetic is, for us, the poetic:

Thou deckest thyself with light as it were with a garment: and spreadest out the heavens like a curtain . . .

Whither shall I go then from thy Spirit; or whither shall I go then from thy presence?

If I climb up into heaven, thou art there: if I go down to hell, thou art there also.

If I take the wings of the morning: and remain in the uttermost parts of the sea;

Even there also shall thy hand lead me . . .

or

By the waters of Babylon we sat down and wept: when we remembered thee, O Sion . . .

But we feel the Psalmist committed an error of taste when he attempted to speak in the same exalted style, and with his singing robes about him, of anything so dry and authoritarian as the Law.

But this, if we are seeking to use the Psalms as a pathway to sympathetic understanding of the Jewish consciousness, is exactly what we must try *not* to feel. The contrast between the Law and the Prophets was no contrast between prose and poetry. The Law, with all its severity, was not Katisha to the righteous Jew; it was Yum-yum herself:

O how sweet are thy words unto my throat: yea, sweeter than honey unto my mouth.

It was written in their hearts:

> *In the volume of the book it is written of me, that I should fulfil thy will,*
> *O my God: I am content to do it; yea, thy law is within my heart.*

They loved it because in their eyes it was lovely. It moved them at times, as music and memories and children move *us* at times. You never knew when it was going to give that little tug at your heart-strings or bring that lump into your throat.

A modern Jew has tried to convey this by means of a comparison. Suppose a well-regulated and affectionate family, living in a district inhabited else by gangsters and hooligans, a family where law and order and routine mean much and are sedulously enforced; where at meal-times, for instance, not only every person, but every salt-cellar and flower-vase have their exactly appointed places; where all must be done 'duly' and ceremonially, one day following another in smooth succession; where none must be late or come with unwashed hands; but where all who belong are welcome and glad. The very table-talk has gradually developed into a private language, intimate, allusive and half-secret. The ritual of bowing to the head of the table on entrance, of holding the knife correctly, chewing properly, passing the dishes to and fro and all the *minutiae* of decent manners, is all-important. Then think yourself a child, a member of this family, coming in out of the street or from a day of harsh contacts with the hooligans outside, who would neither understand nor value these family customs, whose language is crass and vulgar and their conversation larded with jeers and catcalls, who do not bother overmuch with trifles like soap and water. It is not a perfect analogy, but it may help you to feel how it was possible for the Jews, not merely to praise obedience as a duty, but to delight in it as an end in itself, not merely to revere their Law, but to love it:

> *With my whole heart have I sought thee; O let me not go wrong out of*
> *thy commandments.*
> *Thy words have I hid within my heart: that I should not sin against thee.*
> *Blessed art thou, O Lord: O teach me thy statutes . . .*
> *I have had as great delight in the way of thy testimonies: as in all manner*
> *of riches.*

Owen Barfield

I will talk of thy commandments: and have respect unto thy ways.
My delight shall be in thy statutes: and I will not forget thy word.

Human nature does not remain the same. It has developed, and in the course of history quite new potentialities have been added to it. It is indeed often possible to trace how these have been unfolded especially in one place by one people and later spread over a large part of mankind; and the meanings of many common words are living relics of this process. One may trace, for example, how meanings, quite foreign to the original speakers, distinctively *Christian* meanings, were brought into the Greek language, when this was used for writing the literature from which the New Testament canon has been selected, and in that way dispersed, either directly or through the Latin tongue, over a large part of Europe and Asia.

But that is not my purpose here. These Christian meanings had first themselves to be created. How? Not out of nothing. By the Christ Himself then? But even He needed something that would come part of the way to meet Him; some soil prepared and thirsty for the seed He came to sow; some souls for whom His Gospel, though new and startling, would yet, owing to their predisposition, not be so new as to seem wholly meaningless. Such souls He found in Palestine, either Jews themselves or living in intimate communion with Jewish society. There He found what He could have found nowhere else in the world, namely a peculiar quality of love, a tender personal affection, which embraced as its object not persons only but the fountain of righteousness itself. The Greeks, and no doubt other nations also, knew something of this tenderness (στόργη), but only in the family circle as between parent and child or brother and sister. The Jews, as has been already indicated, had come to feel the same *sort* of tenderness for the *Torah*. There is much else besides feeling to be taken into consideration, but it is feeling which I am considering here and it was just *this* feeling which Jesus was able to win for Himself and, by so doing, to transmute it into Christian love and charity.

So much I think any man of reasonably sensitive perception would have to concede, whatever his beliefs about the underlying causes. Is it such a very big step farther to perceive that a metamorphosis so

144

pregnant with meaning for the human race could hardly have taken place by accident, or that it was possible only because the two beloved objects were in substance the same? In loving Christ the first Christians were loving Him whose prevenient shadow the *Torah* (that is, the Law) had always been. Read in the Gospels the remarkably inconsistent references made by Jesus Himself to the Law, which at one moment He ratified to the last jot and tittle and in the next proclaimed to be superseded by Himself. [1] There may well be verbal confusion and paradox, and abrupt changes of heart, where a sharp contrast apparent on the surface springs from identity in the depths. The sudden electrifying perception that this Christ whom, out of his deep reverence for the Law, he had been persecuting so actively in His followers, was not only no enemy, but actually *was* the Beloved, the Law itself—was the very centre and source of its reflected radiance—this surely is the bare concept of St. Paul's experience on the road to Damascus:

> *I will preach the Law, whereof the Lord hath said unto me: Thou art my Son, this day have I begotten thee.*

St. Paul must have known this verse from the Psalms well enough (he was to allude to it later in one of his *Epistles*); but hitherto, we may suppose, he had only taken the one half of it really seriously. Now he realized that both parts must be given equal weight, if the truth was not to slip through his fingers. And at once the old thought became so new that he was temporarily blinded by the revelation. There is no question here of devising a 'rational explanation' for a miracle. Whatever physical disturbance accompanied the *volte face* of consciousness is, for me, of relatively slight importance.

At this point it will probably make my meaning clearer if I say that I personally have long accepted Steiner's account of the Incarnation, according to which it was (*inter alia*) the event which made possible the complete 'descent' of any and every human Ego into a physical body; it is thus at the root of the increasing self-consciousness which, for good and ill, has marked the subsequent psychological history of mankind. The Deity portrayed in the Old Testament, he

---

[1] The dominical utterances on the Law will be found admirably assembled, analyzed and considered in Hort's *Judaic Christianity*.

affirmed (for reasons and with a background into which I need not enter), was related to the Christ as light reflected is to radiant light. For the point which I am seeking to make in this paragraph, however, it is sufficient to suppose that the Old Testament includes a partial or imperfect revelation of certain facts of the spirit which were later to be much more fully expressed in the New—a supposition which, although not now widely accepted, is neither particularly new nor particularly startling. The point is that this fact, if fact it be, is also one of which it is possible to hear both halves, but to grasp and live with one only.

That the Law, and indeed all that is contained in the Old Testament, was *sub specie æternitatis* 'only' a reflection of what is contained in the New—this in this post-revolutionary era is a truth which can be quickly and gratefully grasped by most of those who attach a more than anthropological significance to either document. It is the other half which costs some trouble in the uptake; I mean the at least equally weighty half of the truth, that it *was* a reflection —not, that is, something contrasted and repugnant, but a reflection, with all the faithful likeness of a reflection. Our difficulty, though its solution is less important, is the exact opposite of St. Paul's.

But it is time to return to the Psalms. Keep in mind the special love and tenderness for the Law which I have tried to indicate and suppose a soul imbued and saturated through and through with this tenderness. The Psalms express nothing less than the intimate and personal conversation of such a soul with God. Intimate, because a sense of the actual and immediate presence of God breathes so strongly through them; personal, because the God who is so present is nevertheless so *other*, and therefore so distant. He is addressed indeed as if He were actually another person. He can be argued with:

> *What profit is there in my blood: when I go down to the pit?*
> *Shall the dust give thanks unto thee: or shall it declare thy truth?*

admonished and exhorted:

> *Up, Lord, why sleepest thou: awake, and be not absent from us for ever.*

held to a bargain:

> *O Lord in thee have I trusted: let me never be confounded.*

The trouble here is that, through all the splendour of the diction, we can hardly help feeling faintly uneasy, as we do with the Oxford Groups and those evangelical pastors who inform us readily, and sometimes perhaps a little glibly, that God likes this and does not like that, that He wants us to do so and so and will be disappointed if we do the other; referring to Him rather too much as though He were the Headmistress or Mr. Churchill. In other words, it is above all this imputed personal otherness which constitutes a stumbling-block when, throwing historical imagination to the winds, we turn to the Psalms as we should to a book written yesterday and strive to let them speak afresh to our hearts, and *for* our hearts, as they have done to so many generations of our fathers. I think it is for that reason that for many souls to-day they seem most answerable to its despondent moods. This is certainly the case with those who (like myself) talk, or think much, and also perhaps sometimes a little glibly, of the Ego, thereby identifying ourselves with the spiritual world or at all events affirming ourselves as already its inhabitants. But there may be times when we feel reason to doubt whether, in doing so, we have been speaking with quite the precision which such a subject demands. And then the spiritual world, and the Ego, too, may look quite as over-shadowing and remote and 'other' as did the God of the Old Testament to the Psalmist, when he cried:

> *Take me out of the mire, that I sink not: O let me be delivered from them that hate me, and out of the deep waters.*
> *Let not the waterflood drown me, neither let the deep swallow me up: and let not the pit shut her mouth upon me.*
> *Hear me, O Lord, for thy loving-kindness is comfortable: turn thee unto me according to the multitude of thy mercies.*
> *And hide not thy face from thy servant, for I am in trouble: O haste thee, and hear me.*

Most of those, to whom the presence of the spiritual world is a stark fact and not merely a habit of speech and a voluble assumption, know what it is to feel something of what these words express, that is, to feel how precious little all their talk of the Ego and its divine origin and prospects seems to amount to in practice:

Owen Barfield

By the waters of Babylon we sat down and wept: when we remembered thee, O Sion.

It will be some time yet before there is no longer any place in humanity for writings which affirm in the same moment, and with the beauty and intensity of the Psalms, alike the nearness and the otherness of the Divine Spirit.

How comes it, then, that the Psalms express these two contrasted attributes with such special intensity? Without trying to answer this, let us ask another related question: How comes it that they *lack* something else, something all-important, if we are endeavouring to assess their contemporary value as, let us say, a book of devotion? I mean the sense of the *indwelling* Spirit, of all that is implied in the word 'sacramental'. The second question is really the obverse of the first, for it is implied in that 'otherness', the consideration of which led up to it.

Once again we are brought face to face with the peculiar destiny of the Jewish nation. The gods were immanent in pagan and gentile souls, in the Midianites, the Hittites, the Perizzites and the Jebusites, in a way they could never be, *must* never be allowed to be, in the Jewish. The old sacramentalism represented a direct inflow of the astral and spiritual world into the human astral body and sentient soul. The new sacrament, that is the new *union*, the new transcending of that 'otherness' of which we have spoken, can only take place in and through the Ego itself; and it presupposes the full incarnation of the Ego in the physical body—an event which had not yet taken place when the Jews were making history. But an Ego is not merely, like the astral part of man, a 'soul', it is also a 'self.' Hence, almost by definition, it is 'other' than all that surrounds it, including the Spirit from which it derives its being. The Jews made possible the physical incarnation of the Ego, prepared the physical body in which it first took place. But this was not all. It was they, also, who bore the brunt of the Ego's tragic, almost self-contradictory, task of affirming its separateness from, while maintaining its identity with, the Divine Spirit. I think we are allowed to overhear something of that brunt in the Psalms.

Nor in the Psalms only, but also in the whole of the Old Testament. For the whole history of Israel before the Incarnation is a panorama of the progressive incarnation of the Ego, experienced as a moral problem. They, for the whole human race, were custodians and stewards of that process; tender nurses protecting the nascent Ego and guarding it in their midst. *Egypt, Jerusalem* or *Sion, Babylon, Jordan,* why are they now such colossal and abiding symbols for the experiences of each individual soul on its way? Is it because someone has drawn adroit poetical parallels? Not for a moment. It is because, in the Jews, a whole nation was engaged *as* a nation in solving a moral problem and achieving a moral task, which have since become *the* problem and *the* task facing every individual soul.

I began by endeavouring to approach the Psalms through historical imagination and then I made some attempt to appraise, purposely excluding historical imagination, their value as a book of devotion or vehicle of expression for contemporary religious experience. I am now trying to suggest a sort of *via media* between these two avenues of approach, which if we follow, we may be able to share the poetic and spiritual treasures in the Psalms without being chilled and repelled by that lack, of which I have just spoken. The Psalms lack the peculiar sacramental grace. Inevitably so, because the individual Jew was not able to say 'Now is the Prince of this world cast out', or 'Our lives are hid with Christ in God', or 'No longer I live, but Christ liveth in me'. He could not feel the unfathomed inwardness in himself, because it was not there. But the Jew could and did say to himself: In the world is Judea, in Judea is Jerusalem, in Jerusalem is the Temple, in the Temple's inmost holy of holies is the Ark, and in the Ark is—nothing—everything—the invisible beating of the wings of the Cherubim—a voiceless Breath for ever uttering the unutterable Name, I AM—the two Stone Tables with the Ten Commandments of the Law engraved upon them! Here was *his* mystery of inwardness, not his own, but his nation's; and when he reflected on it, the low mood of despondency beneath the remote and frowning majesty of Jehovah vanished away like smoke, and instead it was:

Sing we merrily unto God our strength: make a cheerful noise unto the God of Jacob.

149

Take the psalm, bring hither the tabret; the merry harp with the lute.
Blow up the trumpet in the new-moon; even in the time appointed, and upon our solemn feast-day.

Having, then, learnt something with the help of historical imagination—that 'peeling away' of the intermediate past of which I spoke earlier—we should abandon the special effort this required but retain in the background of our minds the fruits of meditation on the peculiar destiny of the Jewish people, so that there hovers in our apprehension the picture of the Israelites, wandering long years in the desert, homesick, restless and unhappy, but caring the more tenderly because of that very unhappiness for the Ark and its mystery, which they carried with them in their midst; until they could bring it safe to rest on the holy hill at last and build the Temple to surround it. Then we shall find that the sacramental element, the unfathomed inwardness, is not so entirely lacking as we at first felt. We shall feel its breath stirring over and over again, when the spatial focus of the *Nation's* inwardness is alluded to, that is to say, when Jerusalem or the hills on which it stands are mentioned or poetically invoked:

> *They that put their trust in the Lord shall be even as the mount Sion: which may not be removed, but standeth fast for ever.*
> *The hills stand about Jerusalem: even so standeth the Lord round about his people, from this time forth for evermore . . .*
> *Our feet shall stand in thy gates: O Jerusalem.*
> *Jerusalem is built as a city: that is at unity in itself . . .*
> *As the hill of Basan, so is God's hill: even an high hill, as the hill of Basan.*
> *Why hop ye so, ye high hills? This is God's hill, in the which it pleaseth him to dwell: yea, the Lord will abide in it for ever . . .*
> *Out of Sion hath God appeared: in perfect beauty.*

There are many similar passages, but I must forbear further quotation. The Psalms are not there for any one nation alone; but for the English-speaking peoples they possess this added significance, that there is probably no piece of literature, not even excepting Shakespeare's plays, which has exerted so deep and abiding an influence on their history. Hundreds of those who have played leading parts in that history must have known the Psalms practically by heart. Dig down and you would find their sentiments and cadences intertwined with the roots of the national consciousness. Accordingly, in this time, when there is a strong and growing impulse at work in many quarters to sharply cut off the present and future from their roots in the past, to sabotage all feeling and tradition and to start building the world afresh on a foundation of naked will guided by shallow doctrine, it is well that there should be no unnecessary hindrances in the way of anyone's approach to a document of such ancient and majestic import as the Psalms of David.

PETER TAYLOR

Rain in the Heart

W HEN the drilling was over they stopped at the edge of the field and the drill sergeant looked across the flat valley towards the woods on Peavine Ridge. Among the shifting lights on the tree tops there in the late afternoon the drill sergeant visualized pointed roofs of houses that were on another, more thickly populated ridge seven miles to the west.

Lazily the sergeant rested the butt end of his rifle in the mud and turned to tell the squad of rookies to return to their own barracks. But they had already gone on without him and he stood a moment watching them drift back towards the rows of squat buildings, some with their rifles thrown over their shoulders, others toting them by the leather slings in suitcase fashion.

On the field behind the sergeant were the tracks which he and the twelve men had made during an hour's drilling. He turned and studied the tracks for a moment, wondering whether or not he could have told how many men had been tramping there if that had been necessary for telling the strength of an enemy. Then with a shrug of his shoulders he turned his face toward Peavine Ridge again, thinking once more of that other ridge in the suburban area where his bride had found furnished rooms. And seeing how the ridge before him stretched out endlessly north and south he was reminded of a long street-car ride that was before him on his journey to their rooms this night. Suddenly throwing the rifle over his shoulder he began to make his way back toward his own barrack.

The immediate approach to the barrack of the non-commissioned officers was over a wide asphalt area where all formations were held. As the sergeant crossed the asphalt, it required a special effort for him to raise his foot each time. Since his furlough and wedding trip to the mountains, this was the first night the sergeant had been granted leave to go in to see his wife. When he reached the stoop

Rain in the Heart

before the entrance to the barrack he lingered by the bulletin board. He stood aimlessly examining the notices posted there. But finally drawing himself up straight he turned and walked erectly and swiftly inside. He knew that the barrack would be filled with men ready with stale, friendly, evil jokes.

As he hurried down the aisle of the barrack he removed his blue denim jacket, indicating his haste. It seemed at first that no one had noticed him. Yet he was still filled with a dread of the jokes which must inevitably be directed at him to-day. At last a copper-headed corporal who sat on the bunk next to his own, whittling his toenails with his knife, had begun to sing:

> Yes, she jumped in bed
> And she covered up her head—

Another voice across the aisle took up the song here:

> And she vowed he couldn't find her.

Then other voices, some faking soprano, others stimulating the deepest choir bass, from all points of the long room joined in:

> But she knew damned well
> That she lied like hell
> When he jumped right in behind her.

The sergeant blushed a little, pretended to be very angry, and began to undress for his shower. Silently he reminded himself that when he started for town he must take with him the big volume of Civil War history, for it was past due at the city library. *She* could have it renewed for him to-morrow.

In the shower too the soldiers pretended at first to take no notice of him. They were talking of their own plans for the evening in town. One tall and bony sergeant with a head of wiry black hair was saying, 'I've got a strong deal on to-night with a WAC from Vermont. But of course we'll have to be in by midnight.'

Now the copper-headed corporal had come into the shower. He was smaller than most of the other soldiers, and beneath his straight copper-coloured hair were a pair of bright grey-green eyes. He had a

153

hairy pot-belly that looked like a football. 'My deal's pretty strong to-night, too,' he said, addressing the tall soldier beside him. 'She lives down the road a way with her family, so I'll have to be in early too. But then you and me won't be all fagged out to-morrow, eh, Slim?'

'No,' the tall and angular soldier said, 'we'll be able to hold our backs up straight and sort of carry ourselves like soldiers, as some won't feel like doing.'

The lukewarm shower poured down over the chest and back of the drill sergeant. This was his second year in the army and now he found himself continually surprised at the small effect that the stream of words of the soldiers had upon him.

Standing in the narrow aisle between his own bunk and that of the copper-headed corporal, he pulled on his clean khaki clothes before an audience of naked soldiers who lounged on the two bunks.

'When I marry,' the wiry-headed sergeant was saying, 'I'll marry me a WAC who I can take right to the front with me.'

'You shouldn't do that,' the corporal replied, 'she might be wounded in action.' He and the angular, wiry-headed sergeant laughed so bawdily and merrily that the drill sergeant joined in, hardly knowing what were the jokes they'd been making. But the other naked soldiers, of more regular shapes, found the jokes not plain enough, and they began to ask literally:

'Can a WAC and a soldier overseas get married?'

'If a married WAC gets pregnant, what happens?'

'When I get married,' said one soldier who was stretched out straight on his back with his eyes closed and a towel thrown across his loins, 'it'll be to a nice girl like the sergeant here's married.'

The sergeant looked at him silently.

'But wherever,' asked Slim, 'are *you* going to meet such a girl like that in such company as you keep?'

The soldier lying on his back opened one eye: 'I wouldn't talk about my company if I was you. I've saw you and the corporal here with them biddy-dolls at midway twiest.'

The corporal's eyes shone. He laughed aloud and fairly shouted. 'And *he* got *me* the date both times, Buck.'

'Well,' said Buck, with his eyes still closed and his hands folded over his bare chest, 'when I marry it won't be to one of them sort. Nor not to one of your WACs neither, Slim.'

Slim said, 'Blow it out your barracks bag.'

One of those more regularly shaped soldiers seemed to rouse himself as from sleep to say, 'That's why y'like 'em, ain't it, Slim? Y'like 'em because they know how?' His joke was sufficiently plain to bring laughter from all. They all looked toward Slim. Even the soldier who was lying down opened one eye and looked at him. And Slim who was rubbing his wiry mop of black hair with a white towel muttered, 'At least I don't pollute little kids from the roller rink like some present.'

The naked soldier named Buck who was stretched out on the cot opened his eyes and rolled them in the direction of Slim. Then he closed his eyes meditatively and suddenly opened them again. He sat up and swung his feet around to the floor. 'Well, I did meet an odd number the other night,' he said. 'She was drinking beer alone in Conner's Café when I comes in and sits on her right, like this.' He patted his hand on the olive-drab blanket, and all the while he talked he was not looking at the other soldiers. Rather his face was turned toward the window at the end of his cot, and with his lantern jaw raised and his small, round eyes squinting, he peered into the rays of sunlight. 'She was an odd one and wouldn't give me any sort of talk as long as I sit there. Then I begun to push off and she says out of the clear, "Soldier, what did the rat say to the cat?" I said that I don't know and she says, "This pussy's killin' me."' Now all the other soldiers began to laugh and hollo. But Buck didn't even smile. He continued to squint up into the light and to speak in the same monotone. 'So I said, "Come on," and jerked her up by the arm. But, you know, she was odd. She never did say much but tell a nasty joke now and then. She didn't have a bunch of small talk, but she come along and did all right. But I do hate to hear a woman talk nasty.'

The pot-bellied corporal winked at the drill sergeant and said, 'Listen to him. He says he's going to marry a nice girl like yours, but I bet you didn't run up on yours in Conner's Café or the roller rink.'

Buck whisked the towel from across his lap and drawing it back he quickly snapped it at the corporal's little, hairy pot-belly. The drill sergeant laughed with the rest and watched for a moment the patch of white that the towel made on the belly which was otherwise still red from the hot shower.

Now the drill sergeant was dressed. He combed his sandy-coloured hair before a square hand mirror which he had set on the window-sill. The sight of himself reminded him of her who would already be waiting for him on that other ridge. She with her soft, Southern voice, her small hands for ever clasping a handkerchief. This was what his own face in the tiny mirror brought to mind. How unreal to him were these soldiers and their hairy bodies and all their talk and their rough ways. How temporary. How different from his own life, from his real life with her.

He opened his metal foot locker and took out the history book in which he had been reading of battles that once took place on this camp site and along the ridge where he would ride the bus to-night. He pulled his khaki overseas cap on to the right side of his head and slipped away, apparently unnoticed, from the soldiers gathered there. They were all listening now to Slim who was saying, 'Me and Pat McKenzie picked up a pretty little broad one night who was deaf and dumb. But when me and her finally got around to shacking up she made the most mawkish noises you ever heard.'

With the book clasped under his arm the drill sergeant passed down the aisle between the rows of cots, observing here a half-dressed soldier picking up a pair of dirty socks, there another soldier shining a pair of prized garrison shoes or tying a khaki tie with meticulous care. The drill sergeant's thoughts were still on her whose brown curls fell over the white collar of her summer dress. And he could dismiss the soldiers as he passed them as good fellows each, saying, 'So long, Smoky Joe,' to one who seemed to be retiring even before sundown, and 'So long, Happy Jack,' to another who scowled at him. They were good rough-and-ready fellows all, Smoky Joe, Happy Jack, Slim, Buck, and the copper-headed one. But one of them called to him as he went out the door, 'I wouldn't take no book along. What you think you want with a book this night?' And the laughter came through the open windows after he was outside on the asphalt.

The bus jostled him and rubbed him against the civilian workers from the camp and the mill workers who climbed aboard with their dinner pails at the first stop. He could feel the fat thighs of middle-aged women rubbing against the sensitive places of his body, and they—unaware of such personal feelings—leaned toward one another and swapped stories about their outrageous bosses. One of the women said that for a little she'd quit this very week. The men, also mostly middle-aged and dressed in overalls and shirtsleeves, seemed sensible of nothing but that this suburban bus somewhere crossed Lake Road, Pidgeon Street, Jackson Boulevard, and that at some such intersection they must be ready to jerk the stop cord and alight. 'The days are getting a little shorter,' one of them said.

The sergeant himself alighted at John Ross Road and transferred to the McFarland Gap bus. The passengers on this bus were not as crowded as on the first. The men were dressed in linen and seersucker business suits, and the women carried purses and wore little tailored dresses and straw hats. Those that were crowded together did not make any conversation among themselves. Even those who seemed to know one another talked in whispers. The sergeant was standing in the aisle but he bent over now and again and looked out the windows at the neat bungalows and larger dwelling houses along the roadside. He would one day have a house such as one of those for his own. His own father's house was the like of these, with a screened porch on the side and a fine tile roof. He could hear his father saying, 'A house is only as good as the roof over it.' But weren't these the things that had once seemed prosaic and too binding for his notions? Before he went into the army had there not been moments when the thought of limiting himself to a genteel suburban life seemed intolerable by its restrictions and confinement? Even by the confinement to the company of such people as those here on the bus with him? And yet now when he sometimes lay wakeful and lonesome at night in the long dark barrack among the carefree and garrulous soldiers or when he was kneed and elbowed by the worried and weary mill hands on a bus, he dreamed longingly of the warm companionship he would find with her and their sober neighbours in a house with a fine roof.

The rattling, bumping bus pulled along for several miles over the road atop the steep ridge which it had barely managed to climb in first gear. At the end of the bus line he stepped out to the roadside and waited for his street-car. The handful of passengers that were still on the bus climbed out too and scattered to all parts of the neighbourhood, disappearing into the doorways of brick bungalows or clapboard two-storieds that were perched among evergreens and oak trees and maple and wild sumac on the crest and on the slopes of the ridge. *This* would be a good neighbourhood to settle down in. The view was surely a prize—any way you chose to look.

But the sergeant had hardly more than taken his stand in the grass to wait for the street-car, actually leaning a little against a low wall that bordered a sloping lawn, when he observed the figure of a woman standing in the shadow of a small china-berry tree which grew beside the wall.

The woman came from behind the tree and stood by the wall. She was within three or four steps of the sergeant. He looked at her candidly, and her plainness from the very first made him want to turn his face away toward the skyline of the city in the valley. Her flat-chested and generally ill-shaped figure was clothed with a baglike gingham dress that hung at an uneven knee-length. On her feet was a man's pair of brown oxfords. She wore white, ankle-length socks that emphasized the hairiness of her muscular legs. On her head a dark felt hat was drawn down almost to her eyebrows. Her hair was straight and of a dark colour less rich than brown and yet more brown than black, and it was cut so that a straight and not wholly greaseless strand hung over each cheek and turned upward just the slightest bit at the ends.

And in her hands before her the woman held a large bouquet of white and lavender sweet peas. She held them, however, as though they were a bunch of mustard greens. Or perhaps she held them more as a small boy holds flowers, half ashamed to be seen holding anything so delicate. Her eyes did not rest on them. Rather her eyes roved nervously up and down the car tracks. At last she turned her colourless, long face to the sergeant and asked with an artificial smile that showed her broad gums and small teeth, 'Is this where the car stops'?

'I think so,' he said. Then he did look away toward the city.

'I saw the yellow mark up there on the post, but I wasn't real sure,' she pursued. He had to look back at her, and as he did so she said, 'Don't that uniform get awful hot?'

'Oh, yes,' he said. He didn't want to say more. But finally a thought of his own good fortune and an innate kindness urged him to speak again. 'I sometimes change it two or three times a day.'

'I'd sure say it would get hot.'

After a moment's silence the sergeant observed, 'This is mighty hot weather.'

'It's awful hot here in the summer,' she said. 'But it's always awful here in some way. Where are you from?'

He still wanted to say no more. 'I'm from West Tennessee.'

'What part?' she almost demanded.

'I'm from Memphis. It gets mighty hot there.'

'I onct know somebody from there.'

'Memphis gets awfully hot in the summer too.'

'Well,' she said drawing in a long breath, 'you picked an awful hot place to come to. I don't mind heat so much. It's just an awful place to be. I've lived here all my life and I hate it here.'

The sergeant walked away up the road and leaned forward looking for the street-car. Then he walked back to the wall because he felt that she would think him a snob. Unable to invent other conversation, he looked at the flowers and said, 'They're very pretty.'

'Well, if you like 'em at all,' she said, 'you like 'em a great lot more than I do. I hate flowers. Only the other day I say to Mother that if I get sick and go to the hospital don't bring any flowers around me. I don't want any. I don't like 'em.'

'Why, those are pretty,' he said. He felt for some reason that he must defend their worth. 'I like all flowers. Those are especially hard to grow in West Tennessee.'

'If you like 'em you like 'em more than I do. Only the other day I say to my Sunday School teacher that if I would die it'd save her a lot of money because I don't want anybody to send no flowers. I hate 'em. And it ain't just these. I hate all flowers.'

'I think they're pretty,' he insisted. 'Did you pick 'em down there in the valley?'

'They was growing wild in a field and I picked them because I didn't have nothin' else to do. Here,' she said, pushing the flowers into his hands, 'you take 'em. I hate 'em.'

'No, no, I wouldn't think of taking your flowers. Here, you must take them back.'

'I don't want 'em. I'll just throw 'em away.'

'Why, I can't take your flowers.'

'You have 'em, and I ain't going to take 'em back. They'll just lay there and die if you put them on the wall.'

'I feel bad accepting them. You must have gone to a lot of trouble to pick them.'

'They was just growing wild at the edge of a field, and the lady said they was about to take her garden. I don't like flowers. I did her a favour, and you can do me one.'

'There's nothing I like better,' he said, feeling that he had been ungracious. 'I guess I would like to raise flowers, and I used to work in the garden some.' He leaned forward, listening for the sound of the street-car.

For a minute or two neither of them spoke. She shifted from foot to foot and seemed to be talking to herself. From the corner of his eye he watched her lips moving. Finally she said aloud, 'Some people act like they're doing you a favour to pay you a dollar a day.'

'That's not much in these times,' he observed.

'It's just like I was saying to a certain person the other day, If you are not willing to pay a dollar and a half a day you don't want nobody to work for you very bad. But I work for a dollar just the same. This is half of it right here.' She held up a half-dollar between her thumb and forefinger. 'But last week I pay for all my insurance for next year. I put my money away instead of buying things I really want. You can't say that for many girls.'

'You certainly can't.'

'Not many girls do that.'

'I don't know many that do.'

'No, siree,' she said, snapping the fingers of her right hand, 'the girls in this place are awful. I hate the way they act with soldiers down town. They go to the honky-tonks and drink beer. I don't waste anybody's money drinking beer. I put my own money away instead of buying things I might really want.'

The sergeant stepped out into the middle of the road and listened for the street-car. As he returned to the wall, a negro man and woman rode by in a large blue sedan. The woman standing by the wall watched the automobile go over the street-car tracks and down the hill. 'There's no negro in this town that will do housework for less than two and a half a day, and they pay us whites only a dollar.'

'Why will they pay negroes more?' he asked.

'Because-they-can-boss-'em,' she said hastily. 'Just because they can boss 'em around. I say to a certain person the other day, "You can't boss me around like a nigger, no, ma'am."'

'I suppose that's it.' He now began to walk up and down in front of her, listening and looking for the street-car and occasionally raising the flowers to his nose to smell them. She continued to lean against the wall, motionless and with her humourless face turned upward toward the car wire where were hanging six or eight rolled newspapers tied in pairs by long, dirty strings. 'How y' reckon them papers come to be up there?' she asked.

'Some of the neighbourhood kids or paper-boys did it, I guess.'

'Yea. That's it. Rich people's kids's just as bad as anybody's.'

'Well, the paper-boys probably did it whenever they had papers left over. I've done it myself when I was a kid.'

'Yeea,' she said through her nose. 'But kids just make me nervous. And I didn't much like bein' a kid neither.'

The sergeant looked along one of the steel rails that still glimmered a little in the late sunlight and remembered good times he had had walking along the railroad tracks as a child. Suddenly he hoped his first child would be a boy.

'I'll tell you one thing, soldier,' the woman beside him was saying, 'I don't spend my money on lipstick and a lot of silly clothes. I don't paint myself with a lot of lipstick and push my hair up on top of my head and walk around down town so soldiers will look at me. You don't find many girls that don't do that in this awful place, do ya?'

'You certainly don't find many.' The sergeant felt himself blushing.

'You better be careful, for you're going to drop some of them awful flowers. I don't know what you want with 'em.'

'Why, they're pretty,' he said as though he had not said it before.

Now the blue sedan came up the hill again and rolled quietly over the car tracks. Only the negro man was in the sedan, and he was driving quite fast.

'How can a nigger like that own a car like that?'

'He probably only drives for some of the people who live along here.'

'Yea. That's it. That's it. Niggers can get away with anything. I guess you've heard about 'em attackting that white girl down yonder.'

'Yes. . . . Yes.'

'They ought to kill 'em all or send 'em all back to Africa.'

'It's a real problem, I think.'

'I don't care if no man black nor white never looks at me if I have to put on a lot of lipstick and push my hair up and walk around without a hat.'

The sergeant leaned forward, craning his neck.

'I'm just going to tell you what happened to me down town the other day,' she persisted. 'I was standing looking in a store window on Broad when a soldier comes up behind me, and I'm just going to tell you what he said. He said he had a hotel room, and he asked me if I didn't want to go up to the room with him and later go some-where to eat and that he'd give me some money too.'

'I know,' the sergeant said. 'There's a mighty rough crowd in town now.'

'But I just told him, "No thanks. If I can't make money honest I don't want it," is what I told him. I says, "There's a girl on that corner yonder at Main that wants ya. Just go down there."'

The sergeant stood looking down the track, shaking his head.

'He comes right up behind me, you understand, and tells me that he has a room in a hotel and that we can go there and do what we want to do and then go get something to eat and he will give me some money besides. And I just told him, "No thanks. There's a girl on that corner yonder at Main that wants ya. Just go down there." So there I was looking at a lot of silly clothes, and a man in a blue shirt who was standing there all the time says that the soldier had come back looking for me.'

The sergeant stretched out his left arm so that his wrist watch appeared from under his sleeve. Then he crooked his elbow and looked at the watch.

'Oh, you have *some* wait yet,' she said.

'How often do they run?'

'I don't know,' she said without interest, 'just every so often. I told him, y' see, if I can't make money honest I don't want it. You can't say that for many girls.' Whenever his attention seemed to lag, her speech grew louder.

'No, you can't,' he agreed.

'I save my money. Soldier, I've got two hundred and seven dollars in the bank, besides my insurance paid up for next year.' She said nothing during what seemed to be several minutes. Then she asked, 'Where do your mother and daddy live?'

'In West Tennessee.'

'Where do you stay? Out at the camp?' She hardly gave him time to answer her questions now.

'Well, I stay out at camp some nights.'

'*Some* nights? Where do you stay other nights?' She was grinning.

'I'm married and stay with my wife. I've just been married a little while but we have rooms up the way here.'

'Oh, are you a married man? Where is she from? I hope she ain't from here.'

'She's from Memphis. She's just finished school.'

The woman frowned, blushed deeply, then she grinned again showing her wide gums. 'I'd say you are goin' to take her the flowers. You won't have to buy her any.'

'I do wish you'd take some of them back.'

The woman didn't answer him for a long time. Finally, when he had almost forgotten what he had said last, she said without a sign of a grin, 'I don't want 'em. I hate 'em. The sight of 'em makes me sick.'

And at last the street-car came.

It was but a short ride now to the sergeant's stop. The car stopped just opposite the white two-storey house. The sergeant alighted and had to stand on the other side of the track until the long yellow street-car had rumbled away. It was as though an ugly, noisy curtain had at last been drawn back. He saw her face through an upstairs window of the white house with its precise cupola rising even higher than the tall brick chimneys and with fantastic lacy woodwork ornamenting the tiny porches and the cornices. He saw her through the only second-story window that was clearly visible between the foliage of trees that grew in the yard.

The house was older than most of the houses in the suburban neighbourhood along this ridge top, and an old-fashioned iron fence enclosed its yard. He had to stop a moment to unlatch the iron gate, and there he looked directly up into the smiling countenance at the open window. She spoke to him in a voice even softer than he remembered.

Now he had to pass through his landlady's front hall and climb a crooked flight of stairs before reaching his rooms, and an old-fashioned bell had tinkled when he opened the front door. At this tinkling sound an old lady's voice called from somewhere in the back of the house, 'Yes?' But he made no answer. He hurried up the steps and was at last in the room with his wife.

They sat on the couch with their knees touching and her hand in his.

Just as her voice was softer, her appearance was fairer even than he had remembered. He told her that he had been rehearsing this moment during every second of the past two hours, and simultaneously he realized that what he was saying was true, that during all other conversations and actions his imagination had been going over and over the present scene.

She glanced at the sweet peas lying beside his cap on the table and said that when she had seen him in the gateway with the flowers she had felt that perhaps during the time they were separated she had not remembered him even as gentle and fine as he was. Yet she had been afraid until that moment by the window that in her heart she had exaggerated those virtues of his.

The sergeant did not tell her then how he had come into possession of the flowers. He knew that the incident of the cleaning woman would depress her good spirits as it had his own. And while he was thinking of the complete understanding and sympathy between them he heard her saying, 'I know you are tired. You're probably not so tired from soldiering as from dealing with people of various sorts all day. I went to the grocery myself this morning and coming home on the bus I thought of how tiresome and boring the long ride home would be for you this evening when the buses are so crowded.' He leaned toward her and kissed her, holding her until he realized that she was smiling. He released her, and she drew away with a laugh and said that she had supper to tend to and that she must put the sweet peas in water.

While she was stirring about the clean, closet-like kitchen he surveyed in the late twilight the living-room that was still a strange room to him, and without lighting the table- or floor-lamps he wandered into the bedroom which was the largest room and from which an old-fashioned bay window overlooked the valley. He paused at the window and raised the shade. And he was startled by a magnificent view of the mountains that rose up on the other side of the city. And there he witnessed the last few seconds of a sunset— brilliant orange and brick red—beyond the blue mountains.

They ate at a little table that she drew out from the wall in the living-room. 'How have I merited such a good cook for a wife?' he said and smiled when the meal was finished. They stacked the dishes unwashed in the sink, for she had put her arms about his neck and whispered, 'Why should I waste one moment of the time I have you here when the days are so lonesome and endless?'

They sat in the living-room and read aloud the letters that had come during the past few days.

For a little while she worked on the hem of a tablecloth, and they talked. They spoke of their friends at home. She showed him a few of their wedding presents that had arrived late. And they kept saying how fortunate they were to have found an apartment so comfortable as this. Here on the ridge it was cool almost every night.

Afterward he took out his pen and wrote a letter to his father. He read the letter aloud to her.

Still later it rained. The two of them hurried about putting down windows. Then they sat and heard it whipping and splashing against the window glass when the wind blew.

By the time they were both in their night clothes the rain had stopped. He sat on a footstool by the bed reading in the heavy, dark history book. Once he read aloud a sentence which he thought impressive: 'I have never seen the Federal dead lie so thickly on the ground save in front of the sunken wall at Fredericksburg.' This was a Southern general writing of the battle fought along this ridge top.

'What a very sad sounding sentence,' she said. She was brushing her hair in long, even strokes.

Finally he put down the book but remained sitting on the stool to polish his low-quartered military shoes. She at her dressing-table looked at his reflection in the mirror before her, said, 'It's stopped raining.'

'It stopped a good while ago,' he said. And he looked up attentively, for there had seemed to be some regret in her voice.

'I'm sorry it stopped,' she said, returning his gaze.

'You should be glad,' he said. 'I'd have to drill in all that mud to-morrow.'

'Of course I'm glad,' she said. 'But hasn't the rain made us seem even more alone up here?'

The sergeant stood up. The room was very still and close. There was not even the sound of a clock. A light was burning on her dressing table, and through the open doorway he could see the table lamp that was still burning in the living-room. The table there was a regular part of the furnishing of the apartment. But it was a piece of furniture they might have chosen themselves. He went to the door and stood a moment studying the effect she had achieved in her arrangement of objects on the table. On the dark octagonal top was the white lamp with the urn-shaped base. The light the lamp shed contrasted the shape of the urn with the global shape of a crystal vase from which sprigs of ivy mixed with periwinkle sprang in their individual wiriness. And a square, crystal ashtray reflecting its exotic lights was placed at an angle to a small round silver dish.

He went to the living-room to put out the light. Yet with his hand on the little switch he hesitated because it was such a pleasing isolated arrangement of objects.

Once the light was out he turned immediately to go back into the bedroom. And now he halted in the doorway again, for as he entered the bedroom his eye fell on the vase of sweet peas she had arranged. It was placed on top of a high bureau and he had not

previously noticed it. Up there the flowers looked somehow curi-
ously artificial and not like the real sweet peas he had seen in the
rough hands of the woman this afternoon. While he was gazing thus
he felt his wife's eyes upon him. Yet without turning to her he went
to the window, for he was utterly pre-occupied with the impression
he had just received and he had a strange desire to sustain the
impression long enough to examine it. He kept thinking of that
woman's hands.

Now he raised the shade and threw open the big window in the
bay, and standing there barefoot on a small hooked rug he looked
out at the dark mountains and at the lines and splotches of light that
burned on her dressing table. He knew that it had disturbed her to
see him so suddenly preoccupied, and it was as though he tried to
cram all of a whole day's reflections into a few seconds. Had it really
been the pale flowers that had impressed him so? Or had it been the
setting of his alarm clock a few minutes before and the realization
that after a few more hours here with her he must take up again
that other life that the yellow street-car had carried away with it this
afternoon? He could hear the voices of the boys in the barracks, and
he saw the figure of the woman by the stone wall under the china-
berry tree.

Now he could hear his wife moving to switch off the overhead
light. There was a click. The room was dark and he could hear her
moving toward him. And the room being dark things outside
seemed much brighter. On the slope of the ridge that dropped off
steeply behind the house the dark tree tops became visible. And
again there were the voices of the boys in the barracks. Their crude-
ness, their hardness, even their baseness—qualities that seemed to be
taking root in the very hearts of those men—kept passing like objects
through his mind. And the bitterness of the woman waiting by the
street-car tracks pressed upon him.

His wife had come up beside him in the dark and slipped her arm
about his waist. He folded his arms tightly about her. She spoke his
name. Then she said, 'These hours we have together are so isolated
and few that they must sometimes not seem quite real to you when
you are away.' She too, he realized, felt a terrible unrelated diversity
in things. In the warmth of her companionship, he felt a sudden

contrast with the cold fighting he might take part in on a battlefield that was now distant and almost abstract.

The sergeant's eyes had now grown so accustomed to the darkness inside and outside that he could look down between the trees on the slope of the ridge. He imagined there the line after line of Union soldiers that had once been thrown into the battle to take this ridge at all cost. The Confederate general's headquarters were not more than two blocks away. If he and she had been living in those days he would have seen ever so clearly the Cause for that fighting. And *this* battlefield would not be abstract. He would have stood here holding back the enemy from the very land which was his own, from the house in which she awaited him.

But here the sergeant stopped and smiled at himself. He examined the sergeant he had just imagined in the Confederate ranks and it was not himself at all. He compared the Confederate sergeant to the sergeant on the field this afternoon who had stood a moment puzzling over the tracks that twelve rookies had made. *The sergeant is I,* he said to himself desperately, *but it is not that morning in September of sixty-three when the Federal dead were lying so thick on the ground.* He leaned down and kissed his wife's forehead, and taking her up in his arms he carried her to their bed. *It is only a vase of flowers,* he remarked silently, rhetorically to himself as his wife drew her arms tighter about his neck. *Three bunches from a stand of sweet peas that had taken the lady's garden.* As he let her down gently on the bed she asked, 'Why did you look so strangely at the vase of flowers? What did they make you think about so long by the window?'

For a moment the sergeant was again overwhelmed by his wife's perception and understanding. He would tell her everything he had in his mind. What great fortune it was to have a wife who could understand and to have her here beside him to hear and to comprehend everything that was in his heart and mind. But as he lay in the dark trying to make out the line of her profile against the dim light of the window, there came through the rain-washed air outside the rumbling of a street-car. And before he could even speak the thoughts which he had been thinking, all those things no longer seemed to matter. The noise of the street-car, the irregular rumble and uncertain clanging, brought back to him once more all the incidents of the day. He and his wife were here beside each other, but suddenly he was hopelessly distracted by this new sensation. The street-car had moved away now beyond his hearing, and he could visualize it casting its diffused light among the dark foliage and over the white gravel between the tracks. He was left with the sense that no moment in his life had any relation to another. It was as though he were living a thousand lives. And the happiness and completeness of his marriage could not now seem so large a thing.

Impulsively, almost without realizing what he was doing he sat up on the other side of the bed. 'I wasn't really thinking about the flowers,' he said. 'I guess I was thinking of how nicely you had arranged things on the living-room table.'

'Oh,' she said, for by his very words *I guess* it was apparent that she felt him minimizing the importance of his own impressions this evening and of their own closeness. In the dark he went to the small rocking chair on which his clothes were hanging and drew a cigarette from his shirt pocket. He lit it and sat on the edge of the little rocker, facing the open window, and he sat smoking his cigarette until quite suddenly the rain began to fall again. At the very first sound of the rain he stood up. He moved quickly to the window and put out his cigarette on the sill near the wire screen. The last bit of smoke sifted through the wire mesh. The rain was very noisy among the leaves. He stumbled hurriedly back through the dark and into the bed where he clasped his wife in his arms.

'It's begun to rain again,' she said.

'Yes,' the sergeant said. 'It's much better now.'

JOHN CLARE

Poems and Fragments

By no means all that Clare wrote, either in verse or prose, has been pub-
lished. In the two-volume edition of Clare, published in 1935, Mr. J. W.
Tibble printed 860 poems. More than another 860 are still in manuscript.
Much, but not all, of his prose has been printed by Mr. Edmund Blunden,
and, in their life of Clare, by Mr. and Mrs. Tibble. It is through the kind-
ness of Mrs. Tibble that these additional pieces are published in The Mint.
Although so much has been done, the evaluation and exploration of
Clare are still incomplete. Whatever his limitations, he is the absolute poet,
in a singular purity, little tainted by literature, if too little controlled by
its experience. And as we feel more of Clare, so, without reserve, we
need to know more of what he wrote, and of its considerable curiosities.
These pieces are only a minor instalment. But some of them, whatever
their formal shortcomings, and however touched they are with his madness,
show better than much of his printed verse that glittering purity of
apprehension of Clare's, his natural love intensified into vision.

MOONLIGHT WALK

The Sun like the last look of love
Has smiled farewell on tower and tree
And in the shades of every grove
Has left the calm that pleases me
While all around so pure does seem
I fancy that my God is near
Or think I live in some sweet dream
Where evening's moon is shining clear.

Now evening's dews are falling down
And moonbeams on the gravel stoop
So bright they shine, o'er darkness thrown

They seem as you would pick them up
And   shadows in a group
Darker than dark like coffin'd palls
You're naturally obliged to stoop
To feel where seems no ground at all.

How sweet the bumclocks bagpipes drone
That buzzes by with evening song
He meets the traveller all alone
On furze-clad heath and spinney strong
Now that the busy daylight talk
Has ceased and left this scene alone
I'll wander down the moonlit walk
And call its pleasures all my own.

FRAGMENT

The painted tulip in her bloom begun
Opens her splendid bosom to the sun
The tempted bee hums round with amorous gaze
And in her magic beauty toys and plays
Clouds hide the sun the fair deluder frowns
And in her bosoms gall the plunderer drowns
In vain he buzzes in her bosoms power
And dies self-poisoned in a treacherous flower.

from an
ESSAY ON LANDSCAPE

Real excellence must be its own creator it must be the overflowing
of its own mind and must *make* its admirers willing converts from
its own powerful conceptions and not yield to win them by giving
way to their opinions.

John Clare

NOTE

As we grow into life we leave our better life behind us like the image of a beauty seen in a looking glass happiness only disseminates happiness while she is present and when she is gone we retain no impression of her enjoyments but a blank of cold imaginings and real disappointments unless we are determined to shape our conduct to her approval and then she is ever with us not her picture but her perfection not in shadow but reality—read this over again and profit.

NATURE

from a note on Alexander Pope

As to the foolery of 'indoor' and outdoor nature its not worth the notice of an argument what is good of each is good of both nature is not two persons but one and the same.

'TWAS AT THE HOURS OF EVENING

'Twas at the hours of evening when low descends the dew
When the ring dove seeks the pollard oak and lays a stick or two
And lays her two white eggs aye whiter than the snow
And feeds her young i' golden down from the green pea field below
It was a pleasant evening and the brook in silver moans
Sung its evening song under grass and over stones
Among the pasture whins I will seek for Sally now
Where hangs the red cheeked apple upon the oak tree bough.

I'll meet her when the western cloud burns crimson in the sky
And leaves her mop agen the door and gangs to meet the kye
When the bramble hangs on drops by the old lane side
And the evening star is shining o'er the black woods far and wide

When the daisy turns a bud and the lark is on her nest
When the babe is in the cradle or on the mothers breast
I hide me i' the gloaming and down the green path hie
And meet my bonny sweetheart at the milking o' the kye

I met her in the gloaming—it was but Sunday e'en
Blue ribbons on her white straw hat—her bonny gown was green.
I kissed her bonny cheek and chin and nipped her rosy arms
Frae milking to the gloaming—I feasted on her charms
And now where fireweeds are in flower and the wild thyme scents
    the plain
I'll gang tonight to Sally and see her again
The moth is on the kickses on the teazle sleeps the fly
And I'll gang the dewy evening where Sally milks the kye.

from

'TWAS IN A SUMMER'S MORNING

You've won my heart my dear said I as I sat at her feet
Red was her lip and bright her eye the hay smelt very sweet
I clasped her by the neck so soft like heap of burning twitch
The water rats were nibbling sedge the moonlight hour was rich

The willow tree its shadow flings like brigs across the stream
The owl his hooting ditty sings her bosom white as cream
I kissed she took the homeward track along the meadow ground
Goodnight upon my ear came back in nature's sweetest round.

John Clare

SONG

Long have we parted been
Longsome and lonesome
Noone to cheer the scene
None but Miss Bl–ns–me
Lassie be near me
Love don't live so lonesome
But come and lie near me

I' the Bastilles o' Hell
Bloody and dreary
Bloody tales captives tell
Lonely and weary
I have been where they fell
Wounded and weary
Now I wi' freedom dwell
Lassie come near me

Kisses are sweet my Love
Thy cherry lips cheer me
Sweet as our hope above
Heaven love's near thee
'Tis Hell to be parted thus
Come love and hear me
Give me thy bosom's buss
Lassie be near me

All my heart's anguish
And long I've endured it
In prison to languish
Thy smiles love have cured it
True love and lassie dear
Turn back and hear me
Thy white bosom's near
Lassie come near me

MIND ALONE

from an Essay on False Appearances

I read history and am astonished at the lesson it gives of the vanitys of pride pomp and power—mind alone is the sun of earth—it lives on when the clouds and paraphernalia of pretensions are forgotten.

WILLIAM BLAKE

from an Essay on Honour

Blake is as great a warrior as Nelson the one was honoured with titles the other not.

FRAGMENT OF A NOVEL

There was a small stream went bending in roundabout mazes across the forest and now and then interrupted by a sallow bush that longing to kiss the water had bent its mossy fringed and shaggy rooted branches not only over but into the flood and from these interruptions and the broken down pathways of stones laid by rustics for the benefit of nearer way the waters broke their silence into the beautiful murmuring music that one often hears on suddenly approaching these picturesque rivulets and suddenly lose when we leave their banks—something like the fits and gushes of an eolian harp—here the two girls enjoyed the luxury of drinking the clear water from their white hands—where is the lover who adores beauty that would not have preferred such a necessity to the golden goblet of the splendid banquet and even the nectar cup of Apollo.

John Clare

THE SWEETEST WOMAN THERE

From bank to bank the water roars
Like thunder in a storm
A Sea in sight of both the shores
Creating no alarm
The water birds above the flood
Fly o'er the foam and spray
And nature wears a gloomy hood
On this October day

And there I saw a bonny maid
That proved my hearts delight
All day she was a Goddess made
An Angel fair at night
We loved and in each others power
Felt nothing to condemn
I was the leaf and she the flower
And both grew on one stem

I loved her cheek her lip her eye
She cheered my midnight gloom
A bonny rose neath God's own sky
In one perennial bloom
She lives mid pastures ever green
And meadows ever fair
Each winter spring and summer scene
The sweetest woman there

She lives among the meadow floods
That foam and roar away
While fading hedgerows distant woods
Fade off to naked spray

She lives to cherish and delight
All nature with her face
She brought me joy morn noon and night
In that too lonely place.

BLOOMING MARIA

The sharp wind shivers in the warm gorse blossoms
And trembles in the dead grass over the heath
The silver rain pearls in the wild flower's bosom
And moistens minute flowers of moss beneath
There i' the morning dew I early ramble
What time beneath the fern the weary moth
Hides from the sun in dewdrops hangs the bramble
As down the rabbit track I venture forth

I wander like a sunbeam i' the green
Immortal harmony of Natures love
Her music charms me as a thing unseen
And Hopes emblazoned sunshine gleams above
Blooming Maria is the maid I love
The rosy young and beautiful Maria
She sometimes meets me in the tangled grove
And by her beauty sets my soul on fire

The blackcock hides her dwelling i' the gorse
Wi' curly tail red eyes and shining breast
Among the bracken feeds the weary horse
On the short sward then lays him down to rest
O rosy cheeked and beautiful Maria
The evening is not chill the heavens grey
Drops dew and beauty from all crowds retire
Then why from love's embraces keep away.

THE NURSERY GARDEN

There is a hidden history in the trees
The various shades of green and shapes of leaves
The nursery grounds all stirred with the mild breeze

John Clare

My mind from lonesome weariness relieves
Leaf-shedding some midst evergreen young firs
Whisper and talk to every wind which stirs

I love the nursery calm—or stirred by winds
Sweet chestnut beech and broad leafed sycamore
Fruit trees and shrubs and trees of various kinds
While o'er the various scene the wind waves o'er
That poplar, broom and oak that trees excel
The nursery Oh I love the nursery well

I love the nursery with its trees and bushes
Where gold-beaked blackbirds build their nests and fly
To hear 'neath pine clumps shade the singing thrushes
Hiding their heaven-tint eggs from every eye
I love the nursery with its shades of green
At early morn or in calm eve serene.

The nuts and filberts with their soft broad leaves
Throw shadows on the path of russet brown
The willow grey a summer's chaplet weaves
For night's dull vision when the sun goes down
I love the nursery with its paths and trees
Its songs of birds and summer painting bees

I love the nursery—'tis a pleasant place
To spend one's leisure hours on summer's day
To mark the various trees throughout the space
Noting dark clumps where leaves excludes bright day
I love the nursery where the breezes leave
A whispering song of melody at eve.

H. W. HÄUSERMANN

W. B. Yeats's Idea of Shelley

IT IS not with Shelley's influence upon the work of W. B. Yeats that this paper deals; it has the more limited object of defining the idea of Shelley which Yeats formed for himself in the course of his life. Shelley was never long absent from Yeats's thought, although in later years Swift's figure was clearly in the ascendant. There are numerous passages in the writings of Yeats which refer to Shelley, but three of them are of special interest. The first, an essay on 'The Philosophy of Shelley's Poetry', was written in 1900; the second occurs in the autobiographical *Reveries over Childhood and Youth* composed in 1914; and the last may be found in *A Vision* of 1925, re-edited in 1937.

The three passages mark a gradual change in Yeats's attitude towards Shelley. Judging from such youthful works as *Mosada* (1886) and *The Two Titans* (1889), Yeats in his early twenties merely imitated Shelley's revolutionary poems. But the essay of 1900 shows already signs of a major divergence from Shelley. Later, in the autobiographical book of 1914, we find a curious and indirect statement of the fundamental difference between the two poets' personalities. But it is only in *A Vision* that Yeats fully analyses Shelley's character and gives a complete explanation of his dissension from the ideal of his youth. A study of these three Shelley-portraits contributes more, it is true, to our knowledge of Yeats's personality than of Shelley's; but it may also interest the student of the great Romantic poet himself and the historian of Shelley's literary fame.

I. PORTRAIT OF SHELLEY BY THE POET IN SEARCH OF UNITY OF BEING

The essay on 'The Philosophy of Shelley's Poetry' (1900) comes at the end of Yeats's early period, when he had progressed from *Crossways* (1889) to *The Rose* (1893) and to *The Wind among the*

Reeds (1899), that is, towards an ideal which he called Unity of Being. His father, from whom he borrowed the term, explained it by 'a comparison to a musical instrument so strung that if we touch a string all the strings murmur faintly'[1]. Yeats himself preferred another image: 'I thought that all art should be a Centaur finding in the popular lore its back and its strong legs'[2]. In terms of Yeats's literary development, Unity of Being might be considered as the union of æstheticism, that is, the art of the Rhymers and of the French Symbolists, with the matter of the Celtic Twilight.

Under the influence of Pater and Baudelaire he wanted to give even to the smallest things a deep symbolic value and thus to restore to modern life the mystery and beauty of a former age. The Rhymers impressed him with the necessity of 'conscious, deliberate craft', and in Count Villiers de l'Isle Adam he admired the attitude of aristocratic disdain and artistic concentration. As for the back and the strong legs of the centaur, he found them chiefly in popular Irish mythology. Believing that all individual minds and memories 'are a part of one great memory, the memory of Nature herself'[3], he tried to penetrate into that deeply buried memory through the myths still living among the Irish peasantry and also through various occult studies which seemed to promise a revelation of truths which the modern world has forgotten.

The first part of the essay on 'The Philosophy of Shelley's Poetry' is devoted to the poet's 'ruling ideas' and to an exposition of 'the system of belief that lay behind' those poems, in particular, where Shelley speaks of liberty and political regeneration but means really Intellectual Beauty. In truth, however, Yeats discovers nothing that deserves the name of system. He declares that Shelley 'seems in his speculations to have lit on that memory of nature the visionaries claim for the foundation of their knowledge', that he 'had re-awakened in himself the age of faith', and that 'the flowing forms of his mind' corresponded to what happens 'in the visions of the mystics everywhere and of the common people in Ireland'. Shelley's underlying 'system of belief', therefore, is neither the Platonic nor the Christian

[1] *Autobiographies*, Macmillan, 1926, pp. 235 f.   [2] *Ibid.*, p. 236.
[3] From the essay on 'Magic' (1901) in 'Ideas of Good and Evil' (1896–1903). *Essays*, Macmillan, 1924, p. 33.

system, but Shelley's intuitive discovery of occult knowledge. Had Shelley studied the 'more traditional forms' which this knowledge takes in folklore, some of his poetry would not suffer from 'an air of rootless phantasy'.

Yeats begins his enquiry into Shelley's 'ruling symbols' in the second part of the essay by affirming that, although the poet did not give magic 'any deep study', he nevertheless felt the power of 'the traditions of magic and of the magical philosophy' and that he probably 'brooded over their doctrine of symbols or signatures'. 'One finds in his poetry, besides innumerable images that have not the definiteness of symbols, many images that are certainly symbols, and as the years went by he began to use these with a more and more deliberately symbolic purpose.'

He then distinguishes two principal groups of images or symbols in Shelley's verse. One is formed by all those things which Homer describes in the passage concerning the cave of the Nymphs (*Odyssey* XIII, 102–12) and which, according to the commentary by the Neoplatonist philosopher Porphyry, symbolize the world and what it contains. Thus, a cave stands in Shelley for 'any enclosed life, as when it is the dwelling-place of Asia and Prometheus, or when it is "the still cave of poetry", and it may have all meanings at once, or it may have as little meaning as some ancient religious symbol enwoven from the habit of centuries with the patterns of a carpet or a tapestry'. *The Witch of Atlas* reproduces the cave of the Nymphs with all its details, and the symbolism is the same as in Porphyry. Water symbolizes life, existence; weaving is a symbol of generation because 'the body is a garment'; honey and bees stand for the delights of the senses. Shelley's use of towers as symbols of 'the mind looking outward upon men and things' corresponds to the cave-symbol signifying 'the mind looking inward upon itself'.

The other group of symbols, the Sun, the Moon, the Morning and the Evening Star, represent various forms of the spirit which is always fire. Shelley's favourite spirit-symbol is a star, the most disembodied of all lights, the 'symbol of love, or liberty, or wisdom, or beauty, or of some other expression of that Intellectual Beauty, which was to Shelley's mind the central power of the world'. Yeats sums up its meaning as 'infinite desire'. The Moon, a less pure spiritual emblem, is the favourite symbol of Keats 'with his love of embodied things, of precision of form and colouring, of emotions made sleepy by the flesh'. Shelley did not like the Moon 'because she only becomes beautiful in giving herself, and is no flying ideal, she is not loved by the children of desire'. Still further removed from Shelley's heart is the Sun, the symbol of energy and creative joy. It is the symbol preferred by Blake, but Shelley inclines to identify 'the killing sun' with the abhorred idea of tyrants and priests.

Thus, according to Yeats, Shelley had not attained Unity of Being. It is important to realize the nature of Shelley's weakness as seen by Yeats. Shelley's dominant trait was 'infinite desire', a longing to escape from the limitations of mortal existence. Because this trait was not sufficiently balanced by a corresponding strength of Shelley's physical and instinctive being, he lacked unity. Matthew Arnold's Shelley lacked ethical strength; Yeats's Shelley lacked the religious belief of the primitive man. Yeats too, though for a different reason, saw Shelley as a 'beautiful and ineffectual angel, beating in the void his luminous wings in vain'. If Shelley had added to his intuitive knowledge of truth, the study of popular mythological tradition, then he would have attained Unity of Being. The use he makes of age-old symbols, such as caves and rivers and towers, suggests that he had come very near to that goal: 'His poetry becomes the richer, the more emotional, and loses something of its appearance of idle phantasy when I remember that these are ancient symbols, and still come to visionaries in their dreams'. Yeats believes that Shelley read Porphyry (which is not improbable) and consciously made use of the old commentator's allegorical system (which is very unlikely). But Porphyry alone was not enough to give Shelley's 'infinite desire' the necessary counterpart of popular, primitive mythology.

In his twenties, when Yeats wrote *Mosada* and *The Two Titans* under the influence of *The Revolt of Islam* and of *Queen Mab*, he would have seen such a counterpart to the poet's 'infinite desire' in his political thought. But under the influence of Pater, Rossetti, and of the Rhymers, he gradually emptied his own political aspirations of their former content of passion and practical purpose. In his volume of poetry *The Rose* (1893), he tried to express as one and the same emotion the love of Ireland and the love of beauty and holiness. The

W. B. Yeats's Idea of Shelley

Fenian leader John O'Leary, it is true, had made of Yeats a Nationalist whose patriotism was not the longing for some ever-fleeing ideal: 'The Rose differs from the Intellectual Beauty of Shelley and of Spenser in that I have imagined it as suffering with man and not as something pursued and seen from afar.' [4] But the difference is not very great, for in the essay of 1900 he identified Shelley's desire for Intellectual Beauty with his hatred of tyranny, and Shelley's feeling for the oppressed was certainly not less deep than Yeats's sympathy with his countrymen. It is only in his later works that Yeats distinguished between the two sources of inspiration, personal and impersonal, and through this very distinction was able to advance further towards true Unity of Being.

II. SHELLEY AND THE POLLEXFENS

Yeats's *Reveries over Childhood and Youth,* written in 1914, speak of a desire which haunted the child and the youth to identify himself with Shelley or one of Shelley's poetic characters. Even in his mature reveries Yeats seems to be following this boyish aspiration. The parallels between the two men's boyhoods are, as such, not very remarkable: they bear on actions and events that may be found in many a young poet's life. Yeats, however, in his narrative, places a peculiar emphasis upon them. Thus we are told that he did not willingly bear the discipline of the school he was sent to. 'Shelley the atheist' was ostracized at Eton much as 'the mad Irishman' was made unhappy at the cheap school in Hammersmith. The part played by Dr. Lind in Shelley's education corresponds to the influence of J. B. Yeats, the clever and original Irish portrait-painter, upon his son. Both men encouraged their charges' eccentricity, and both were to represent later on that type of spiritual authority which the grown-up poets respected but would not accept. As schoolboys they united an interest in science with a curiosity about spirit-lore, and this dual interest considerably modified their thought in riper years. The violent criminals and heroes of *Zastrozzi* and *St. Irvyne* find their counterpart in the characters peopling Yeats's mind when, at fifteen, he climbed the hills, visited caves and ruined castles, or wandered about the harbour of Sligo, and 'the world seemed full of monsters

[4] See *Collected Poems,* Macmillan, 1933, p. 438.

H. W. Häusermann

and marvels'[5]. With the awakening of sex both poets abandoned their dreams of power and violence, and they are filled with strange new emotions as with a sense of consecration. Shelley relates in the Dedication to *The Revolt of Islam* how

> there came upon my mind
> A sense of loneliness, a thirst with which I pined.

Similarly, Yeats began to cultivate a sense of noble solitude 'I had many idols', he wrote, 'and as I climbed along the narrow ledge I was now Manfred on his glacier, and now Prince Athanase with his solitary lamp, but I soon chose Alastor for my chief of men and longed to share his melancholy, and maybe at last to disappear from everybody's sight as he disappeared drifting in a boat along some slow-moving river between great trees. When I thought of women they were modelled on those in my favourite poets and loved in brief tragedy, or like the girl in *The Revolt of Islam*, accompanied their lovers through all manner of wild places, lawless women without homes and without children'[6].

Yeats's conception of Shelley as a poet who is by nature gentle and sociable but who in his poetry creates proud, solitary, and violent men is clearly the outcome of his thinking about his father's and his mother's families. A considerable part of the *Reveries over Childhood and Youth* is devoted to the Pollexfens, his mother's family. The awe-inspiring figure of the poet's grandfather, William Pollexfen, whom the little boy confused with God[7], is the first and most important character in this autobiographical retrospect. He was a silent and solitary man, and 'he had a good deal of pride and disliked his neighbours'[8]. One of Yeats's earliest experiences of the supernatural is connected with his grandfather. The child had dreamed that the boat in which his grandfather had sailed the day before was ship-wrecked. It must have been second sight, for the ship had really sunk and William Pollexfen had saved himself and others by swimming[9]. The figure of this powerful man made a lasting impression on the poet. 'Even to-day when I read *King Lear* his image is always before me and I often wonder if the delight in passionate men in my plays

[5] *Autobiographies*, p. 63.   [6] *Ibid.*, pp. 78 f.   [7] *Loc. cit.*, p. 9.
[8] *Ibid.*, p. 11.   [9] *Ibid.*, pp. 14 f.

and in my poetry is more than his memory'[10]. Then there was his mother's brother, George Pollexfen, a well-to-do, elderly man, but gloomy and inactive, 'in whom the sap of life seemed to be dried away', but who 'had a mind full of pictures'[11]. He had been a great hunter and the best rider in Connaught. Under the influence of his second-sighted servant, Mary Battle, he came to believe in the super-natural world. Yeats spent most of his holidays from school with this uncle, and even much later, when the poet was nearly thirty, he stayed with him and introduced him to cabalistic symbolism[12]. The two men exchanged letters on astrology in which science George Pollexfen was an adept. He died in 1910.

The family of the poet's father, however, counted among its members no adventurers, mystics, or astrologers. They were respect-able people, high officials, rich merchants, and clergymen. When the influence of J. B. Yeats upon his son, William, was at its height, he used to read poetry to him, for instance the 'first speeches of the *Prometheus Unbound*, but never the ecstatic lyricism of that famous fourth act'[13]. He was a clever, sensitive man, but his mind was empirical and practical. 'He thought Keats a greater poet than Shelley, because less abstract, but did not read him, caring little, I think, for any of that most beautiful poetry which has come in modern times from the influence of painting'[14]. The fundamental difference between the two families was described by J. B. Yeats in these words: 'Inarticulate as the sea-cliffs were the Pollexfens, lying buried under mountains of silence. They were released from bondage by contact with the joyous amiability of my family, and of my bringing up, and so all my four children are articulate, and yet with the Pollexfen force '[15].

Yeats suggests in his *Autobiographies* that his youthful dreams of noble solitude, of pride and power, came from his Pollexfen blood. Shelley is introduced into this autobiographical narrative mainly because he furnished an example of a similar dualism of character.

[10] *Ibid.*, p. 10.   [11] *Ibid.*, p. 85.
[12] See 'Hodos Chameliontos', in *Autobiographies,* pp. 319 f.
[13] From 'Reveries over Childhood and Youth'. *Autobiographies*, pp. 79 f.
[14] *Ibid.*, p. 80.
[15] *J. B. Yeats's Letters to his Son W. B. Yeats and others, 1869–1922,* ed. with a memoir by Joseph Hone and a preface by Oliver Elton, Faber, 1944. From the memoir, p. 29.

H. W. Häusermann

Only those Shelleyan traits which speak of violence and pride are described. Yeats discovers Shelley's kinship with the Pollexfens, those lonely hunters and fishers; and a long passage from *Hellas* is quoted for the sole purpose of illustrating this dream of proud, God-like solitude dreamt by gregarious Shelley and gregarious Yeats [16]. The icy rocks in the Indian Caucasus, Count Axel's castle in the Black Forest, and the sea-cliffs to which J. B. Yeats compared the Pollexfens, are alternative symbols. Those books were sacred, they had the power to make Yeats feel 'for certain hours or months' that he was 'partaking in some incredible romance' [17]. They inspired him with the wild hope that one day he might 'create some new *Prometheus Unbound*; Patrick or Columbkil, Oisin or Fion, in Prometheus' stead; and, instead of Caucasus, Cro-Patric or Ben Bulben' [18].

The Shelley-portrait in the *Autobiographies* reflects two stages in Yeats's thought about the poet. There is again the 'occultist' Shelley in search for Unity of Being who wrongly chooses a classical myth as the subject-matter of his poem instead of choosing some legend in folklore. And there is also the Shelley whom a Pollexfen created in his own likeness. Nothing, however, or very little is revealed in this book of a third and earlier conception of Shelley. Just as Yeats excluded from his *Collected Poems* the numerous works which appeared in the *Dublin University Review* and elsewhere about 1885, so he omitted from his *Reveries over Childhood and Youth* a portrait of the Shelley who inspired *Mosada, The Two Titans*, and other contemporary compositions. These poems and plays clearly derive their revolutionary and heretic tendency from *Queen Mab* and *The Revolt of Islam*. But Yeats soon outgrew this mask of a cosmopolitan and philanthropic Shelley. Referring to the meetings of the nationalist 'Young Ireland' club which he attended, Yeats lays stress upon the radical character of his reaction against all forms of humanitarianism: 'From these debates, from O'Leary's conversation, and from the Irish books he lent or gave me has come all I have set my hand to since' [19]. The Shelleyan earnestness of *Mosada* now seemed to him mistaken in its object and falsifying his own intention: 'When I re-read those early poems which gave me so much trouble, I find little but

[16] Lines 152–85. *Autobiographies*, pp. 212 f.   [17] *Ibid.*, p. 394.
[18] *Ibid.*, p. 240.   [19] *Ibid.*, p. 125.

romantic convention, unconscious drama. It is so many years before one can believe enough in what one feels even to know what the feeling is' [20]. When, with this riper knowledge, he drew another Shelley-portrait in *A Vision*, he no longer suppressed the poet's humanitarianism. This new objectivity, which was not a new tolerance—for Yeats still condemned that aspect of Shelley's personality—is a measure of the realistic outlook which was his in his later period.

III. SHELLEY AND YEATS'S VISION OF EVIL

Before one rejects *A Vision* for its fantastic terminology and irresponsible attitude, one should recognize the amount of perfectly rational experience and serious study which Yeats put into this work. It might be shown, I believe, that the rational element predominates largely over the occultist features in 'Book I: The Great Wheel', and that the terms and images drawn from alchemy and similar sources are in the nature of a poetical metaphor. When he summed up, arranged, and edited what he had found in 'some fifty copy-books of automatic script' and in 'a much smaller number of books recording what had come in sleep' [21], he not only used in the process the fruit of his own and his wife's wide reading in philosophy and biography, but he also gave his work the benefit of a lifetime's keen observation of human nature. The public and private disappointments he had experienced since 1900, together with the growing sense of his mastery as a poet, convey to his System an air of ripeness and authority in spite of those of its aspects which are inacceptable to the common-sense critic.

The Great Wheel has been wrongly called a form of determinism. In reality, Yeats admits free will. Man is free to struggle against adversity, to affirm his will in opposition to external circumstances, or to refuse that struggle and, for weariness or weakness, to escape into a world without conflict. In an essay published posthumously [22], Yeats declares that there was in Shelley (as there was also in Wordsworth and Ruskin) 'a constant resolution to dwell upon good only',

---

[20] *Ibid.*, p. 127.
[21] *A Vision*, Macmillan, 1937, p. 17. All quotations are from this edition.
[22] Quoted by M. D. Zabel in 'The Thinking of the Body: Yeats in the Autobiographies', *The Southern Review*, Louisiana, 1941, p. 587.

and that this was the cause of Shelley's lack of dramatic sense. 'Is it that these men', Yeats demands, 'who believe what they wish, can never be quite sincere and so live in a world of half-belief? But no man believes willingly in evil or in suffering. How much of the strength and weight of Dante and of Balzac comes from unwilling belief, from the lack of it how much of the rhetoric and vagueness of all of Shelley's poetry that does not arise from personal feeling?' This idea of the acceptance of evil is one of the leading conceptions of Yeats's later life. He called it the Vision of Evil, and it largely superseded the earlier idea of Unity of Being. It is this Vision of Evil to which his System contains the key, for that System helped him 'to hold in a single thought reality and justice'[23]. Shelley did not attain Unity of Being because he had no folklore, and he could not sustain the Vision of Evil because the explanation of it had not been revealed to him. The Shelley-passage in *A Vision* can only be understood in the light of this new conception.

We must now try, with the help of this idea, to translate that strangely worded description of Shelley as an example of Phase 17 into the language of ordinary experience.

Most of what is unsatisfactory in Shelley's poems and questionable in his life may be attributed to his failure 'to conceive of the world as a continual conflict'. Thus his hatred of tyrants and priests compensates his thwarted desire for universal love. The objects of his hate, Yeats says, 'are monstrous, meaningless images. And unlike Byron . . . he can never see anything that opposes him as it really is'. His hallucinations, nightmares, monstrous phantasies, and other abnormal states of mind are symptoms of escapism. Another form of evasion of the Vision of Evil consists in a quixotic activity: he 'writes pamphlets, and dreams of converting the world, or of turning man of affairs and upsetting governments'. Speaking of his own political work, Yeats had confessed in 'Ireland after Parnell'[24]: 'It was many years before I understood that I had surrendered myself to the chief temptation of the artist, creation without toil . . . But now I had found the happiness that Shelley found when he tied a pamphlet to a fire balloon'. In his longer poems Shelley tended towards mechanical creation, to a flow of 'fantastic, constructed images'. This auto-

[23] See *A Vision*, p. 25.   [24] See *Autobiographies*, p. 249.

matonism, as Yeats called it, permitted him to maintain his irrational hatred of priests and tyrants because that hatred remained, as it were, outside his personality.

One of the most striking examples of Shelley's flight from the Vision of Evil is a passage in *Prometheus Unbound* which Yeats must have thought of in his condemnation of the poet. It is from the Fury's speech in Act I, lines 625–31:

> The good want power, but to weep barren tears,
> The powerful goodness want: worse need for them.
> The wise want love; and those who love want wisdom;
> And all best things are thus confused to ill.
> Many are strong and rich, and would be just,
> But live among their suffering fellow-men
> As if none felt: they know not what they do.

Shelley could not master this revelation of essential evil. For thus Prometheus counters it with a vague hope:

> The sights with which thou torturest gird my soul
> With new endurance, till the hour arrives
> When they shall be no types of things which are.

Yeats's Vision of Evil comprises the three main aspects of violence, pride, and animalism; and in each of them he is opposed to Shelley. The Pollexfen in him refused more and more to be identified with a Shelleyan figure. His later conception of poetry is the direct negation of Shelley's famous definition: 'Poetry is the record of the best and happiest moments of the happiest and best minds'. Take these lines from 'The Tower' (1926):

> I mock Plotinus' thought
> And cry in Plato's teeth,
> Death and life were not
> Till man made up the whole,
> Made lock, stock and barrel
> Out of his bitter soul.

In a letter dated March 24, 1909, J. B. Yeats had written to his son: 'I think the reason you have the popular gift is because your

talent is benign. That is its essential quality—[word indecipherable]
are *malign*; so are aristocracies and pessimists . . . but so were not
Shakespeare or Shelley. Had the latter lived he would have proved
it. His "passion to reform the world" which he himself avowed made
him quarrelsome, but later on, the quarrels over, he would have been
wholly benign . . . This benign quality you get from me; I say this
remembering my father's family. They all of them in every fibre of
their being were "the Good people", in a sense the fairies are not. For
that reason people loved them but did not fear them, so they passed
making no mark'. Yeats's whole later life and work disproved his
father's theory. He did not want to be of 'the Good people', he
wanted to be of the fairies and Furies. Thinking of the inferior part
Shelley made the Fury play in *Prometheus Unbound*, he exhorted
Dorothy Wellesley to let herself be inspired by the spirit of violence:

> What climbs the stair?
> Nothing that common women ponder on
> If you are worth my hope! Neither Content
> Nor Satisfied Conscience, but that great family
> Some ancient famous authors misrepresent,
> The Proud Furies each with her torch on high.[25]

And in his own vision of the modern anarchy he denounces Christian charity as a form of evasion of reality, and he prophesies the
advent of a new dispensation in which the impossible Christian love
is replaced by brute force:

> Things fall apart; the centre cannot hold;
> Mere anarchy is loosed upon the world,
> The blood-dimmed tide is loosed, and everywhere
> The ceremony of innocence is drowned;
> The best lack all conviction, while the worst
> Are full of passionate intensity.
>
> . . . .
>
> The darkness drops again; but now I know
> That twenty centuries of stony sleep

[25] *Last Poems and Plays,* Macmillan, 1940, p. 21. See also the author's *Textbook of Modern English Poetry*, Berne, 1943, pp. 68 f.

> Were vexed to nightmare by a rocking cradle,
> And what rough beast, its hour come round at last,
> Slouches towards Bethlehem to be born? [26]

The poem, entitled 'The Second Coming', appeared in 1921, a year before Mussolini's 'march on Rome'. The Pollexfen inheritance counts for something in Yeats's sympathy with the Fascist movement. Yeats's pride, too, is un-Shelleyan. Whereas Shelley identified himself with the oppressed, Yeats declared in 'The Tower' that his spiritual progeny should inherit his pride,

> The pride of people that were
> Bound neither to Cause nor to State,
> Neither to slaves that were spat on,
> Nor to the tyrants that spat.

J. B. Yeats's belief in the 'solitary' nature of the 'superior' man became also one of his son's deepest convictions [27]. According to Yeats, Shelley 'returns again and again to these two images of solitude', a wandering lover and an inaccessible sage; but Shelley's gregariousness is explained either as a sign of weakness or as a heterogeneous element in his personality. Thus Shelley becomes an 'antithetical' man, that is, a man developing 'towards Nature' rather than 'towards God', who values the inner world of desire and imagination more highly than 'actual fact', who seeks 'subjectivity, unity of being, beauty' rather than 'objectivity, passivity, plasticity', in one word, who is 'passionate' rather than 'reasonable'. Shelley is an antithetical man whose condition is aristocratic, as opposed to 'primary' men whose condition is democratic. Yeats considers himself as a man of the same phase as Shelley, but whereas Shelley lost his self to gain humanity, Yeats esteemed his self more highly than a humanity which was for him only an abstraction. When he said that Shelley

---

[26] Quoted from *Collected Poems*, Macmillan, 1933, pp. 210 f. The difference between Yeats's and Shelley's conceptions of history and Christianity, as illustrated by the comparison of 'The Second Coming' with the passage from *Prometheus Unbound* quoted above, may also be studied in the first of the 'Two Songs from a Play' and the final chorus in *Hellas*. See E. M. W. Tillyard, *Poetry Direct and Oblique*, Chatto & Windus, 1934, pp. 196 f.

[27] J. B. Yeats, *loc. cit.*, p. 33. From the memoir by Joseph Hone.

lacked the Vision of Evil, he meant, among other things, that Shelley would never resign himself to his individuality, but must always sacrifice it to a collective ideal.

Nothing could be further removed from Shelley than the animalism of the Crazy Jane poems. The lifelong struggle between Yeats's Soul and Self was not won finally by the Shelleyan ideals of a prematurely aged youth or an inaccessible sage, but by an astonishingly rabelaisian old poet who frankly admitted his animal delights [28]:

> You think it horrible that lust and rage
> Should dance attention upon my old age;
> They were not such a plague when I was young;
> What else have I to spur me into song?

This rehabilitation of the senses is also the reason for Yeats's praise of Donne at the expense of Shelley: 'Donne could be as metaphysical as he pleased, and yet never seemed unhuman and hysterical as Shelley often does, because he could be as physical as he pleased; and besides, who will thirst for the metaphysical, who have a parched tongue, if we cannot recover the Vision of Evil?' [29] Yeats here participates in the revival of interest in Donne during the Post-War period, but his own approach is different from that of T. S. Eliot or Herbert Read who prefer the metaphysicals to the romantics, not because Donne could be physical, but because he showed that poetry could be subtle and profound without being uniformly sublime and serious.

To conclude this description of Yeats's Shelley-portraits it may be said that Yeats probably had in his mind two entirely different conceptions of Shelley. One conception was that of a great popular poet who expresses, as it were, the age-old wisdom of humanity. Comparing himself to a sort of Taillefer, he writes thus in a letter to Dorothy Wellesley: 'We stride ahead of the crowd, its swordsmen, its jugglers, looking to right and left. "To right and left" by which I mean that

[28] See 'The Spur' in *Last Poems and Plays*, p. 37. In 'The Bounty of Sweden', 1925, Yeats is amused by the thought, 'now I am old and rheumatic, and nothing to look at, but my Muse is young'.
[29] From 'The Trembling of the Veil' (1922), book IV, 'The Tragic Generation', *Autobiographies*, p. 402.

we need like Milton, Shakespeare, Shelley, vast sentiments, generalizations supported by tradition ' [30]. This was the Shelley-portrait which was also in the mind of Yeats's father. Yeats himself identified his own image with the Shelley-Taillefer ideal when he felt physically strong and healthy.

The opposite Shelley-picture occurred to him when his health was low. He recounts in 'The Tragic Generation' how the Rhymers taught him 'that violent energy, which is like a fire of straw, consumes in a few minutes the nervous vitality, and is useless in the arts. Our fire must burn slowly, and we must constantly turn away to think, constantly analyse what we have done, be content even to have little life outside our work, to show, perhaps, to other men, as little as the watch-mender shows, his magnifying glass caught in his screwed-up eye' [31]. It was in periods of low health that Yeats usually lost himself on the *Hodos Chameliontos* which he describes in these terms: 'But now image called up image in an endless procession, and I could not always choose among them with any confidence; and when I did choose, the image lost its intensity, or changed into some other image.' [32] Perhaps the traditional Celtic style of book ornamentation as seen in the seventh-century Book of Kells and its successors illustrates this imaginative process described by Yeats. There is the same ebullient motion, excitement, passion, and the same absence of a simplifying rational principle. Thought does not go straight to its object; it moves in spirals, curves; it lacks rigour and direction.[33] In *A Vision* Yeats tends to see Shelley as a man who was denied the power of deep and constructive thought. His 'mental images . . . flow, change, flutter, cry out, or mix into something else; but without . . . breaking and bruising one another . . . The *Will* is falling asunder, but without explosion and noise. The separate fragments

[30] *Letters on Poetry from W. B. Yeats to Dorothy Wellesley*, O.U.P., 1940. Letter dated April 20, 1936.
[31] See *Autobiographies*, p. 392. Compare also Yeats's note to 'The Winding Stair and other Poems', in *Collected Poems*, 1933. In a letter to Dorothy Wellesley of August 5, 1936, Yeats speaks, not of an alternation of high and low vitality influencing his poetry, but of an unconscious conflict between emotional calm and emotional tension.
[32] *Autobiographies*, p. 335 and p. 462.
[33] See the article on Illuminated MSS. in *Encycl. Brit.*, and Dagobert Frey, *Englisches Wesen in der bildenden Kunst*, Stuttgart und Berlin, 1942.

H. W. Häusermann

seek images rather than ideas, and these the intellect . . .must synthesize in vain, drawing with its compass-point a line that should but represent the outline of a bursting pod.' It probably never occurred to Yeats that he must choose between these two ideas of Shelley. Feeling himself alternately a Taillefer or a Byzantine gold-smith, he conceived of Shelley, too, as either the one or the other type of artist. Perhaps he may claim to have discovered the 'real Shelley' with as much right as those critics who explain the poet's elusive personality by an all too simple formula.

JAMES T. FARRELL

The Language of Hollywood

IN America, a tremendous commercial culture has developed as a
kind of substitute for a genuinely popular, a genuinely democratic culture, which would re-create and communicate how the
mass of the people live, how they feel about working, loving, enjoy-
ing, suffering, and dying. This culture has become a big business. It
is capitalized at hundreds of millions of dollars, returns many
millions in annual profits, rent, and interest, and employs thousands
of men and women to whom it pays additional millions more in
wages and salaries. At times, the apologists and propagandists for
the cultural industries proudly boast of the 'cultural' achievements of
these industries: on other occasions, however, they assert that these
industries produce entertainment, not culture. Let not us quibble
over words. The products of these industries (motion pictures, songs,
radio plays and soap operas, cartoons, and so on) re-create images of
life: they communicate feelings, no matter how banal these may be;
they externalize reveries; they fix ideals; they embody and illustrate
moral attitudes; they create tastes which in turn influence how objects
are regarded—in brief, directly and by lesson, suggestion, innuendo,
fable, story, they tell huge masses of people how and what to believe.
And all this is done in terms of the most powerful artistic inventions
and media of all time. If the performance of such functions be
described as something other than cultural, then the plain meaning
of words is being inexcusably debased.

Usually, the debates concerning these industries—and most
especially the motion picture industry—are concerned with the problem of commercial versus artistic values. Critics of the motion
picture industry generally claim that pictures are not artistic enough;
their adversaries then reply that pictures are as artistic as they can be
made, considering the fact that they must be produced for a profit.

James T. Farrell

The claim that the function of pictures is to produce entertainment serves as a justification of the simple and the admitted fact that the fundamental purpose of the motion picture studios is to make money. All this is common knowledge. It is clear that business considerations play a decisive rôle in all these fields. However, we will gain little in understanding if we merely protest the harmful effects of capitalism on culture in general, in the abstract. Art which we call good, art which we call bad, art which we call counterfeit—all this is sold on the commodity market. Due to basic economic causes, something of the most profound significance has happened in American culture: it has been invaded by finance capital. American commercial culture is owned and operated by finance capital. The motion picture industry is dominated by a few huge studios; the same is the case in radio. The success of *Reader's Digest* and the Luce publications reveals the same tendency triumphing in journalism. Some of the consequences of this fact must be noted. It is seemingly paradoxical but true that the bigger a corporation producing for the consumer market, the more must it depend on good will. Due to the investments in Hollywood, for instance, risks must be minimized. Thus, the facts show us that the Hollywood studio can permit less freedom in the treatment of subject than the Broadway producer; he, in turn, can allow less freedom than the book publisher. The bigger our cultural industries become, the greater are the restrictions they must impose on the choice and the handling of subject matter. Economic necessities dominate all else. The aims, the tastes of the men controlling the industries must be harmonized with them. One producer may be more sincere, more artistic than another. But all must adjust themselves; all must work within this system. It allows relatively little real individualism of taste, daring, experiment. One act of daring experiment and bold honesty may cost a million dollars. Similar actions by book publishers can be more easily sustained because the risks are not as great. Those who really control the studios are big capitalists. They think and act according to their class interests. It is folly to expect them wilfully to produce art (and even to lose money on it) that will endanger their class interest. Honest art often threatens that interest. This means that there is a double restriction imposed on the character of what is produced in motion picture.

Besides promising a profit, a picture must not seriously threaten the class interests of the owners.

Genuine works of art have something new and individual to convey. They reveal new aspects of life, of human feeling. They make us conscious of what had been hitherto hidden, concealed, not clearly grasped in our own consciousness. To assimilate them is painful, disturbing, difficult; we must make an effort; we must expand our boundaries of feeling, thinking. Growth and assimilation are almost always painful, disturbing, demanding. For we are then forced to change, to alter the force of habit. It is a truism that in a shoddy culture shoddy art generally gains quicker acceptance than genuine art does. The time required for the assimilation of new, more honest, more revealing pictures would be too long and, during that period, large losses would have to be sustained.

Now and then, it may happen that a good picture is produced. This is exceptional, often accidental. Usually, bad pictures are produced. Here is the explanation of why this is the case. The aim of the studios is to get a return on investment, and to get profits, rent, and interest. If returns on investment permit the studios to produce great art, then, and *then only,* will they do it; otherwise, the artistic values, the truth and artistic values embodied in pictures, are and will remain merely secondary. In order to be a business man in this system, you must do what business requires; in order to be an artist, you must meet the demands and responsibilities required by art. An artist must be sincere, honest, clear, and for his work he must draw on his own inner life and inner tensions. A business man must stay in business. *Q.E.D.!*

My analysis can be extended to encompass the economic relationships which play an important role in other fields of culture, as well as in the motion picture industry. I use the latter as an illustration. Hollywood is not a cause; it is a consequence. And it reveals tendencies now at work in American culture with such relative purity that it serves me as a most illuminating illustration of what I want to convey. The rise of Hollywood to the realm of culture is a phenomenon somewhat analogous to that of the triumph of machine production during the industrial revolution developed to an advanced degree. We have social methods of production carried on for private profits. But those who contribute to this production do not (with rare exceptions) control it. They lose their independence as artists and craftsmen, and become employees. Their economic relationships thereby change. Most writers, for instance, become the wage-working writer. It is true that their wages are generally fantastically higher than those of factory workers, but this is not the decisive factor here. In the economic sense, most writers have a relationship to their employers similar to that of the factory worker to his boss. Just as the worker sells his labour power, so does the writer sell his skill and talent. What he then receives is a wage. All control over the product of his work resides in the employer. Thus, the writer suffers from the same kind of alienation, the same kind of self-estrangement, as does the factory worker. He is alienated from control over his means of production, and over what he produces.

And there is a singular character to the alienation of the writer. His real means of production is his skill, his feelings, his needs which feed his work, his way of seeing life; in other words, his real means of production is his soul. This is what he sells. As a consequence of his economic relationships, the writer may write what he feels and wants to write, only if his employer allows him to do so. But he does not determine whether he will or will not do this.

Culture, art, is the most powerful means invented by mankind for preserving the consciousness of civilized man. It externalizes and communicates that in human life which is most important—man's inner life. But here, the writer who plays the rôle of the artist, who is ostensibly the creator, sells his very ability to create as a commodity. There is a clear-cut difference between freely creating out of inner need and then selling the creation, and selling the very faculty of creating instead of the results of that creation. The writer may thus write out of his inner self, only when his own needs, feelings, and attitudes coincide with the demands of his employer. The nature of these demands have already been uncovered in this analysis. Under such conditions, free creation is not a conscious act of will; it is merely accidental, coincidental. Such being given it is, however, not accidental that so many Hollywood writers, once they become inured to their work, reveal a retrogression in consciousness. When they write they cannot fully draw on their needs and emotions. Much of their writing is reduced to the level of literary carpentering. They are fettered. And the fettered consciousness must retrogress. Here is the real situation. Here is the essential mechanics concerning how they who should be artists are turned into mere purveyors of entertainment. Let each make what he can of this situation in accordance with his values, his moral outlook, and with what he wants in life for himself, and for his fellow men.

Just as there is a huge investment capital in the production end of the industry, so is there in its distribution end. America (the world in fact) is almost glutted with motion picture theatres, each of which also must return its profit, its rent, its interest. In many instances, these are also organized into chains. Taken together they constitute a huge and voracious mouth for ever crying for commodities to be consumed. And they must be fed. They must stay open; they must have customers parading continually to the box office. The studios must supply them. Halt this flow of commodities and bankruptcies will follow. This need, more than any other, conditions the production schedules of the studios. Gigantic blocs of capital are involved in the total structure of the industry. Consequently, it must find the widest possible market. This means, the largest possible audience is necessary. Such an audience can be only a most heterogeneous one, encompassing all age, emotional, and mental levels. Such an audience will alone permit this industry to continue. There is no time to waste in educating the tastes of this audience. That would be too costly. Staple commodities based on the lowest common denominator of the mentality and the emotional life of the audience must be produced. Staple commodities in art, produced in this way, and in order to meet such requirements must mean, in the main, counterfeit art. This is one of the decisive reasons why the masses of the American people really 'need' so much Hollywood 'entertainment'.

Actually, the motion picture industry needs the money of the American masses as much as they need its entertainment. We get, thus, an endless barrage of Hollywood publicity, of Hollywood advertising which almost batters the intelligence of the nation into insensibility. Hollywood must do this in order to give the public what Hollywood wants it to want. The audience cannot directly

James T. Farrell

choose. It is not given proper alternatives. Usually, it may choose one of various absurd pictures, or none of them at all. When choice is so restricted, it is meaningless to argue that the public really gets what it wants. Also, the contradictions which we have observed in the motion picture industry are apparent in American society as a whole. The conditions of American life create alienated and truncated personalities, a fact which has already engaged the attention of more than one generation of sociologists, political scientists, psychologists, judges, social workers, and others. The conditions of earning one's bread in this society create the self-estranged modern man.

It is such conditions which explain the need, sometimes feverish, for an entertainment which so repetitively presents the same reveries, the same daydreams, the same childish fables of success and happiness. So much of the inner life of men is dried up that they tend to become filled with yearnings and to need the consolation of these reveries about people who are happy, healthy, and who always succeed. Tastes are thus conditioned. Increasingly deprived of proper alternatives from which to choose, the American masses have also become habituated to this taste for the movies. The movies have, thereby, become a social habit. The kind of profitable commercial culture which we now have would have demanded conditions which would aid in the creation of the necessary audience. The two have developed more or less harmoniously. Hence, parallel to the retrogression of consciousness in, say, the Hollywood writer, there is a more widespread and also more pernicious retrogression of consciousness in the motion picture audience. Social and economic conditions have established the basis for this; the motion picture further enforces it. But such a process can continue only so far. Eventually a limit must and will be reached. Eventually, there will be a profound revulsion of popular taste. But this will depend not only on the audience being saturated with what it is given; more than this, it will depend on fundamental changes which are economic, political, and social in character.

Most motion pictures enervate rather than energize. They distract the masses of the people from more clearly becoming aware of their real moral, æsthetic, spiritual needs; in other words, they distract from what are the real and most important problems of life. As such,

The Language of Hollywood

they offer what William James aptly characterized as 'a moral holiday'. Moral holidays are necessary, but when so much time is used up in a nation in having these moral holidays, we have a social problem to define. The gap between the realities of life in our time, and the way that these are represented on the screen is a wide one. However, the masses of the people do not lose their real needs merely because these are not fulfilled in motion pictures.

It should now be clear that this commercial culture is a safety valve. Here, I offer in opposition to the conceptions, the apologetics, the theorizations of such a culture, a different idea of what a culture should do. It should help to create those states of consciousness, of awareness of oneself, of others, and of the world, which aid in making people better, and in preparing them to make the world better. Hollywood films usually have the precisely opposite effect; most of them make people less aware, or else falsely aware. This is, to me, the sense in which Hollywood films do not fulfil the real cultural needs of the masses of the people. For really to try and achieve that, one must not merely envision them as they were in the past, and as they are now; one must also envision them as they might be; one must establish as a premise their great potentiality. In other words, one must think in terms of the future as well as of the past and of the present. Such a premise is essential if one has the ideal of a culture that is truly human, a culture that is truly free. Here, in essence, is the great ideal of a free, a human, a socialist culture expressed by Friedrich Engels when he spoke of the possibility of mankind escaping from the kingdom of necessity, and entering the kingdom of freedom.

The content of motion pictures is so familiar that it need not be analyzed here in great detail. The values which pictures generally emphasize are those of rugged individualism. The lessons which they inculcate are those which imply that the world we have, and have had, is the best of all possible worlds. The major qualities embodied in most motion picture heroes are those of the pioneer, plus those of the present which are either consistent with the practices, the standards, the mores of bourgeois America, or are else in no vital contradiction with them. The past is re-created in the accents of weak nostalgia; the present glorified. The future is promised as no different. All history is, in fact, being gradually revised on the screen until it

201

begins to seem like some glamorous fable. Further, pictures often embody within their very context a kind of visual and illustrative argument that the function of the motion picture is entertainment; thus the reliance which is placed on entertainment within the picture, which is itself an entertainment.

But there is no essential change in the pattern, or in the moral, or in their implications. What characterizes almost all Hollywood pictures is their inner emptiness. This is compensated for by an outer impressiveness. Such impressiveness usually takes the form of a truly grandiose Belasco realism. Nothing is spared to make the setting, the costumes, all of the surface details correct. These efforts help to mask the essential emptiness of the characterizations, and the absurdities and trivialities of the plots. The houses look like houses; the streets look like streets; the people look and talk like people; but they are empty of humanity, credibility, and motivation. Needless to say, the disgraceful censorship code is an important factor in predetermining the content of these pictures. But the code does not disturb the profits, nor the entertainment value of the films; it merely helps to prevent them from being credible. It isn't too heavy a burden for the industry to bear. In addition to the impressiveness of the settings, there is a use of the camera which at times seems magical. But of what human import is all this skill, all this effort, all this energy in the production of effects, when the story, the representation of life is hollow, stupid, banal, childish? Because a mass of people see these films, they are called democratic. In addition, there is often a formal democratic character embodied in the pictures. Common speech is often introduced; an ambassador acts like a regular guy named Joe; poor working girls are heroines and, now and then, they continue to marry rich men; speeches are introduced propagandistically in which the common man is praised, democracy is cheered for, and the masses are flattered with verbiage. The introduction of such democratic notes is an additional way of masking the real content of the picture; these merely are pressed into the service of glorifying the *status quo*.

Granted that, now and then, an unusual picture is produced, one different from those which I have characterized. Let us not forget that once we saw a picture called 'The Informer'. But does one, or do even ten such films, justify a greater number of their opposites?

One might ask a theologian—if a man steals money, and uses some of it to have masses said for the suffering souls in Purgatory, will he thereby redeem his guilt for theft? To argue that because we once in a while get a picture such as 'The Informer', Hollywood is thus justified, is to argue that you are forgiven for theft because you use some stolen money for the souls in Purgatory. I leave those who argue in this manner to the theologians who can explain what is wrong with their argument. And similarly, the argument that bad pictures are necessary to make money which will permit the use of profits for good pictures is a fallacious one. The reason that this happens, when it does, is because of the social organization of the industry, and I have already indicated what that is.

Hollywood has not created all of this counterfeit culture. It borrowed most of what it has given us from tendencies which antedate its appearance on the cultural scene. In fact, other than in the technical realm, it has invented very little. It has used the powerful inventions of the cinema to repeat most of the cheap stories, the cheap plots, the counterfeits which have long been printed as stories in commercial magazines. Many of its jokes were even familiar to our fathers, and perhaps our grandparents. Here Hollywood is significant mainly because it is a clear cut example of the development of commercial culture in the period of finance capital. Due to its size, its wealth, its ability to reach such a mass audience, it has a penetrating influence in the whole field of culture, one which far exceeds that which was exerted in the commercial culture of which it is the heir.

Its penetrating influence has long been observed in the drama and the novel. At present, novels are even sold for pictures before they are written. One can guess what most such books will be like; or if one wishes to know without trusting to a guess, then one can read Louis Bromfield. Another penetrating influence of Hollywood in the novel is the stimulation which it has given to a kind of hard-boiled realism which imitates all of the manners of serious realistic writing, but contains none of the inner meaning, the inner protest against evils, the revelation of social mechanisms and social structures which we perceive in serious realism. This tendency is illustrated by such books as The Postman Always Rings Twice. The influence of the film industry is to be observed, also, in an incalculable way. For instance, there is the diversion of talent, the fettering of talent, in brief, the retrogression in consciousness about which I have already commented. A large proportion of the literary talent of America is now diverted into Hollywood and radio writing. In many instances, there is a certain inevitability in this. For with the rise of these industries, the situation for writers is such that, on the whole, the book market can support relatively fewer of them. By and large, talent flows towards the highest bidder. A writer represents more than an individual talent; he represents so much social labour which had to be performed in order that he may have developed his talents. This social labour has been expended for the development of literary talents in America. Instead of these talents then returning honest work for this social labour which permitted them to develop, they are used up, burned out in scenario writing. This is a positive social loss. And there can be little doubt of the fact that a correlation exists between the success of this commercial culture, and the loss of æsthetic and moral vigour in so much contemporary writing. Such must be a consequence when talent is fettered and sold as a commodity, when audiences are doped, and when tastes are confused, even depraved.

The culture of a society ought not to be viewed as a mere ornament, a pastime, a form of entertainment. It is the life, the consciousness, the conscience of that society. When it fails to serve as such, then, it moves farther and farther away from the real roots of life. Such is precisely and unmistakably the situation in America where we have this tremendous commercial culture spreading itself like an octopus. And consider how many lives, how much labour power, how much talent, how much of social goods is poured, not only into Hollywood, but into American commercial culture as a whole. The social cost is fabulous. We are familiar with the news telling us of the financial costs of pictures. A million dollars. More than that. And then, we go once again and see what has been produced at such cost. Once again, we see a picture so silly that it insults one's intelligence. Once again, the same old stupid and inept story of boy meets girl, framed, mounted, glorified until it becomes a monumental absurdity. And so inured are most people to this that they do not even see anything wrong in it.

The Language of Hollywood

This entire structure can be metaphorically described as a grandiose Luna Park of capitalism. And if the serious artist enters it, he well may quote these words from Dante: 'All hope abandon, ye who enter here.'

This is a culture which does not serve men; on the contrary, it makes men its servants. Its highest measure of worth is revealed in little numerals, written in black and red ink on sheets of paper which record profits and losses. Let those who favour this masquerade try to justify it. Far better is it to see it for what it is, and to renounce all of the ideals and aims which it embodies. For the writer to do this places him in that category which one motion picture executive has described as 'the irresponsible literati'. Correct! Irresponsible to this system; responsible to an ideal of trying to show men what life is like now, of seeking to do what one can in the necessary effort of creating in men that consciousness of their problems, their needs, and their future which will help to create a better society.

CHRISTOPHER SALMON

Broadcasting, Speech, and Writing

'*I want to tell you a tale—just one tale—out of many hundred sights and atrocities I saw. I myself was driving a milk stall, and round this milk stall was a screaming crowd of women with babies. I kept picking a few babies out and feeding them. One woman who was—I think she was mad—kept kissing my feet, hands and clothing. So I took the baby from her, and when I looked at the baby its face was black—it'd been dead for a few days. I couldn't convince her it was dead—so I pressed the lips open and poured the milk down its dead throat. The woman crooned, gibbered with delight. I gave her the baby back and she staggered off, and lay in the sun. And when I next looked she was dead with the baby in her arms, and so I put her with a stack of other dead bodies—two or three hundred dead, and I turned away.*'—BROADCAST IN THE HOME SERVICE, MAY 1945*

'*The deceitful and dangerous experiment of the criminal* quæstio, *as it is emphatically styled, was admitted, rather than approved, in the jurisprudence of the Romans. They applied this sanguinary mode of examination only to servile bodies, whose sufferings were seldom weighed by those haughty republicans in the scale of justice or humanity; but they would never consent to violate the sacred person of a citizen till they possessed the clearest evidence of his guilt. The annals of tyranny, from the reign of Tiberius to that of Domitian, circumstantially relate the executions of many innocent victims; but, as long as the faintest remembrance was kept alive of the national freedom and honour, the last hours of a Roman were secure from the danger of ignominious torture.*'—DECLINE AND FALL OF THE ROMAN EMPIRE

IN these two passages two men, having something to communicate, have made use of English. And since they both express themselves in the same language, if the advantage goes to one of them rather than the other, can it be for any other reason than that one of them uses the language more skilfully than the other? They have both drawn their words from one dictionary. They use many of the same words and spell them alike with letters from the same alphabet. Their sentences show subjects, verbs, and objects, so that we may look to the same grammar for the key to both. But I believe that when all this is admitted, these apparent similarities cover a world of different intentions. I believe that though they did both deliver themselves in English, the man who spoke the first, without any preparation, but under urgent need to speak, to his interlocutor at Belsen Concentration Camp, and Gibbon, writing in his study for posterity, were pulling at English from different situations and driving its import towards different ends.

What may be properly attempted with language in speech is different from what may properly be written; and what is required of language in prose is different from what speech requires, though the distinctions are commonly obscured. I can write, it is true, I can actually set down in visual symbols, without restatement, anything that I have spoken, and I can, though not always without difficulty, speak, that is to say, represent in audible symbols, without restatement, anything that I write; but more is involved between speaking and writing than equivalent meanings, and if I have originally written or spoken successfully, I shall not express myself successfully in any literal translation.

I believe that language, like a plant with two sexes, includes two principles of life. I believe, indeed, that the functions of writing and speaking are specific enough to warrant our saying, with less danger of ambiguity, of ourselves, and of the French, and the Dutch and the Norwegians and of every people, that we all have command in our own right of two languages rather than of one, and that we shall only keep French, English, Dutch and the rest in health, and hand them on to our children with undiminished prospects of life, if we continue to practise them in both their modes, speaking them with one set of intentions and in one idiom, and writing them in another, and not allowing either our eye or our ear to prevail in the other's kingdom. For that is what is involved here, two separate kingdoms, each deriving from a different sense and owning a different quality of meaning and a different order of possibilities.

Languages are instruments. That they should last is a condition of the continuity of societies and cultures. But that we should continue individually to speak and listen, and to write and read, is of crucial importance to ourselves, for these two uses of language are incomparably the most subtle and effective means we possess for developing our contacts with the world outside us and our relations with one another. Now, as long as the two modes in any one language are adequately practised in their own right, the language which includes them will benefit by the developments of both. Those who write the language will find it quicker and more flexible through the efforts of those who speak it, and those who speak it will find their resources more subtle and far-reaching for the efforts of the writers. But if ever the writers of a language take too readily to the mode of speech, or those who speak it consent too widely to the idioms of the eye, the body of the language will sicken, lacking the fertility to maintain for long even the mode which the speakers or the writers are erecting to take possession of it; and the people who own the language will lose, not only the way of life they have made for themselves through their private intercourse, but the objective environment they have built round them with their truth finding and their science. In no language and in no society can writing take over for long, with impunity, the offices of speech or speech those of writing.

Languages which are no longer spoken we call, significantly, dead. All living languages reveal health-giving and morbid tendencies. I believe it would be possible to find traces in the final condition of a dying language of most of the social and political influences which have contributed to its death. For this reason, also, to advance the matter from the other end, a language is an excellent index, at any given time, of the health of the society it serves. But a dead language leaves only visible remains, and these are inadequate to a post-mortem. They do none the less reveal more than the functions of their writers. For if a language has ever been spoken, the bones it leaves, words and grammar, belonged to its body and were partly the product of those who spoke it. It is for that reason that we cannot now assess even the literary capacity of Latin and classical Greek unless we can recover their authentic sound.

I suppose it is possible that over-speech, which may in the past have arrested languages, we now know nothing of, on the margin of primitive life, might yet attack some modern language like Italian whose aural architecture is still a European glory. But most contemporary languages, if they have not like English in the British Isles already done so, are likely to run into the opposite danger of being over-read. The invention of printing was what first made this possible. The extension of literacy is what makes it likely.

So long as the majority of people could not read, the care of the spoken word was safe in their hands. They had to live by its means. They were obliged to discover what they could do with it, and what they did with it was original. They used it as a native art, as the countryman still does, and found it a medium in which they could express themselves and develop personal relations between them which were both unique and sincere. It was within the experience exclusively of the educated for the way a man wrote to influence the way he spoke. Sometimes, as in England in the eighteenth century, this influence was very marked and led to some stiffening of manners. But this was only among the minority, and outside polite circles writing could still only influence speech indirectly through the impact on the people of professionals like the actor and the priest. This kept the body of the language in rude health, so that when Wordsworth and Coleridge were looking for means to refresh their art they knew where to look and found what they wanted. But nowadays, when we are all literate, if the exercise of writing does not affect us all, what we read certainly does; and it is here the danger lies. For while the writer is likely to know what he is trying to do, the reader is apt simply to be letting something happen to him, and what this is he may not know, or that it is threatening to rob his speech of its direction and authority. The fact that we all of us now spend so much of our time in reading, and that newspapers and advertisements are mostly what we read, more than offsets the opportunities our secretaries, our typewriters and our dictaphones might otherwise have given us recently to start some influence moving in the other direction from our speech to our writing. It is clear, I think, that the Americans have made a better use of these chances than we have.

Now it would be very absurd if, in all this, I was trying to belittle what in the past, at any rate, we have owed to our writers. If, as I argue, we shall always, lacking telepathy, have to depend on the spoken word for our personal relations, we should never, but for the written word, have been able to establish an order of society within which we could develop them.

Originally, in the far backward reaches where language was born, we have, I suppose, to imagine the creatures we then were, labouring through all sorts of uncouth roaring and mewing towards some positive expression. Heaven knows through what dreadful oppression of spirit we had to bring up the weight of what we felt to the transforming kindness of our lips and tongues; but somehow, I suppose, as we struggled to our feet and contracted our muscles into uprightness, we did succeed in exchanging with each other primitive messages of gradually increasing complexity. Under the pressure of situations which threatened several of us together we did, I suppose, arrive at as much common understanding as we needed to escape from them. One man expressed, perhaps, something that the rest of us could follow.

But it was the draughtsmen who took the first decisive step. When they found means to scratch shapes on the walls of their caves, they had started the process moving on which thereafter all of us were going more and more to have to depend. They had stumbled on that miraculous transformation of one element into another by which presently we were to come to a method by which we could spread out and fix meanings once and for all in front of our eyes. We could then discover identities and refine upon them, and, in the confidence this gave us, fairly start to push back the dark of superstition, and afterwards build solidly round us, and as far from us as might be convenient, a dependable objective world. Thereafter, we have to imagine the clerks gradually breaking down, first into established sequences, next into words, and finally, in some societies, into letters, the continuity which the rest of us were all the time learning better and better to speak. Gradually so the unsegmented worm of all that was within us began its long evolution towards its ultimate vertibrate and articulate condition.

The written language was nothing less than our means to all objectivity, and out of it came gradually order and law, science, and status, and contract. As languages differentiated themselves, it mattered very much what symbols the clerks found for them. The alphabet was an enormous advance on the ideograph and put into the hands of the people who used it an unprecedented reach. It mattered also how much emphasis the clerks might lay on the act of writing. Where, as in China, the gesture of writing became too important in itself, those who had not the skill were forced to revolt with a vernacular which thenceforth they had to use, for their personal intercourse, entirely without benefit of clergy. But in every language the tendency was naturally enough for the official patronage and the advantages of authority to be laid more and more upon the visible mode. For some time the herald and the bard might continue to exact reverence for the divine rights of speech, but the printing press finally took even poetry into its custody. And it is not, I believe, until the invention, in the last twenty years, of broadcasting, that we come to anything powerful enough to alter the direction in which things were moving.

I wish to make this a plea for standing back, for weighing things and examining opportunities. We cannot afford to take the first course of any invention or any new technique for granted. The essence of specifically human affairs, we should have to admit, is that we can never afford to say afterwards, merely, Look, this is what happened! The more prodigious inventions are, the farther and faster they reach, the more likely they are to escape in the train of their effects anything so shy as a critical attention. Too many people are busy too soon drawing out the consequences which already show as possible in the direction in which the invention happens to have been applied. Too many others are engaged in involving, often for cash, as many people as possible in the general consequences. In an instant the process sets and becomes a part of all those irresistible tendencies whose force is only that we never question them.

Our opportunities are easiest to see in matters of taste. We are likely to demand of our writers and our artists, our theatre men, or film producers, or musicians, more only, if better, of what they happen already to have taught us to like. But look at Chinese music in the East and European in the West. From inside either body of music now it would be impossible to guess at or work one's way to the other. May there not be, then, indefinite numbers of unexplored systems of sound still hanging in silence?

That the past always seems to lead straight to the present is because we look back at it from where we are. Look away once and one can no longer convince oneself that where one is, or ever will arrive, is all the place, or even the best place, one might have come to. It is open to us to convince ourselves from our own experience, that wherever a man or woman has stood, he or she might always have interfered. We are all meeting-places and places of issue, and the actual roads events travel away from us are not the routes down which they need have gone.

Now I have planted the difference between speaking and writing where I believe they should be planted, on the different senses from which they spring and to which they give systematic opportunities for active and receptive exercise. But if anything in the world could be left to look after itself it might be thought the exercise of our senses could. Our senses seem so native and peremptory. But we have only to remember that we have already, as compared with the dog or the fox, as good as thrown away our sense of smell, and that the blind man, by merely trying, is able almost magically to enlarge the sensibility of his touch and hearing. Most of us do, I believe, make much less use than we need to of the openings our senses give us.

We should do quite well to think of the senses as competing with one another, as it were on their own, for our attention. How we balance their findings is very much our individual business, and partly responsible for our particular personalities. Certainly we can never afford to take our sense-habits for granted. What a jaded view, after all, our eye is apt to take of the world! How quick it is to snap a look at things, not for themselves, but only for their practical uses! And because there are vested interests in use, had it not been for the artist, we might have lost ourselves quicker than we have in our prejudices, wanting refreshment from things as they are.

I see no reason why we should not now get our broadcasters to do something for our ears. They might induce the loudspeaker to do to fifteen minutes' worth of time what the painter's frame does to his square feet of space—isolate it from its surroundings and make it more important to us in its own terms. Music, perhaps, is out of mortal danger, but the spoken word needs help. Speech has its own patterns and its own sequences which we have forgotten. Broadcasting might make us re-aware of them. It possesses the necessary formal opportunities. But we have to break old habits. We have to listen afresh. And we must see to it that our broadcasters no longer introduce to the loudspeaker conventions which derive from the requirements of the eye.

The requirements of the ear and the eye turn out, even under superficial examination, to be radically different. The first obvious difference is one of scale. The range of the eye compared with the ear is immensely extended. I take the canvas of the eye to be not less than six hundred words, as many as you will find on the two pages of a book held open, counting thirty lines to each page and ten words to a line. I do not pretend, of course, that the eye concentrates equally at once on all the six hundred. The size of the central focus of the eye varies very much with the skill of the reader. But whether the central group of words is larger or smaller, the eye always sets it as the reader then interprets it with reference to its particular place within the whole field. As I read, I add to the sense of the words I take in at the focus all sorts of implications which I pick up from the field. Half-way down the right-hand page I have already seen, one chapter ends and another begins. Lower down on the left-hand page, I can see, narrative or description will give place to dialogue. The dialogue, I take in, is to be shared between three people. But of these three I recognize that one will do most of the talking, and this answers to what I might have expected since it is appropriate to their characters. Or it may be an argument I am reading. My eye watches its development. I see that in his opening section the author means to lay thesis against antithesis, but in the next section he is to offer me a view of several connected arguments which already I can see spread out in the proportions and relations which on their first impact they already roughly deserve. Assumptions, negations, hypotheses, all these with all manner of other subtler amplifications and qualifications, strike my eye even as I embark, and pique my expectation on. Without the pleasure or ruffle of these anticipations I could not take up my author's meaning. Without the preparation of my eye's extended view, without its backward and forward ranging, I could not carry the long significance of what I read.

Now it is precisely this large scope of the eye which gives the writer his chance. It defines his art. If he knows his medium, he will use the eye's scope to the full. He will study to refine more and more upon meanings, to balance, to oppose, to qualify, to draw the eye, and through the eye the intelligence, on and on, puzzling, satisfying, tantalizing, surprising, as the stops and the commas give his reader pause or lead him on. He will know how to vary and develop moods in his reader through the protracted flow of sentences in contemplation, through abrupt suspense, through dramatic transition, through interrupted beats of episode. But he will require a skill in his reader to match the range of his art, and it is very far from everyone who, in this refined and educated sense, can read. Most of us leave the masters on their shelves because, before there is any question of our mind's inadequacy, our eye cannot move quick enough or take in enough at a time. On the other hand, in the service of the skilled reader how the eye does enjoy itself! With what pleasure it stretches itself forward to the limit of the elaborately articulated sentence, how it answers to all the shocks the author offers it of inversion and juxtaposition, how it lingers, contracts, and shuts down, in a perfectly qualified and fully exercised perceptive act!

Prose, and not poetry, is the original art of the written word. Poetry, though it has now for a long time consented to use the eye, still really depends on the ear; it is, indeed, speech exalted to its highest capacity and given a permanent form. But prose, as the art of saying exactly everything that is meant, and of excluding from what is written everything, exactly, that is not meant, is the characteristic art of the written word and the most developed use of language in visible form.

But, now, contrast with the scope of the eye the scope of the ear. We listen to a sequence of sounds. How much can we hear? How many words do we seize at once as they pass? How large is our field? Like the eye, the ear has an immediate focus and a surrounding field, but how much smaller! We actually hear two words perhaps, and remember two, and can anticipate two. We can be made to stretch out our hearing a little, but the consequences of this are significant. If the speaker stretches it backwards, if he requires us to hold on to sentence beginnings, or subjects of phrases, a long way back, and later much qualified, he will certainly turn our attention away from what he is saying towards the way he is saying it. He will not then be setting up a very direct or personal relation between himself and you, but if he is an orator he will have his own reasons. A speaker can also stretch our hearing forward in expectation, but, if we can anticipate too much and too exactly what he is going to say, we shall be bored and cease to listen.

It must be evident already that, to correspond to the radically different conditions of its reception, the art of speech must be very unlike the art of prose. I believe there is no escape from one conclusion, that speech cannot carry what prose does, and should not attempt it. Speech must reconcile itself to being relatively a subjective medium. This will strike most people, I believe, as a hard doctrine, at odds with a good deal which they have been accustomed to look for to speech by way of instruction in lecture and exposition. It may relieve others as providing an explanation for the failure of so many lecturers. But if anyone still doubts that the content of prose is not a content which speech can contrive, let him carry out a simple experiment which will enable him to receive a passage of prose through the eye under the conditions in which he would have to receive it through the ear. He has to substitute for a continuous extension a sequence of small groups of words isolated, as by silence in speech, from one another. All he has to do is to cut out on a visiting card just as much space as will let through six words but no more in a line. Let him then cover the rest of the page and set out to read by moving the visiting-card forward slowly along the lines, confining his eye only to the little group of words which, one after another, the hole in the card will disclose. If he has chosen a passage by any modern master of prose, he will not, I am sure, be able to read farther than a line or two; and this will be because the little nucleus of words he is confined to will not contain enough life to support his interest or sustain it through the pause while he moves his card to the next. Try this on Proust or Henry James! It is the nature of speaking to deliver its impact by breaking silence with little episodes of sound, but the eye cannot make sense of this interrupted procession of words. Why, otherwise, does not the cinema give us the written word, when it has to, not spread out but in sequences, as it gives us the rest of its visible context?

It is because the writer is able to deliver his material to us in a continuous and extended field that he has his chance to be explicit. It is characteristic of explicit meaning that it cannot, in fact, be compressed. If a writer had to make do, like the speaker, with fewer words at a time, he would have to allow his meaning to become by that much more implicit and less actually expressed. This is what the poet so gladly does in his verse. He loses in explicit meaning, but gains enormously in suggestive power. It is a bargain of essentially the same sort that the speaker has to make with his words. He has to set out to provoke by suggestion what he would bore his listener by even trying actually to state.

It is worth looking at this also from the receiving end. Reading is an engrossing occupation in which the elaborate organization of the perceptive act is matched by that of the understanding. Our conscious apprehension, the interpretation we are putting upon the words, keeps, as it were, in step with the movements of the eye. But the act of hearing is relatively primitive and careless. Where the eye itself moves, the ear is fixed. In music, of course, there are whole columns of sound to be entertained at once, and the two ears between them must provide the imagination with material which it can balance in depth. But in listening we have but to hear a single thread of speech which the understanding can immediately and quite flatly take over. Compared with reading, the simple act of hearing requires little attention, as again anyone can prove for himself. Unless I am provoked into adding to, modifying, enlarging, and improvising through all sorts of imaginative exercise, the material with which I am presented, a good deal of the attention I have, at any given moment, at my disposal will stray to, and begin to make sense of, other stimuli as well. If we are to understand what we read, we must, as we well know, give ourselves very completely to it. But in listening we are not at all necessarily engrossed. How much of my attention I shall in fact give to my neighbour will depend on how much of it he is at any moment demanding and refuses to dispense with. Indeed, unless he speaks with more knowledge and a better practice of his art than most people, I shall find that while I am doing quite everything which is necessary for me to understand what he says and even to answer him, I shall be entertaining at the same time a whole series of other sequences of sound, the tune on a piano in the opposite house, perhaps, a conversation at the next table, the clock on the wall, and the noise of the traffic in the streets. The ear may be a light listener, but it insists, often in the most provoking manner, on collecting, however variously, its earful; and unless our imagination manages to keep it in check, it is likely, always, to embarrass us with a superfluity of irrelevant material.

I come back to this, then—that it is the essence of the spoken word to suggest rather than to state. And this is something which not only the act of hearing requires, but also the situation of the speaker. When we write, we must do what we can for our meaning while we write. For once we have printed it or posted it, we have sent it out to where it must stand on its own legs. If it succeeds by itself in expressing to the reader what we intended it to express, we shall have written it well. But how utterly different is our situation when we speak! We are then never at any moment having to set something or establish something where we must leave it. The essence of speaking is that we are not normally alone, we are face to face with someone and can continue to improvise and add to what we have said for as long as our hearer will listen to us. What we are after is only to start in his mind some ferment of thought or imagination. What we must do at all costs, if we are to speak successfully, is to provoke him to some response. If our listener responds by talking himself, we shall submit ourselves contentedly in turn to his influence. But if his response is silent, we shall be equally content to adapt what we say next to what we guess is the direction of his thought, correcting and adding to his impressions as we choose. But, verbal or silent, some response is always what we speak for. The jump we want is back to ourselves, and not to independent conclusions. We speak to keep our man, to establish between us all sorts of relations. Our speech must be as quick as our sympathy, as flexible as our personalities. For the words we speak are to be bridges we swarm across, and the entrances we shall gain over them are, barring physical contact and whatever carpet the eye can lay, the most personal and rewarding access we can have to each other.

Now it is not easy to convince English people of all this, for in our country we not only make light of talking but think ourselves the better because we do. Certainly it is for ourselves, and not for anyone abroad, to decide whether we can really afford to leave talking to those who make too free with their feelings or those who, because without any trouble they find it easy, have nothing significant to say. Personally, I am not convinced that talking is bound to do so much less than justice to what we want to exchange with each other; nor do I, if it comes to that, rate feeling in itself so highly that I think we should do anything but gain by giving it as much mental scrutiny as will be involved in our trying to find a counterpart, and a means of communication for it, in words. We do not, after all, live any longer in the forest and in society, it seems to me, we might as well admit that we can profit by polite exchange. Part of the trouble for us is that speech includes voice, for in England we are shy of the voice as well. We are apt to take anything like a full-bodied use of the voice as an exhibition which the noble character is bound to disdain. I believe myself that our present contempt of the voice is contributing no small influence to the decline of English and the contemporary weakness with which we speak it. But if we are to continue to neglect speech and its adjuncts, we must recognize that we are preparing to dispense with by far the most subtle and quick instrument we possess for originating and developing personal relations. Where there is no language the people perish.

When I say this I do not intend any slight on character. Mere words, I agree, cannot help us. We are not after words when we talk but the stuff they root in. When I approach someone, I can only open my communication with him from where I am. Where I am is my character. And when I open my mouth to speak, the only resources I have to offer him are the sum of my experiences to date and any use I have so far been able to put them to. I can follow the bias of my disposition as it inclines me naturally towards him or away, I can take advantage of any excitement I find in his presence. But however packed my own mind may be, or how ready my inclination, I shall not have anything which is properly my own to give him, and no manner of my own with which I can hope to supply it, unless I have learnt how to speak and to speak for myself. Now speaking is not something that we can simply lazily do. We cannot, like the art of writing, practise it by ourselves; but this makes it all the more important that we should come up to every opportunity of speaking in an attitude of absolute integrity.

If we tender our neighbour merely the current phrase, we shall be turning a private into a public occasion. But if the idiom we proffer him is not only public property, but lifted from print, we shall be opposing our neighbour, not with a bridge, but with a wall to climb. What we need between us is material we can work on, stuff of speech, not print, suggestive stuff we can adapt and adopt from each other. Print can only be a forswearing and denial, for if it comes between us at all, it can only say things for itself and renounce us.

When we speak, we should be trying to convey ourselves to each other. But since we have all been taught to read, we have ceased to attach any proper importance to what we hear. Under the influence of the advertisement hoardings and the newspaper we are now, most of us, stopping short of each other even when we make love, exchanging clichés which are not only penny-common but eye-received. And the eye which received them is probably one which has never been taught to read prose. The newspapers and the hoardings which have captured it, have been written specifically for those who cannot in this sense read. The journalist's mode is a nondescript. The journalist uses a set-up of language which does not exact enough from the eye to arrive at prose. His idiom is a hybrid which cannot breed.

Perhaps we have already begun to watch the deterioration of our language from a condition of health in which the two idioms of speaking and writing act separately on the common English words and grammar, into a uniform and fruitless state where, instead of two forms of expression, we have only one crossbred which can adequately serve neither of our purposes. Cheap printing and the spread of literacy were bound to run enormous risk. The risk was that, while the eye became the universal organ of appeal, writing itself might be debased to accommodate the relatively uninstructed eye of the new readers. From that point, unless an unexpected influence was brought to bear, a universal decadence of the language would be inevitable. What is required to save English now is a vehicle which can carry back to the ear some of the burden of the overloaded eye. And this vehicle must maintain itself for at least as long as our schoolmasters need to turn the newly literate into properly instructed readers. Our general education is recent. That more of us have not yet acquired a literary taste is not surprising. On the evidence of booksellers and librarians our taste has begun to improve. As it does improve, we may count on our growing correspondingly disinclined to put up with a slackness in print which does no sort of justice to our new powers. But as the style of the printed word grows, then, as it will, in characteristic extension and complexity, it will grow less and less amenable to the uses of speech, and we shall find ourselves less and less inclined to adapt it to our personal intercourse.

Well, isn't broadcasting the very vehicle that can save us? Our ears have become accustomed to receiving the alien idiom outside, but broadcasting is still new enough to startle us, and it has the éclat. Since we can do nothing but listen to broadcast talks, we cannot grumble if our speakers ask us to listen more specifically. There is a chance they will.

It remains to be shown that in passing the authentic spoken word through the loudspeaker the broadcaster in his lonely studio can still contrive to speak as if he were not alone, and exact from his listener the response he would have to exact if he were face to face with him. I believe it can be shown. I believe that broadcasters have already come some way to doing it. But that is another story and too long to be added here.